RATIONALITY AND REASONING

Rationality and Reasoning

Jonathan St.B.T. Evans
University of Plymouth, UK

David E. Over
University of Sunderland, UK

Psychology Press
An imprint of Erlbaum (UK) Taylor & Francis

Copyright © 1996 by Psychology Press
an imprint of Erlbaum (UK) Taylor & Francis

Psychology Press, Publishers
27 Church Road
Hove
East Sussex, BN3 2FA
UK

British Library Cataloguing in Publication Data

A catalogue record for this book is available from the British Library

   ISBN 0-86377-437-7

Cover by Clearwater Design, Hove.
Printed and bound by TJ Press (Padstow) Ltd.

Contents

Foreword   vii

Preface and acknowledgements   ix

1. **Rationality in reasoning**   1

   The rationality paradox   2
   Two kinds of rationality   7
   The limitations of logical reasoning   16
   Form and objectives of this book   21
   Notes   23

2. **Personal goals, utility, and probability**   25

   Goals and decisions   25
   Problems with normative decision theory   29
   Epistemic goals and utility   36
   Conclusions   43

3. **Relevance, rationality, and tacit processing**   45

   Relevance and rationality   46

Relevance in reasoning   54
Relevance in decision making and judgement   62
Conclusions   68
Notes   70

4. Reasoning as decision making: The case of the selection task   71

The deontic selection task   73
Indicative selection tasks   83
Conclusion   93

5. Prior belief   95

Use and neglect of Bayesian priors   97
Confirmation bias   103
Belief bias   109
Conclusion   115

6. Deductive competence   119

Competence and bias in reasoning:
   The evidence   120
The mechanism of deduction:
   Rules or models?   129
Note   139

7. A dual process theory of thinking   141

Dual processes in reasoning: Sequential, parallel,
   or interactive?   144
The nature of tacit thought processes   147
The nature of explicit thought processes   153
Conclusions and final thoughts   161
Note   162

References   163

Author index   173

Subject index   177

Foreword

There has been a dramatic increase, on both sides of the Atlantic, in contributions to the psychology of reasoning: research into how people actually think rather than how they ought to think. It has even justified a new journal, *Thinking & Reasoning*, devoted exclusively to this topic. Incidentally, the editor of the journal is the first author of this book. It is of passing interest to note that the origins of this research have been due to luck and play, not, as some authorities assume, a concerted attack on the grasp of deductive reasoning. What started as a perplexing puzzle has now been polished and consolidated into a wide variety of complex theories.

The bored psychologist glancing at the shelves marked "cognition" in the local bookshop, might catch sight of this book and inwardly exclaim, "Not another book on reasoning!". Such a dismissive reaction would be plausible, but entirely wrong. In my view, there are at least three features in this book which merit more than a cursory glance.

First, the book is a collaborative effort between two people who have different backgrounds in psychology and philosophy. Jonathan Evans is a distinguished experimental psychologist whose work has spearheaded research on reasoning for some time. David Over was originally a philosopher who has increasingly worked with psychologists on decision theoretic analyses of what had been seen as pure problems in reasoning. His papers with Ken Manktelow have helped to illuminate deontic versions of the Wason selection task. Even more recently, he and Jonathan Evans have started to integrate work on reasoning and decision making in new ideas about indicative versions of the task, the most formidable and intractable of all the problems in the field.

What has been achieved by this collaboration is a liberation from the conventional wisdom of the dominant group, and an appeal to regard reasoning behaviour in a wider focus. Johnson-Laird and I have always invoked propositional logic as the normative standard for judging performance, but the present authors distinguish between "Rationality$_1$" which is basically a "generally reliable" way of achieving goals, and "Rationality$_2$" which is achieving a goal sanctioned by a normative theory (e.g. logic).

The second reason for commending this book is that it draws not merely on the "reasoning" literature but on the "decision making" literature. Decision making is concerned intrinsically with probability rather than deduction. It has acquired its own sophisticated mathematical methodology, but to invoke both traditions to tackle the same empirical data may be regarded as a daring step. We like to keep our nests immaculate, and not muddied by a different tradition, even if we are totally unaware of this penchant.

A third point of interest lies in a study in which I was privileged to work with Evans (Wason & Evans, 1975), discussed in the final chapter of this book. Its results show a marked discrepancy between the causes of people's actions or decisions and the explanations that they offer for them. This has similarities to the annotations of a chess master which claim to be objective but are frequently rationalisation of a line of play already accepted (or rejected). The concept of rationalisation originates, of course, in a psychoanalytic context where it is regarded as justifying unconscious wishes, demands, etc. In such cases the choice, or decision, is invested with prior meaning or emotion. However, the results which Evans and I obtained in two experiments were based on that trivial material (circles, triangles, etc.) so beloved by the cognitive psychologist. Furthermore, the written protocols in our experiment suggest that what looked like a fluctuation of insight from one test to another, was really governed by a prior non-verbal choice. While the limits of such "dual processing" have not yet been fully established, the current volume contains new and valuable discussion of the role of tacit and explicit thinking.

Not all of us in the firm will agree with everything claimed by the authors. How could it be otherwise? For instance, I am inclined to agree with some "criticisms" recently made about an experiment of mine published nearly 40 years ago, but such criticisms overlook an unanticipated, qualitative result which makes the study a unique example of obsessional thinking under controlled conditions. However, this was a "one-off" experiment which has led only to methodological debate. Nevertheless, I hope enough has been said to show that this book is a fertile ground for others interested in cognition and epistemology. May it meet with the success it deserves.

Peter Cathcart Wason
Oxford, February 1996

Preface and acknowledgements

Readers may be interested to know how a collaborative book between a psychologist and a philosopher living some 400 miles apart came to be written. The first author (JE) has been active in researching the psychology of reasoning since the early 1970s and has made a particular study of biases in reasoning, the subject of an earlier book in this series (Evans, 1989). To his continuing puzzlement he found that many authors in the field were attributing to him a claim that such biases implied that human beings were irrational. Not only were such claims absent from JE's publications, but some pretty clear statements to the contrary had actually been provided. For example:

> The view that I wish to argue here is that errors of thinking occur because of, rather than in spite of, the nature of our intelligence. In other words, they are an inevitable consequence of the way in which we think and a price to be paid for the extraordinary effectiveness with which we routinely deal with the massive information-processing requirements of everyday life. (Evans, 1989, p.111.)

The second author (DO) is a philosopher who has been active in the psychology of reasoning for some years and who regularly defies the rules of the philosophers' union by running experiments. His interest developed through collaboration with the psychologist Ken Manktelow, and, in 1993, he and Ken edited a volume on rationality to which a number of leading researchers, including JE, were asked to contribute (Manktelow & Over, 1993). In his chapter, JE took the opportunity both to respond to some reviewers of the 1989 book who had criticised it for avoiding the issue of rationality, and to deal with the broader question of what implications research on reasoning biases has for human rationality. This led to the first presentation of the distinction between two definitions of rationality—rationality$_1$ and rationality$_2$—which are discussed at length in this book. The basic idea is that one may be rational in terms of achieving personal goals (rationality$_1$) without being rational in the sense of conforming to a normative system such as logic (rationality$_2$). DO had been working for some time on the idea that behaviour on some reasoning tasks could be better viewed in terms of decision processes rather than as logical reasoning. JE's distinction thus struck an immediately sympathetic chord and instigated a series of discussions that led first to some collaborative papers and eventually to the current volume.

With a title like *Rationality and Reasoning*, readers might wonder whether this book is intended as a work in philosophy or psychology. The answer is both. The primary focus of the work is on the interpretation of the psychological literature on reasoning and decision making—hence publication in this "Essays in Cognitive Psychology" series. However, we deal also with philosophical issues and bring these to bear on the interpretation of the psychological evidence. In the early part of the book we concentrate mostly on conceptual issues, attempting to clarify thinking about the concept of rationality in psychological research and exploring the limitations of normative theoretical analysis. As the book progresses, we increasingly develop our psychological theory of reasoning and decision processes. Although our differing backgrounds were obviously helpful in this endeavour, we would like to stress that every part of this book has been drafted or redrafted by each of us. We both wrote all of it.

Although a relatively short book, the curent volume was written over the deliberately protracted period of two years in order to allow full consideration of some very complex questions. During this period both authors benefited from periods of fellowship leave, which made the task a lot easier than it might have been. We would like therefore to acknowledge our employers—the Universities of Plymouth and Sunderland—for their support in this enterprise. DO would also like to acknowledge the Psychology Department of Princeton University where he was a Visiting Fellow while on leave and where he benefited particularly from discussions with Phil Johnson-Laird, Danny Kahneman, and Dick Jeffrey. JE spent part of his leave as Visiting

Professor to CREPCO in the University of Provence, France where he had many relevant discussions with Paolo Legrenzi and Vittorio Girotto.

There are a number of other colleagues whose assistance we would like to acknowledge. First, we must especially thank those who read and commented on the entire book in draft manuscript form: Dan Sperber, Paolo Legrenzi, Jonathan Lowe, and John Clibbens. We made significant changes in response to each of these commentators. Next, we acknowledge that our thinking about these issues has benefited from discussions with various collaborators in our recent work on the psychology of reasoning and decision making—in particular Ken Manktelow, Rosemary Stevenson, Steve Newstead, Ruth Byrne, Simon Handley, and David Green. Finally, there are those with whom we have not formally collaborated, but with whom we have discussed some of the ideas that feature in this book; in particular we would like to mention Kris Kirby, Patricia Cheng, Mike Oaksford, and Nick Chater.

CHAPTER ONE

Rationality in reasoning

Reasoning and decision making are topics of central importance in the study of human intelligence. Reasoning is the process by which we can apply our vast stores of knowledge to the problem at hand, deducing specific consequences from our general beliefs. Reasoning also takes place when we infer the general from the specific, by formulating and then testing new ideas and hypotheses. Rules for correct reasoning have been laid down by great thinkers in normative systems (principally logic and probability theory) and it is tempting to define, and evaluate, human rationality by referring only to these rules. However, we shall argue in this book that this approach is mistaken. The starting point for any understanding of human rationality should be behavioural: we must ask how decisions taken and actions performed serve the goals of the individual. Formulating and making use of logical and other rules has always had to rest on a more fundamental human ability to achieve behavioural goals.

The psychology of thinking has a long history, but the past 25 years or so have witnessed an explosion of research effort in the areas of decision making, judgement and reasoning, with many hundreds of experiments reported in the psychological literature. These studies are reviewed in detail in several recent textbooks (e.g. Baron, 1988; Evans, Newstead, & Byrne, 1993a; Garnham & Oakhill, 1994) and we will make no attempt to repeat the exercise here. In this book our purposes are theoretical and integrative: we seek to make sense of research in these vast literatures and to resolve some central theoretical issues of importance concerning rationality and the nature of human thinking. Hence our discussion of the published studies will be highly selective, although we believe focused on findings that are both important and representative of the area as a whole.

The aims of this book are three-fold. First, we address and attempt to resolve an apparent paradox of rationality that pervades in these fields. The issue of rationality is central to the first two chapters and underpins much of our later discussion. Next, we seek to achieve integration between the study of reasoning and decision making. Despite some recent efforts to bridge the gap, research in these two areas has proceeded largely in isolation. It seems to us that the mental processes of reasoning and decision making are essentially similar, although we shall see how an emphasis on rule-following as the basis of rationality has rendered this resemblance less than self-evident. Finally, we shall present a dual process theory of thinking which advances understanding of the phenomena we discuss and the psychological mechanisms underlying the kinds of rationality that people display in their reasoning and decision making.

THE RATIONALITY PARADOX

The human species is far and away the most intelligent on earth. Human beings are unique in their cognitive faculties—for example, their possession of an enormously powerful linguistic system for representing and communicating information. They have learned not only to adapt to the environment but to adapt the environment to suit themselves; and they have organised vastly complex economic, industrial, and political systems. They have also developed a capacity for abstract thinking that has enabled them, among other things, to create logic and other normative systems for how they ought to reason.

What happens when representatives of this highly intelligent species are taken into the psychological laboratory to have their processes of thinking, reasoning, and decision making studied by psychologists? The surprising answer is that people seem to make mistakes of all kinds, as judged by the normative rules that human beings have themselves laid down. Many of these rule violations are systematic and arise in cases where a bias is said to exist. Some psychologists use this term as a necessarily pejorative one, but for us it will be descriptive, meaning only a departure from an apparently appropriate normative system. We are not talking here about minor aspects of human performance: systematic deviations from normative principles have been identified and reported in many hundreds of published studies within the past twenty years alone. Although we discuss the issues in general terms in this chapter, a number of specific examples of reasoning and decision biases will be discussed throughout this book. Lest this chapter be too abstract, however, we present a single example of the kind of thing we are talking about.

In syllogistic reasoning tasks, subjects are presented with two premises and a conclusion. They are instructed to say whether the conclusion follows logically from the premises. They are told that a valid conclusion is one that must be true if the premises are true and that nothing other than the premises is relevant to this judgement. Suppose they are given the following problem:

1.1   No addictive things are inexpensive
      Some cigarettes are inexpensive
      Therefore, some addictive things are not cigarettes

On the basis of the information given, this syllogism is invalid. In other words, the conclusion does not necessarily follow from the premises. The class of cigarettes might include all addictive things, thus contradicting the conclusion. Of course, those cigarettes that were inexpensive would not be the ones that were addictive, but this is quite consistent with the premises. However, the majority of subjects given problems like 1.1 state erroneously that the conclusion does follow logically from the premises (71% in the study of Evans, Barston, & Pollard, 1983). Now suppose the problem is stated as follows:

1.2   No cigarettes are inexpensive
      Some addictive things are inexpensive
      Therefore, some cigarettes are not addictive things

The logical structure of 1.2 is the same as 1.1; all we have done is to interchange two of the terms. However, with problems of type 1.2 very few subjects say that the conclusion follows (only 10% in the study of Evans et al., 1983). What is the critical difference between the two? In the case of 1.1 the conclusion is believable and in the case of 1.2 it is not believable. This very powerful effect is known as "belief bias" and is discussed in detail in Chapter 5. It is clearly a bias, from the viewpoint of logic, because a feature of the task that is irrelevant given the instructions has a massive influence on judgements about two logically equivalent problems.

There seems to be a paradox. On the basis of their successful behaviour, human beings are evidently highly intelligent. The psychological study of deduction, on the other hand, appears to suggest that they are illogical. Although some authors in research on biases have been careful to qualify their claims about human behaviour, others have made fairly strong claims that their work shows people to be irrational (see Lopes, 1991, which discusses a number of examples). It is perhaps not surprising that research on biases in reasoning and judgement has come under close scrutiny from philosophers and psychologists who simply cannot accept these findings at face value and who take exception to the inferences of irrationality that are often drawn from the studies concerned. These criticisms mostly come from authors who take human rationality to be obvious, for the reasons outlined above, and who therefore conclude that there is something wrong with the research or its interpretation.

Evans (1993a) has discussed the nature of this criticism of bias research in some depth and classified the arguments into the following three broad groupings:

- the normative system problem;
- the interpretation problem; and
- the external validity problem.

The first major critique of bias research by a philosopher was that of Cohen (1981) whose paper includes examples of all three types of argument. The normative system problem, as Cohen discusses it, is that the subject may be reasoning by some system other than that applied in judgement by the experimenter. For example, psychologists studying deductive reasoning tend to assume a standard logic—such as extensional propositional logic—as their normative framework, whereas many other logics are discussed by logicians in the philosophical literature. Cohen (1982) suggested further that people might be using an old Baconian system of probability based on different principles from modern probability theory. We find this suggestion implausible—substituting, as it does, one normative system for another. However, the idea that rationality is personal and relative to the individual is important in our own framework as we shall see shortly.

A different slant on the normative system problem is the argument that conventional normative theories cannot be used to assess rationality because they impose impossible processing demands upon the subject. We would not, for example, describe someone as irrational because they were unable to read the text of a book placed beyond their limit of visual acuity, or because they could not recall one of several hundred customer addresses, or were unable to compute the square root of a large number in their heads. For this reason, Baron (1985) distinguishes normative theories from prescriptive theories. The latter, unlike the former, prescribe heuristics and strategies for reasoning that could be applied by people within their cognitive processing capabilities. For example, people cannot be expected to internalise probability theory as an axiomatic system and to derive its theorems, but they can learn in general to take account of the way in which the size and variability of samples affects their evidential value.

In the case of deductive reasoning, this type of argument has been proposed in several recent papers by Oaksford and Chater (e.g. 1993, 1995). They point out that problems with more than a trivial number of premises are computationally intractable by methods based on formal logic. For example, is is known that to establish the logical consistency of n statements in propositional logic requires a search that increases exponentially with n. Oaksford and Chater go on to argue that the major theories of deductive reasoning based on mental logic and mental models (discussed later) therefore face problems of computational intractability when applied to non-trivial problems of the sort encountered in real life, where many premises based on prior beliefs and knowledge are relevant to the reasoning we do. In this respect the argument of Oaksford and Chater bears also upon the external validity problem, also discussed later.

The interpretation problem refers to the interpretation of the problem by the subject, rather than the interpretation of the behaviour by the psychologist. The latter is a problem too, but one which belongs under the third heading, discussed below. The interpretation argument has featured prominently in some criticism of experimental research on deductive reasoning. For example, in a very influential paper, Henle (1962) asserted that people reason in accordance with formal logic, despite all the experimental evidence to the contrary. Her argument is that people's conclusions follow logically from their personalised representation of the problem information. When the conclusion is wrong, it is because the subject is not reasoning from the information given: they may, for example, ignore a premise or redefine it to mean something else. They might also add premises, retrieved from memory. Henle illustrates her argument by selective discussion of verbal protocols associated with syllogistic reasoning. There are some cases, however, in which her subjects appear to evaluate the conclusion directly without any process of reasoning. These she classifies as instances of "failure to accept the logical task".

Another version of the interpretation problem that has received less attention than it deserves is the argument of Smedslund of a "circular relation between logic and understanding" (see Smedslund, 1970, for the original argument and 1990 for a recent application of it).

Smedslund argues that we can only decide if someone is reasoning logically if we presume that they have represented the premises as intended. Conversely, we can only judge their understanding of the problem information if we assume that they have reasoned logically. Smedslund's surprising conclusion from his discussion of this circularity is that "the only possible coherent strategy is always to presuppose logicality and regard understanding as a variable". This argument was scrutinised in detail by Evans (1993a) who refuted it by discussion of the specific example of conditional inference. He showed that subjects' reasoning in such cases is not logically consistent with any interpretation that can be placed upon the conditional sentence and nor is there logical consistency between reasoning on one problem and another.

Perhaps the most potentially damaging critique of bias research is that based on the external validity problem. In its least sympathetic form, as in Cohen's (1981) paper, the argument can aim to undermine the value of the research fields concerned on the basis that they study artificial and unrepresentative laboratory problems. Consider, for example, the Wason selection task (Wason, 1966), which we discuss in some detail later in this book. Devised as a test of hypothesis testing and understanding of conditional logic, this problem is solved— according to its conventional normative analysis—by less than 10% of intelligent adult subjects, and has become the single most studied problem in the entire reasoning literature (see Evans et al., 1993a, Chapter 4, for a detailed review). Cohen attempted to dismiss the phenomenon as a "cognitive illusion", analogous to the Muller-Lyer illusion of visual perception. If he is right, then many researchers have chosen to spend their time studying a problem that is wholly unrepresentative of normal thinking and reasoning and that presents an untypically illogical impression of human thought. We disagree with Cohen, but we will nevertheless consider in some detail how performance on this particular task should be interpreted. Where we will agree with him is in rejecting the notion that the selection task provides evidence of irrationality. However, unlike Cohen we believe that study of this task has provided much valuable evidence about the nature of human thought.

Other aggressive forms of the external validity argument include suggestions that bias accounts are proposed to accord with fashion and advance the careers of the psychologists concerned and that researchers create an unbalanced picture by citing disproportionately the results of studies that report poor reasoning (see Berkeley & Humphreys, 1982; Christensen-Szalanski & Beach, 1984). A milder version of the argument has been presented by such authors as Funder (1987) and

Lopes (1991) who, like us, are sympathetic to the research fields but concerned by interpretations of general irrationality that are placed upon them. Experiments that are designed to induce errors in subjects' performance are valuable in advancing our theoretical understanding of thought processes. It is a mistake, however, to draw general inferences of irrationality from these experimental errors. As an analogy, consider that much memory research involves overloading the system to the point where errors of recall will occur. This provides useful experimental data so that we can see, for example, that some kinds of material are easier to recall than others, with consequent implications for the underlying process. Such research is not, however, generally used to imply that people have bad and inadequate systems of memory. So why should explorations of cognitive constraints in reasoning be taken as evidence of poor intelligence and irrationality?

Our own theoretical arguments stem from an attempt to resolve the problems outlined in this section and to address some of the specific issues identified. In doing this we rely heavily upon our interpretation of a distinction between two forms of rationality, first presented by Evans (1993a) and by Evans, Over, and Manktelow (1993b).

TWO KINDS OF RATIONALITY

Human rationality can be assessed in two different ways: one could be called the personal and the other the impersonal. The personal approach asks what our individual goals are, and whether we are reasoning or acting in a way that is usually reliable for achieving these. The impersonal approach, in contrast, asks whether we are following the principles of logic and other normative theories in our reasoning or decision making. Flanagan (1984, p. 206) gives a good statement of an impersonal view of rationality:

> Often rationality is taken as equivalent to logicality. That is, you are rational just in case you systematically instantiate the rules and principles of inductive logic, statistics, and probability theory on the one hand, and deductive logic and all the mathematical sciences, on the other.

Taking this approach, we would say that people are rational if they have reasons for what they believe or do that are good ones according to logic or some other impersonal normative system. But this way of looking at rationality should be combined with a personal view, which sees an individual's mental states or processes as rational if they tend to be of reliable help in achieving that individual's goals. Nozick (1993, p.64) comments that neither the personal nor impersonal view taken on its own "... exhausts our notion of rationality."

As a simple example of the need for both views, consider a man who tries to dismiss a woman's ideas about economics by arguing that women are incapable of understanding the subject. We could rightly, from the impersonal point of view, call this irrational and charge that the man does not have a good reason for dismissing these ideas. Invoking normative principles to justify ourselves, we would point out that he is committing an *ad hominem* fallacy. This should not, however, be the end of the story. It is probably not even in the woman's interest to stop thinking about this man. For what is his underlying goal, and is he likely to achieve it? To ask this question is to take the personal view, which can be of great practical importance. Perhaps the man is a politician who is trying to advance his own position at the expense of the woman's. He may succeed in this by appealing to the prejudices of a section of the electorate if the woman takes no steps to stop him. It is foolish in itself to assume that someone who violates some normative principle does not know what he is doing nor how to achieve the goal he has in mind. The man in our example could be rational from the personal point of view. We should keep this in mind if we do not want to underestimate him, but do want to predict what he will try to do, so that we can stop him from doing it. Of course, one way to stop him may be to go back to the impersonal view and point out in public that he is violating normative principles. This would be, in effect, to show that his private, personal goal is not at all that of discovering the best economic theory.

To avoid confusion, we shall introduce a terminological difference between these two ways of looking at rationality, and try to make the distinction between them more precise. We shall use "rationality$_1$" for our view of personal rationality, and "rationality$_2$" for our view of impersonal rationality. Until recently, most research on deductive reasoning has presupposed a version of impersonal rationality and almost totally ignored personal rationality. Our object is to explain how we think this distinction should be made, and to bring out its importance for future work on reasoning. As a first step, we adopt the following rough introductory definitions:

Rationality$_1$: Thinking, speaking, reasoning, making a decision, or acting in a way that is generally reliable and efficient for achieving one's goals.
Rationality$_2$: Thinking, speaking, reasoning, making a decision, or acting when one has a reason for what one does sanctioned by a normative theory.

Returning to our example, we can now describe it as one in which someone is not rational$_2$ but may be rational$_1$. The male politician tries to achieve a selfish personal goal by using an invalid argument, and yet he could still be rational$_1$ if his attempt to appeal to prejudice has a good chance of success. Of course, the principles of valid inference from logic are properly used for a specific purpose—that of inferring what must follow from premises assumed to be true. Logicians sometimes have this purpose as an end in itself, but most of us use valid inferences to help us achieve some further end—say, that of advancing scientific knowledge about economics or psychology. In our example, the politician did not have this goal; his only goal was his personal political advantage. Fortunately, he could not openly acknowledge this in our society and still hope to attain it. The use of logic could also have some utility in a political debate with him, as people do have some deductive competence without special training (Chapter 6). As we shall see later in this chapter, however, the usefulness of logic has its limits even in science.

An important contrast in the aforementioned definitions is between the use of "generally reliable" in the first and "when one has a reason" in the second. Both phrases are there to indicate that one cannot properly be said to be rational or indeed irrational, in either sense, by accident or merely as a result of good or bad luck. To possess rationality$_2$, people need to have good reasons for what they are doing, which must be part of an explanation of their action. They have to follow rules sanctioned by a normative theory: this is what makes the reasons "good" ones. In this book, we are only concerned with normative theories (mainly logic and decision theory, including probability theory) for manipulating propositional representations. For example, people would have a good reason for concluding that it will rain by following an inference rule, *modus ponens,* which permits them to infer that conclusion from the propositions that the barometer is falling and that it will rain if this is so. If people are being rational$_2$, we expect the existence of such reasons to be indicated in their protocols, where they are asked to give a verbal report of their thinking or reasoning while they do it.

The rational$_1$ perspective is a different one. What makes people more or less rational in this sense is the extent of their ability to achieve their goals. People will usually be aware of a goal they have and may have some awareness of some of the steps required to attain it. But they will usually be unaware and unable to describe the processes that do much to help them achieve their ordinary goals. Still less will they have good reasons for the way these processes work. People may know, for example, that they are going out to buy a newspaper at a shop, but will know next to nothing about how their visual system works to enable them to get there. The working of this system is beyond their knowledge or control, and so they can hardly be said to have good reasons for making it produce representations of the world in one way rather than another.

We believe that human cognition depends on two systems. What we shall call the tacit or implicit system is primarily responsible for rationality$_1$, while what we shall call the explicit system mainly affects the extent of people's rationality$_2$. The latter system is employed in sequential verbal reasoning, which people consciously engage in and can give some report about.[1] On the other hand, tacit systems operate in parallel, are computationally extremely powerful, and present only their end-products to consciousness. Such systems may have an innate basis—as many psychologists and linguists now believe to be the case with linguistic learning and understanding—but are always extensively shaped by interactions with the environment. In the case of reasoning and decision making, tacit processes are largely responsible for the selective representation of information—what we term *relevance* processes—and hence the focus of attention of the reasoner. We will see evidence in Chapters 2 and 3 that many basic decisions are largely determined by such implicit processes, with conscious thought contributing little more than some overall justification for the actions. The nature of these dual thought processes—the implicit/tacit one and the explicit one—will be discussed in more detail in the final chapter of this book, though the distinction really calls for a book in itself. For the time being we note that some philosophers have argued for such a duality (Harman, 1986, pp. 13–14), and that strong evidence for it may be found in the literature on implicit learning (see Reber, 1993, and Berry & Dienes, 1993). Sloman (1996) also argues for a similar distinction between what he calls associative- and rule-based reasoning.

Contemporary reasoning theories are addressed to several different objectives which Evans (1991) has analysed as the explanation of (a) deductive competence, (b) errors and biases observed in experiments and (c) the dependence of reasoning upon content and context. In the course of this book we shall be examining all of these issues and the associated theories, but for the moment we confine our attention to deductive competence which links directly to rationality$_2$. The major theories that have addressed the issue of deductive competence are those of mental logic (or inference rules) and mental models.

Mental logic and mental models

Rationality$_2$ is most obviously presupposed by the theory that people reason by use of an abstract internalised logic. The notion that the laws of logic are none other than the laws of thought enjoys a long philosophical tradition and was popularised in psychology by the

Piagetian theory of formal operational thinking (Inhelder & Piaget, 1958) and by the paper of Henle (1962) already mentioned. These authors did not propose computational models of the kind expected by today's cognitive scientists, however, so contemporary advocates of mental logic have attempted to provide better specified accounts of precisely how people reason (see for example, Braine & O'Brien, 1991; Rips, 1983, 1994).

Formal logic provides a normative standard for deductive inference. Valid deductions are inferences that add no new semantic information, but derive conclusions latent in premises assumed to be true. Deductive systems (such as expert consultant systems programmed on computers) are powerful in that they can store knowledge in the form of general principles that can be applied to specific cases. However, such systems must have effective procedures for making deductions. Furthermore, if the system in question is a person rather than a computer, we require a psychologically plausible and tractable account of this reasoning process.

Propositional logic, as the basic formal logic, deals with propositions constructed from the connectives *not, if, and* and *or*, and provides several alternative and equivalent procedures for inferences containing these propositions. Premises consist of such propositions: for example, the premise "if p then q" connects two propositions, p and q, by the conditional connective. One way of establishing the validity of an argument is by a method known as truth table analysis. In this approach, all possible combinations of truth values of the premises are considered in turn. If no situation can be found where the premises are all true and the conclusion false then the argument is declared valid. This exhaustive algorithm neatly demonstrates the exponential growth of logical proof spaces as one must consider "2 to the power of n" situations, where n is the number of propositions.

In fact, no one seriously suggests that human reasoning resembles a truth table analysis. Mental logic theories are built instead upon the other main proof procedure provided by logic—abstract inference rules, known in philosophical tradition as "natural" deduction. An example of such a rule is *modus ponens*, which takes the general form:

If p then q
p
Therefore, q

A rule of this kind is abstract and therefore general purpose. The idea is that particular verbal reasoning problems are encoded in an abstract manner and then rules like this are followed. So on encountering the propositions "If the switch is down the light is on" and "the switch is down" one would encode "the switch is down" as p, and so on, and follow the rule. This leads to a conclusion q, which is translated back into the context as "the light is on". There are a number of mental logic theories differing in detail about the number and nature of the inferences and rules and the procedures for applying them. One of the best known—and best specified—is the ANDS model of Rips (1983, renamed PSYCOP by Rips, 1994), which is a working computer program.

The theory of mental logic is self-evidently committed to the idea that people often display rationality$_2$: they have the best of reasons—logical ones—for the inferences they perform. The hypothetical mental system has its limitations, of course, but there are supposed to be many valid inference rules, like *modus ponens*, that people systematically use in their reasoning: this is the force of saying that they have a mental logic. Notice how this theory implies that people explicitly follow logical rules, in a step-by-step or sequential pattern of manipulating propositional representations. People are supposed to follow *modus ponens* because their mental or verbal representations of a conditional and its antecedent match the conditions for the application of the rule, with the result that they perform the inference. People do not merely come to the same conclusion that logic would sanction but in some other way: they are held to do more than just passively comply with or conform to logic.[2] Indeed, people's grasp of the meaning of *if* and the other connectives supposedly consists in their ability to follow logical rules. Moreover, the supporters of mental logic hold that people can give some report, in verbal protocols, of the inferences they are drawing from conditionals and other logical forms.

The other contemporary theory to address the issue of deductive competence is the highly influential view which holds that people reason by constructing mental models—i.e. mental structures that are similar to the situations they represent (Johnson-Laird & Byrne, 1991). People are supposed here to have some understanding of validity, some grasp that an inference cannot be valid if its premises are true and its conclusion false in some model, and that the inference is valid if there is no model of this kind. However, it is not proposed that people go through an exhaustive truth table analysis, examining all logical possibilities. Rather they are held to set up models in which the premises are *true*, and aim to discover what else must be true in those models. The effort at deduction is achieved by focusing on a putative conclusion and making some attempt to find a counter-example to the claim that its supporting argument is valid—i.e. a model in which the premises all hold but the conclusion does not. People draw as deductions those conclusions that hold in all the models constructed, and their understanding of the connectives consists in their ability to construct and manipulate mental models in the right way. Fallacious inferences will typically result when there are too many possible models for them all to be considered. Hence this theory incorporates its own specific notions of cognitive constraint—especially due to limited working memory capacity.

As an example, the equivalent of *modus ponens* is achieved by model construction. On receiving a proposition of the form "if p then q", the reasoners set up a model that looks like this:

[p]   q
...

Each line represents a possible situation in which the propositions are true, and the square brackets mean that a proposition is exhausted in that model. Hence the first line means there may be a situation in which a p is linked with a q and this will be true of every p. The second line, the "...", means that there may be other situations as well—ones where by implication of the exhausted representation of p in the explicit model, p does not hold. On receipt of the second premise of the *modus ponens* argument, i.e. the assertion that p is true, the first, explicit line of the model allows the immediate inference of q. Were the second premise to be of the form not-q, however, the reasoning would be more difficult as the other line of the model would need to be made explicit.

The theory of mental models may itself be viewed as a form of mental logic, albeit based upon a semantic rather than inference rule approach to logic (see Lowe, 1993; Rips, 1994). It requires some understanding of the meanings of the connectives and of validity. It also requires some general and abstract rules for processing propositional representations that may be used to describe the mental models themselves. The relevant normative theory would be a formal logical system known as semantic tableaux (Jeffrey, 1981)—people would follow all the rules formalised in this theory if they searched in the logical way for counter-examples to arguments. Actually, Johnson-Laird and Byrne do not hold that a mental tableaux system exists in this very strong form (see Chapter 6). But in their proposal, people's reasons for accepting or rejecting an inference as valid would depend on whether they had found a counter-example in their mental models. We shall take the theories of mental logic and of mental models to be our prime examples of what it would be to follow rules sanctioned by a normative theory in one's inferences—i.e. to have good reasons for these inferences.

In our terminology, the theories of mental logic and of mental models both imply that people ought to and often do display rationality$_2$. That this is so follows from the fact that these theories have some deep similarity to each other. They both take a normative theory—a formal natural deduction system in one case, and a formal semantic tableaux system in the other—and modify it for the limited processing powers and memory of human beings. They then postulate that the result is the means by which people understand the logical connectives and perform their deductive inferences. We shall have more to say about these theories throughout this book, but especially in Chapter 6 where we focus on the issue of deductive competence.

Theoretical and practical reasoning

We can begin to see the strengths and weaknesses of the theories of mental logic and mental models by noting that they cover only a part of what philosophers would call theoretical reasoning. This does not just refer to reasoning about theoretical entities, like electrons and quarks, but more generally to reasoning that has the object of inferring true beliefs, which we do when we hope to describe the world accurately. It is contrasted in philosophy with practical reasoning, which has the object of helping us decide which actions to perform to try to achieve some goal. We do this when we want to bring about some change in the world to our advantage. For example, we would use theoretical reasoning to try to infer what the weather will be like in the next month, and practical reasoning to decide, in the light of what we think we have discovered about the weather and other matters, where we should go on holiday during that time. (Audi, 1989, has more on this distinction and is an introduction to the philosophical study of practical reasoning.)

This distinction rests on the psychological fact that beliefs are not actions, and acquiring a belief, such as that it will rain tomorrow, is a different process than performing an action, such as picking up an umbrella. Good theoretical and practical reasoning, however, do depend on each other. We have little chance of achieving most of our goals if we cannot describe the world at least fairly accurately. On the other hand, to describe the world accurately we need to perform actions, such as opening our eyes to begin with, looking at objects, and manipulating them, and also identifying, interacting with, and communicating with other people. Note that, if people were not rational$_1$ in basic activities like these, there would be no grounds for holding that they had any beliefs at all, accurate or inaccurate.

To engage in good practical reasoning is to have rationality$_1$, which—as we have already indicated—involves much implicit or tacit processing of information. In practical reasoning we need, not only to have identified a goal, but to have adopted a reliable way of attaining it, which for the most part is accomplished almost immediately with little awareness on our part of how it is done. Our eyes identify, say, an apple we want to pick up or a person we want to talk to. If we are not experts in perception, we have little idea how this is done. We then choose some way to get to the apple or person, avoiding any obstacles that may be in the way, and we are largely unaware of how we do this. Finally, we pick up the apple with ease, or with almost equal ease speak to the person and understand what the individual says in reply. Such simple acts of communication require significant computations, many of which are tacit. These commonplace abilities are really remarkable, as we realise if we have any knowledge of how difficult it has been to program computers to display them in crude and simple forms.

When most psychologists talk about "reasoning", they mean an explicit, sequential thought process of some kind, consisting of propositional representations. As our examples reveal, however, we do not think that what has traditionally been called practical reasoning in philosophy always requires much "reasoning" in this sense. The psychologists' use of the term—which is linked with their endorsement of rationality$_2$—is much closer to what a philosopher would call theoretical reasoning. Certainly much of practical thought, as it would be better to call it, does not depend on conscious step-by-step inferences from general premises we believe or know to be true. It requires more than performing inferences that we have good reasons for, and the rationality$_1$ displayed in good practical thought cannot in some way be reduced to rationality$_2$.

Anderson (1990) has made a distinction similar to ours between rationality as "logically correct reasoning", and rationality as behaviour that is "optimal in terms of achieving human goals". This is clearly a distinction between an impersonal idea of rationality and a personal one. He holds that the latter sense should be the basic one in cognitive science, which should be guided by what he calls the General Principle of Rationality: "The cognitive system operates at all times to optimise the adaptation of the behaviour of the organism" (p. 28).

For example, Anderson argues that our ability to categorise objects, such as when we recognise an apple tree, is rational in his personal sense. This adaptive sense of rationality is obviously close in some respects to what we mean by rationality$_1$, and we have been influenced by much of what he says. However, we are unhappy with talk of human beings "optimising" or "maximising" anything in their behaviour; we shall say more about this in the following chapter on decision making (Chapter 2). Note that Anderson is himself somewhat uncomfortable with this idea, and that there is considerable doubt that natural selection can be said to optimise adaptations in a very strong sense.

It is easy to see why this should be so. Our hands, for example, can still be used effectively for climbing trees, though there would be better designs for this. They are also fairly effective at using computer keyboards, though they could have a better design for this as well. Perhaps they have the "optimal" design, given what evolution initially had to work on, for the kind of life style that they were originally evolved to serve in one of our hominid ancestors. That was a long time ago, and it is hard to say for sure. However, our hands are quite well designed for many practical purposes, as are the mental processes we use in our practical thought to guide our hands to do their work. Our hands and most of these mental processes have been shaped by evolution from the time even of our pre-human ancestors. Our more conscious and explicit cognitive processes, of the type we use in our most theoretical reasoning, can be less effective, as we shall see in this book. These processes are of more recent origin, and yet are sometimes called on to try to solve problems in the contemporary world for which evolution did not prepare them.

THE LIMITATIONS OF LOGICAL REASONING

Our ability to reason, whether theoretically or practically, did not evolve for its own sake. We do not naturally reason in order to be logical, but are generally logical (to the extent that we are) in order to achieve our goals. Of course, very sophisticated thinkers, beginning with Aristotle, have reflected on our ordinary deductive reasoning and identified the rudiments of a formal system that can be abstracted from it. Such thinkers can have the abstract goal of using this system as an end in itself to prove theorems, or as the foundation of mathematics and science, which themselves can be pursued for the goal of acquiring knowledge that is seen as an intrinsic good. But even logicians, mathematicians, and scientists have practical goals in mind as well when they use logic in their academic work, such as finding cures for serious diseases and making money from consultancy work.

Formal logic, whether axiomatised as a natural deduction or a semantic tableaux system, begins with assumptions. It does not specify where these assumptions come from, and it takes no interest in their truth in the actual world. To say that they are assumptions is, in effect, to treat them for the moment as if they were certainly true. Logic as an axiomatic system was set up by mathematicians, who could think of their premises as certain because these embodied abstract mathematical truths. But in ordinary reasoning we are mainly interested in performing inferences from our beliefs, few of which we hold to be certain, or from what we are told—in little of which we have absolute confidence. Arbitrary assumptions that are obviously false, or highly uncertain, have no utility for us when we are trying to infer a conclusion that will help us to achieve a practical goal. What we need for such a purpose is an inference from our relevant beliefs in which we have reasonable confidence, or at least an inference from suppositions that we can make true ourselves, as when we try to infer whether we shall have good weather supposing that we go to France for a holiday.

We have already illustrated the form of inference known as *modus ponens*. Consider, now a second and more interesting (i.e. less apparently trivial) inference associated with conditionals, known as *modus tollens*:

If p then q
not-q
Therefore, not-p

In each case, we have an inference form with two premises, the major premise being conditional and the minor one categorical. Except where these premises depend on earlier assumptions, they are to be assumed true, at least until some further inference form discharges them. Both *modus ponens* and *modus tollens* are valid: their conclusions must be true given that their premises are true.

In experiments on conditional reasoning, however, people have a substantially greater tendency to perform or endorse *modus ponens* than *modus tollens* (Evans et al., 1993a, Chapter 2). To supporters of mental logic and mental models, with their eyes fixed only on rationality$_2$, the failure to make *modus tollens* is seen as an error, though one to be excused by the limited processing powers of human beings. Hence believers in mental logic simply hold that people do not have *modus tollens* as an underived inference rule in their mental natural deduction systems. Thus this inference can only be drawn by "indirect reasoning" which is prone to error (see Braine & O'Brien, 1991). Believers in mental models claim that people tend not to construct an initial model in which the consequent of a conditional is false (see above) and hence that "fleshing-out" is required for this inference. Neither theory has an explanation of why people have these limitations considering that very little processing power would be needed to overcome them.

We can start to see the difference between these two inference forms in a new light by using an example about ordinary reasoning from our beliefs. Suppose we see what looks very much like an apple tree in the distance. It looks so much like other apple trees that we have looked at before that we are highly confident that we have identified it correctly. We cannot tell from this distance whether it has apples on it hidden among its branches, but it is the autumn and we are confident enough to assert:

If that is an apple tree then it has apples on it.

But now someone we trust coming from the tree replies:

That does not have apples on it.

In this case, we would be most unlikely to apply *modus tollens*, and we would hardly display rationality$_1$ by doing so. If we did assume that the above two statements were true, we could apply *modus tollens* as a valid inference form, inferring "That is not an apple tree". But in actual reasoning we would be concerned to perform an inference from our relevant and sufficiently confident beliefs, with the object of extending those beliefs in a way that would help us to achieve our goals. To acquire the belief that we are not seeing an apple tree would be to reject the evidence of our eyes, and this could force us to try to modify our recognition ability for apple trees. That might not be easy, and if we succeeded in doing it, we might be less able to recognise apple trees in the future, to our disadvantage when we wanted an apple. To use Anderson's terms, we should be cautious in rejecting the output of an adaptive system that, if not optimal, has at least served us well in the past.

What we would probably do in a real case like this would be to reject the conditional above, at least if we continued to trust our eyes and the person who made the second assertion. More precisely, we would lose our moderate confidence in what was conveyed by the conditional, and would perhaps become confident that it was a bad year for apples on that tree. In general, we would tend not to apply *modus tollens* to a conditional, after learning of the falsity of its consequent, if we were then more confident of its antecedent than of the conditional itself. Instead of performing this inference, we might well give up holding the conditional. In contrast, the cases in which we would decline to perform *modus ponens* are much rarer. One such exception would be when we had asserted a conditional like, "If what you say is true, then I'm a monkey's uncle", which has the pragmatic point of indicating that we think the antecedent is false. (Stevenson & Over, 1995, has more on these points, and a study of inferences when the premises are made uncertain.)

It often seems to be forgotten in experiments on deductive reasoning that logic itself allows us to perform an infinite number of inferences from any premises. In more technical terms, any one of an infinite number of conclusions validly follows from any premises, and, as a normative theory, logic should be thought of as telling us what we may infer from assumptions, rather than what we have to infer from them. As an analogy consider the distinction between the rules of chess and the strategy of chess. Someone who merely knows the rules, does not know how to play, except in the sense of producing a legal game. Choosing from among the large number of legal moves those likely to advance the goal of winning the game, requires a *strategy* based upon both a relevant goal hierarchy and sound understanding of the semantics of chess positions. In the same way, the use of logic itself in ordinary reasoning requires good practical judgement to select a conclusion that is relevant to a goal we hope to attain. Logic no more provides a strategy for reasoning than do the laws of chess tell you how to be a good chess player.

Even more practical judgement is necessary to have the right degree of confidence in our beliefs to help us to attain our goals, and to know when to extend our beliefs with an inference, and when to give up one of them instead. Of course, logic can give us some help with this through the use of the *reductio ad absurdum* inference, which allows us to reject, or technically discharge, one of our assumptions when an inconsistency follows from them. People sometimes use this form of argument to attack positions they disagree with, and then they will do what is rare in ordinary reasoning and use premises they have no inclination to believe. But logic is of limited help even here. It does not tell us which assumption to give up when we derive an inconsistency; we must make a judgement on this ourselves, in the light of what we think will best serve our goals. Again, *reductio ad absurdum* as a logical inference applies to assumptions and inconsistent conclusions, and not to the general case, in which we are trying to extend or modify beliefs, and to make good judgements about the degree of confidence we should have in our conclusions.

Sometimes we can express our confidence in, or in other words our subjective probability judgement about, a proposition precisely enough for probability theory to apply. Using this in conjunction with logic, one can prove that our degree of uncertainty in the conclusion of a valid inference should not exceed the sum of the uncertainties of the premises (Adams, 1975; Edgington, 1991). Here the uncertainty of a proposition is one minus its subjective probability, and so a proposition that has high, or low, probability for us has low, or high, uncertainty. To be rational$_2$ we should follow this principle about uncertainty and others that can be derived from probability theory, which can be of more help than logic alone in our practical thought. Still, this help also has its limits. These principles generally allow us an unlimited number of ways of adjusting our degrees of confidence in the premises and the conclusion of a valid argument. Going beyond them, we have rationality$_1$ when we raise our confidence in certain propositions, and lower it in others, in a way that helps us to achieve our goals.

Johnson-Laird (1994a, b) has recently started to attempt a combined account of deductive and inductive reasoning in terms of mental models, but the standard theory of mental logic is very limited indeed by the fact that it takes no account of subjective probability judgements. The limitations of both theories are well illustrated by what they say about *modus tollens*. For them, people make a mistake, and reveal a limitation that they have, when they do not perform this inference in experiments on reasoning. Mental logic and mental model theorists have yet to take account of the fact that almost all ordinary reasoning is from relevant beliefs, and not from arbitrary assumptions. They could claim that this is beside the point in their experiments, in which the subjects are supposed to say what follows from the given assumptions alone. But the main object of study should be subjects' ordinary way of reasoning, which may anyway interfere with any instructions they are given. In the interpretations of psychological experiments that we provide throughout this book, we shall argue repeatedly that habitual methods of reasoning are based largely on tacit processes, beyond conscious control. Hence, they will not easily be modified by presentation of verbal instructions for the sake of an experiment.

We shall argue generally in this book that psychologists of reasoning should move beyond their narrow concentration on deductive logic, and investigate the relevance of probability judgement and decision making to their subject. Much research on deductive reasoning has uncritically applied a simple Popperian view of rationality, which is a type of rationality$_2$ defined only in terms of deductive logic. According to this, there is no rational way of confirming hypotheses—i.e. making them more probable. Deductive logic alone should be used to derive empirical conclusions from a theory, and if these conclusions turn out to be false, then the theory is falsified and should be rejected. Hypotheses and theories can never be confirmed in any legitimate sense, from this point of view. Ordinary people do apparently try to make their beliefs more probable, and consequently they have been said to have an irrational confirmation bias by psychologists influenced by Popper (see Popper, 1959, 1962; and Evans, 1989, Chapter 3 for a discussion of the psychological literature on confirmation bias).

Popperian philosophy of science, however, has been heavily criticised in recent years, in part just because it allows no place for confirmation. Background assumptions, e.g. about the reliability of our eyes or of experimental equipment, are needed to derive testable predictions from scientific theories. Our eyes sometimes do deceive us, and the best equipment can fail to be accurate, and so we can rarely be certain about what we derive from a theory plus some background assumptions. If a prediction turns out to be false, this means that we may be uncertain that the theory itself, or even some part of it, is at fault and should be declared falsified. For this and other reasons, there are good grounds for preferring a non-Popperian framework that allows hypotheses to be confirmed (Howson & Urbach, 1993). In this book, we shall discuss the probability of hypotheses to support our case that human thought and reasoning should not be condemned because it departs from the limited confines of deductive logic. We develop these points in Chapter 2.

FORM AND OBJECTIVES OF THIS BOOK

We have laid out in this chapter the fundamentals of our theory of rationality and begun to explore the implications that it has for the study of human reasoning, and for reasoning theory. In the next chapter, we develop further our distinction between rationality$_1$ and rationality$_2$ and begin our discussion of the other major topic of interest—the psychology of decision making and judgement. Throughout this book, we shall argue that a rational$_1$ analysis is the crucial starting point and one which provides a perspective from which we can understand much apparently puzzling behaviour in the literature on reasoning and decision making. People should be rational$_1$—though not necessarily rational$_2$—within broad cognitive constraints provided by such limitations as finite memory capacity and limited ability to process information.

It is most important, however, to appreciate that this kind of rational analysis is not in itself a descriptive psychological theory. What it provides is rather an important *constraint* upon a psychological theory of reasoning: any mechanisms proposed must have the property of achieving outcomes that are broadly rational$_1$ in nature. The reason that we need to start with a rational$_1$ analysis is to be able to identify the cognitive constraints upon reasoning and hence to develop our theory of the underlying processes. It is by probing the limits or bounds upon rationality$_1$ that we begin to develop our understanding of the psychological mechanisms of inference and decision making.

Our descriptive psychological theory is developed from Chapter 3 onwards and is focused on the nature of the cognitive processes underlying reasoning and decision making. Our theory rests critically on the distinction between implicit and explicit cognitive systems. In particular we shall argue for a relevance theory account in which attention to selective features of problem information, together with retrieval of information from memory, is determined by rapid, preconscious processes of a connectionist nature. Such tacit processes are often primarily responsible for judgements and actions. In general, our personal rationality depends more on tacit or implicit processes than on our conscious ability to form explicit mental representations and apply rules to them. Even our ability to manipulate propositional representations, in a way justified by impersonal normative rules, requires the selection of relevant premises, which is mainly the result of implicit processes.

Much of this book is taken up with providing rational$_1$ accounts of behaviour normally classified as constituting error or bias and hence, by definition, irrational$_2$. Rationality$_2$ requires compliance with experimental instructions: for example, if subjects are told to reason deductively, draw only necessary conclusions and disregard prior beliefs, then they are irrational$_2$ if they fail to achieve these goals. However, because we believe that rationality$_1$ resides in the tacit cognitive system we regard it as reflecting habitual, normally adaptive processes that may not always generalise effectively to an arbitrary experimental task. We consider in some detail the Wason selection task (see Chapters 3 and 4) on which behaviour is highly irrational$_2$ from a logicist perspective. We will show that when viewed as a decision task strongly influenced by preconscious judgemental processes, the extensive research on this problem reveals surprising evidence of adaptive thought. In Chapter 5 we look at the influence of prior belief in reasoning and decision making, and critically examine the various claims that people are irrational by taking either insufficient or too much account of prior knowledge.

Nozick (1993, p.76) speculates that what we have called tacit processing may be a better way for human beings to think than the conscious application of rules. He even suggests that philosophers could become "technologically obsolescent" if this is so. We do not support such a sad prediction, nor the extreme conclusion of Harman (1986, p. 11) that "... logic is not of any special relevance to reasoning", which could make logicians redundant. Explicit logical thinking—conscious, verbal and sequential—affects some of our decisions and actions and is of some value. In Chapter 6 we review the evidence for deductive competence, concluding that people do possess an abstract deductive competence—albeit of a fragile nature—and that the processes responsible for this are explicit. In that chapter we also return to the debate about whether mental logic or mental model theorists have the more plausible explanation of how such competence occurs. Finally, in Chapter 7 we explicate our dual process theory of thinking in detail and consider the general nature and function of both the tacit and explicit systems of thought.

NOTES

1. The extent to which conscious verbal processes can be reported is a subject of great theoretical and methodological debate. The relevant issues are discussed in Chapter 7.
2. See Smith, Langston, and Nisbett (1992), Sloman (1996), and Chapter 7 on the distinction between following rules and complying with or conforming to them.

CHAPTER TWO

Personal goals, utility, and probability

In the previous chapter we discussed the distinction between rationality$_1$ or personal rationality, and rationality$_2$, or impersonal rationality, and introduced our argument that the rationality of human thought and reasoning is not sensibly to be judged by the strictures of formal logic alone. Because we have emphasised instead the idea of successful goal-directed behaviour, it might seem that rationality could be judged instead by decision theoretic principles referring to subjective probabilities and utilities. But we will show that whereas normative decision theory—an impersonal system—deals with the objects of a rational$_1$ approach, such as degrees of belief and utilities, it has serious deficiencies in accounting for behaviour that leads to the achievement of personal goals.

GOALS AND DECISIONS

One has personal rationality when one has a reliable way of achieving one's goals, but there is much more to be said about goals and ways of attaining them. We have a goal when we aim to reach some state of affairs—i.e. to make some proposition true—by means of our actions. We prefer this state of affairs to other possible outcomes of other actions and believe that we have some chance of reaching it. The means that we use to try to get there may include a strategy and tactics that we have carefully thought out, consciously and explicitly, in great detail. But even if this is so, we will still rely to a large extent on preconscious and automatic processes in the action or actions we take to try to attain our goal. We will have more to say in Chapter 3 about the nature of these tacit processes and their connection with relevance theory.

Consider making a decision about where to go on holiday. Let us say that we prefer warm and sunny weather and think that the best chance of getting that, out of all the places where we can go, will be in Provence. Going to Provence then becomes our goal, and we make plans about how to get there. No matter how much we plan the trip, we will have to leave to automatic processes a great deal of the mental work for achieving the necessary steps or sub-goals for getting there successfully. We must, for example, walk out to our car, start it up, drive off, identify the right route, and avoid any hazards on the way. These sub-goals themselves have sub-goals (that are achieved, say, by turning our heads and looking in a certain direction) that constitute the essential steps on the way to Provence.

People tend not to be as impressed as they should by their ability to achieve the basic goals we have been referring to as the sub-goals for going to Provence. The computer at the Automobile Association can perhaps plan our route over the roads in France better than we can at our conscious level of thought, but no existing computer can drive a car safely a very short distance on ordinary roads. No existing computer can even observe the traffic as well as we can, as a first step towards controlling a car properly. Our personal rationality, our ability to achieve goals, is seen at its very best in these basic abilities, including linguistic ones, which we would display by asking someone the directions and understanding the reply. By contrast, we may fail to attain some high level goal, such as starting a successful business to make enough money to retire to Provence, because we violate some impersonal normative principles. Perhaps we believe that interest rates will go down on grounds that are highly irrational$_2$, but that would not mean that we had failed to display rationality$_1$ in many of our basic actions. Just to start up a business, which is later to fail, we would have to accomplish successfully many basic sub-goals. The processes by which sub-goals are generated and achieved can operate at a tacit level, below the threshold of consciousness.

In the previous chapter we discussed the limitations of logic as a standard for how we ought to conduct our theoretical reasoning. Some would claim, however, that we have an adequate normative theory for how we ought to engage in practical thought, which is to do with achieving goals in our actions. Normative decision theory is sometimes seen as the standard for choosing goals to pursue and the best actions for trying to get them (for detailed exposition of formal decision theory, and its application to real world decision making, see von Winterfeldt & Edwards, 1986). Certainly this theory is more useful for this purpose than logic on its own, but there are a number of reasons why it also cannot provide a full account of rationality[1].

Decision theory tells us that we ought to *maximise subjective expected utility* in the choices we make. To simplify grossly, suppose that we have the ability to perform just one of two incompatible actions, such as turning left or turning right, each of which has a number of possible outcomes, such as getting to Provence by alternative routes in different times, depending on the traffic. To follow this theory explicitly, we begin by reflecting on our preferences among these outcomes. At the highest level, in this example, we have already determined that we prefer going to Provence rather than to any other place, and have decided to have that as our highest goal. Now we might prefer further to get there in the shortest possible time. From such preferences, utilities in the technical sense can be assigned to outcomes. These numbers are just a technical device and do not represent anything in the world or in our mental states, except the relative strength of our preferences. Nor does their use imply that our preferences are somehow explicitly labelled with numerals. In this example, the highest utility is to be assigned to the shortest time, and the lowest to the longest, with the utilities of the other times in between.

The next step for us to take, according to normative decision theory, is to make subjective judgements about the probability of each of the outcomes given each of the actions. Perhaps if we turn left and it rains, we will have the longest journey, as the traffic will slow down on busy roads. But if it does not rain, then turning left will get us to Provence in the shortest time. From the strength of our confidence that it will rain, a number between 0 and 1 can be assigned to represent our subjective belief in the proposition that it will rain. That is again a technical device that does not imply that our beliefs or propositional representations have explicit numerals attached to them. However, once we have the numbers for our utilities and the propositions we believe to some degree, we should multiply them together and add them up. Technically, subjective expected utility (SEU) is calculated by following the formula:

2.1
$$SEU = \sum_i s_i U_i$$

where s_i represents the subjective probability of the ith outcome and U_i represents its subjective utility, and where i ranges over a finite set of mutually exclusive and exhaustive outcomes. If we further have j possible actions open to us, we should—according to the principles of decision theory—compute the SEU for each of the actions and then choose an action that maximises SEU. That is, we choose the j option whose SEU computes to the highest positive quantity. Conventionally such reasoning is modelled via decision trees that have branches for actions we can control and different kinds of branches for outcomes whose probabilities we can only estimate.

Consider this normative approach in the case of our example. For turning left, we multiply our subjective probability that it will rain and the utility for us of having the longest journey, and then add that to what we get by multiplying our subjective probability that it will not rain and the utility for us of having the shortest journey time. This sum gives us the subjective expected utility of turning left. We go through the same process of multiplying and adding up to get the subjective expected utility for turning right. We maximise subjective expected utility by choosing the action with the highest sum. This may be turning left, and then according to normative decision theory, that is what we should choose to make our sub-goal at this point.

Even in such a simple example, matters can be more complex. We may fail to achieve our goal of turning left because trying to do so causes us to collide with a bus. To have taken this into account in our decision, we would have made judgements about the probabilities of having this accident when trying to turn left and alternatively when trying to turn right. The relevant utility in each case would be the cost to us of having the accident. Multiplying the appropriate probability and the utility, and adding the results to the sums for turning left and for turning right, might have given us a different answer. The new sum might show that we should turn right. Clearly, we cannot follow decision theory explicitly and consciously every time we have to turn left or right in car. Nor could preconscious implicit or tacit processes make calculations about every possibility that faces us in many of our choices.

We do, however, make some basic choices that conform to what normative decision theory would recommend, and as a matter of fact, other animals can do this. Even apparently primitive animals like bumble-bees are able to maximise, within certain constraints, the food energy they get in their foraging behaviour (Real, 1991). They learn to adjust this behaviour appropriately to the frequency with which they get a certain quality of food from particular sources. These bees have a need for food, process information about where to find it, and reliably get it. In the light of this, it is appropriate to say that the bees display goal-directed behaviour that is rational$_1$. Such behaviour could not of course be viewed as rational$_2$, because the bees do not have mental representations of probabilities or utilities to manipulate according to the principles of decision theory—they do not follow these principles in their behaviour and hence do not have a good reason for it in this sense.

Human foraging, and the sharing of food collected, can be equally efficient, though naturally far more complex (Cosmides & Tooby, 1992). Human beings will learn where to go to have a good chance of finding high quality food, and can communicate this information directly to each other (as can honey-bees to some extent). Again, if people could not do this sort of thing reasonably well, satisfying their basic desires, such as ones for food, with the help of their beliefs about the world, it would not make sense to say that they had desires and beliefs at all. Human beings, unlike bees, can usually give some kind of verbal report about their real life goals: they have explicit knowledge, say, that they are trying to find food. Their knowledge of the processes that help them to achieve these goals, such as those that produce reliable perception of the world and help them to learn from it, is usually much more restricted. Like the bees we rely largely on implicit processes in our perception and much of our learning. To help us learn how to satisfy many of our basic desires to a reasonable extent, we do not have to have mental representations of probabilities and utilities, make calculations at any given point of all the possibilities before us, nor rely just on explicit learning. Tacit or implicit processing is highly characteristic of this kind of personal rationality, and can sometimes comply with decision theoretic principles without following them, by producing the same outcome in a different way.

PROBLEMS WITH NORMATIVE DECISION THEORY

To say that human beings and other animals sometimes comply with normative decision theory is obviously not to say that they can always do this, and still less that they can often do it explicitly by following rules. In the terms we are introducing in this book, this normative theory could only give us another version of rationality$_2$. We will show that it is both too strong in some respects and too weak in others to capture our notion of rationality$_1$. To begin with, it sets standards that are far too high for our probability judgements or degrees of belief; indeed its standards here could be said to be infinitely high. This follows from its requirement that these judgements satisfy the principles of probability theory, which requires in turn that all logical true propositions have a probability of one. There are infinitely many logical truths, and there is no effective way of deciding, beyond propositional logic, whether an arbitrary proposition is a logical truth or not. Similarly, the conclusion of any valid argument would have to have a probability of one given its premises. Probability theory depends on logic and inherits all its impossibly high abstract ideals.

Constrained knowledge and the problem of invariance

Normative decision theory presupposes that we know all the actions that are within our power, and all the possible states of affairs or worlds that could result from performing them. But we cannot be expected to have this knowledge most of the time in ordinary affairs. Some of our own abilities are so hidden from us that extensive scientific research would be required to get an idea of what they are. There are also unlimited possible consequences, impossible for us to anticipate in advance, of even very simple actions. Moreover, we are not always able, before we make ordinary decisions, to give precise preferences among the possible outcomes of our actions we do know about. Our preferences are not always the expression of immediate drives, but sometimes have themselves to be inferred from complex moral, legal, or other reasoning. Even if these other problems did not exist, we have already illustrated that we cannot make efficient choices in real time (even simple ones like whether to turn left or right in a car) by applying normative decision theory. We can learn to conform to this theory, without ever following its rules for manipulating propositions and making calculations, in simple but important cases. That is why most of us can turn left or right safely. In general, however, we cannot live up to the highest standards of this theory.

The theory also presupposes that people's preferences have a property that has been called invariance, which means that these preferences are not affected by how the outcomes are described (Tversky & Kahneman, 1986). It is obviously wrong to make invariance too strong a requirement. Suppose we are asked whether we prefer our best friend to get a kick or our worst enemy to get one. It would be easy to say that we prefer the latter, but if we are then told that we are our own worst enemies, we would change our preference. This should not happen given a strong invariance standard, as this preference has depended on how an object—ourselves in this case—has been described. The point is that people cannot be reasonably expected to tell, in all cases, when two linguistic or mental representations refer to the same object or outcome in the real world. They also cannot be expected to tell when any two representations necessarily refer to the same outcome, as there is no way to decide generally whether two statements are logically equivalent.

People's tendency to violate any invariance requirement will depend on how they represent objects and outcomes. They will tend to have less trouble if these are presented to them perceptually. Their preference for not colliding with a bus, for example, will not usually be affected by their visual point of view. Seeing a bus from different angles or perspectives does not make it any more or less desirable as an object to run into. But it is often far from easy to identify the referent of a term like "one's worst enemy". We should expect fewer violations of invariance when people are expressing preferences for basic goals, achieved in simple actions, rather than higher level ones, described only in language.

Bounded rationality and satisficing

The founders of normative decision theory knew that they were proposing an idealised standard for rationality (Savage, 1954). However, not all their followers in economics, psychology, and other social sciences spoke as if this were so, and it was in response to them, in part, that Simon (1957, 1983) introduced what he called "bounded rationality". We have been influenced by Simon in our view of normative decision theory as far too strong to be the standard of rationality$_1$ in ordinary decision making. To accept it as the only measure of rationality would itself violate the principle that "ought" implies "can", as moral philosophers say. It is impossible for people to live up to such a standard all the time, and so they can hardly be required to do so. Sometimes people can do no better than to have vague preferences, based on just partial knowledge of what their language refers to, and can only make vague and limited probability judgements. Sometimes they can only consider a very restricted number of the options before them, and choose one that is reasonably satisfying. That is, they have an understandable tendency to aim at what is *satisficing*, to use the technical term, rather than what is maximal (see Slote, 1989, on satisficing). Learning often helps us to get satisficing outcomes, without requiring calculations that are really beyond us.

A good example of satisficing has been discovered in some recent studies of engineering design processes using observational methods and studying engineers working on real design problems (Ball, 1990; Ball, Evans, & Dennis, 1994). The study was focused on electronic engineers in the early and high level of design rather than on implementation. Engineering design is a very complex process involving the search of large problem spaces to satisfy typically ill-defined goals. To make things more difficult, the technical design problems are constrained by a number of practical considerations including cost, time, customer and market needs. Although expert engineers adopted more efficient breadth-first approaches to design, in common with the less experienced designers in Ball's studies they rarely attempted to optimise solutions to any of the many sub-problems they generated, settling instead for any solution that was simply good enough. We believe this to be representative of effective problem solving and decision making in the real world.

Confidence, calibrations and the principal principle

Not only is normative decision theory too strong to describe real decision making, but in other respects it is too weak. For example, whilst it is too strong in always requiring our probability judgements to be coherent, i.e. to satisfy probability theory, on the other hand it allows them to be totally subjective: our subjective probability judgements do not have to correspond even approximately to objective probabilities, i.e. chances or frequencies. We have satisfied the normative theory by choosing the course of action with the highest subjective expected utility for us, even if there is no objective chance that we will get what we want by performing this action. This would be so even though, by ordinary standards, we should have known about this objective probability. With absurd optimism, we can be highly confident that the safest way to drive is with our eyes closed, and still be rational by this theory.

For a better account of rationality, one might hope to add to normative decision theory good rules for finding out about objective chances or frequencies, and then for basing subjective probability judgements on these. There is a rule for relating objective probability to subjective probability, much discussed by philosophers of science, that is usually called the "principal principle" (Howson & Urbach, 1993). Given that a coin is fair—i.e. one with an objective probability of 0.5 of coming up heads when spun—this principle tells us that our subjective confidence that it will come up heads on some particular occasion should equal 0.5. Given that the coin is biased, with a higher or lower objective probability of coming up heads when spun, the principle would tell us that our subjective confidence should be equally high or low that this will happen at some point.

The principal principle thus tells us what subjective confidence to have about an outcome of a single case, such as the spinning of a coin at some particular time and place, given some supposition about the objective properties of the coin. These properties of the coin determine the general chance that, or frequency with which, it will come up one way or the other when spun again and again. We might make the supposition that the coin is fair, and then spin it again and again. Following the principal principle, our confidence that it will come up heads each time should be 0.5. Of course, the coin may not have a tendency to come up heads half the time, but in that case, we can systematically lower our confidence in the statement that the coin is fair. We are told how to do this by a result in probability theory known as Bayes' theorem, which we shall discuss in more detail later in this chapter.

Researchers on reasoning have not so far investigated whether people conform to the principal principle in their inferences about probability. Related to this question, however, is extensive research on subjective confidence in the literature on decision making and probability judgement. In that research, people would be said to be well calibrated about a coin that tended to come up heads half the time, if their subjective probability judgement that it would do so on each occasion equalled 0.5. They would be said to be overconfident, or underconfident, about this coin coming up heads, if they thought it was more likely, or less likely, than 0.5 to come up heads. There is much research on the extent to which people are overconfident or underconfident at times, and controversy about how far these tendencies show anything about their rationality (Gigerenzer, Hoffrage, & Kleinbölting, 1991; Griffin & Tversky, 1992; McClelland & Bolger, 1994). Unfortunately, most of this research does not directly address the question of how being well calibrated, or being overconfident or underconfident, in real life affects people's ability to achieve their ordinary goals.

There is evidence that entrepreneurs are more confident of the success of their own enterprises than would seem to be justified, on the basis of the principal principle, by their knowledge of the failure rate for similar enterprises (Cooper, Woo, & Dunkelberg, 1988; Griffin & Tversky, 1992). However, it is unclear if these people are actually violating the principal principle, or how their apparent overconfidence is affecting their attempts to succeed. As we have already indicated, any overconfidence could not have affected their ability to attain many of the basic sub-goals necessary to starting and running businesses. Moreover, one should not assume that it is always rational[1] to be well calibrated. Overconfidence at least can perhaps be justified in some circumstances. Being highly confident that one is going to recover from a life threatening illness, for instance, may actually increase the objective chance that one will get better, though perhaps not to a level as high as one's confidence. Trying to be more realistic in such a case and well calibrated may progressively decrease one's chance of recovery, by making one more and more depressed. Continuing to pursue realism might cause increasing depression that might in turn have an increasingly adverse effect on one's chance of recovery. Of course, a few people might have realism as their only relevant goal, but for those whose only aim was good health, getting into such a vicious circle would not be rational$_1$. It would be better for them to ignore or forget what they knew about the objective probability of recovery.

Some research does suggest that a lack of realism about some matters can be beneficial, and that depression is associated with greater realism and "mental health" with some unrealistic optimism (Ackerman & DeRubeis, 1991; Taylor & Brown, 1988). Now one must be careful not to assume that depression is invariably a bad thing. It may be that a dynamic combination of initial overconfidence, with the drive this supplies, and then more realism if we fail to reach a goal, so that we can set our sights lower the next time, is often the best way to reach many ordinary goals. For this reason, mild depression after a failure in life could have its advantages, making us indeed "sadder but wiser". Physical pain has the benefit of helping us to avoid physical injury, and it may be that some mental pain, in the form of depression, has an analogous function for our cognitive states. People could have some tendency to overconfidence or depression because these states were adaptive, and these could still have some benefits for us.

Of course, in many cases realism about objective chances is indisputably advantageous, and research does show that people can, sometimes with little or no conscious attention, be good at recording frequencies in the real world (Hasher & Zacks, 1984). It is interesting that the evidence of overconfidence which is frequently claimed in the psychological literature (see Lichtenstein, Fischhoff, & Phillips, 1982) is based on experiments in which people make explicit judgements about probability. Studies of implicit learning of probabilities, by contrast, show that people can learn very rapidly and accurately the contingencies to which they are exposed (see Reber, 1993). It is of course the implicit or tacit cognitive system that we view as the main source of rational$_1$ behaviour. The ability to detect contingencies and covariations is also shared by most animals whose survival may depend upon detection of the inherent predictability of events in their environment. Gigerenzer (e.g. 1993) has argued that for evolutionary reasons we are good judges of frequency but not of probabilities of individual events. He shows, even on quantitative word problems requiring explicit judgements, that performance can be greatly enhanced by when problems are expressed or judgement required in frequency rather than single-case terms.

Subjective goals and personal rationality

Normative decision theory has also been attacked for being too weak on the grounds that it does not give us the means to evaluate our ordinary goals and their relation to our preferences (Sen, 1990). Can a serial killer, for example, be called completely rational if his preference is for murdering people and he chooses the optimal way of doing this? The totally personal view of rationality would accept that he can be. Of course, his goal could be condemned on other grounds, e.g. its cruelty, and it may be important for the police to think of his having personal rationality so that they do not underestimate him. Still, it is hard to accept that any goal, no matter how bizarre, can be rational in every sense, and this is a place where $rational_2$ principles may be appropriate. These principles would obviously go far beyond deductive logic, which cannot tell us that any goal is irrational.

The other point is that our longer-term goals may not be reflected in our short-term choices, which are usually taken in the application of decision theory to reveal our preferences. Our goal of good health, for example, might be in conflict with our apparent day-to-day preference for cigarettes. Although we want to be happy, we might discount the future, living only for the moment, and fail to grasp what will make us happy next week or next year. It may well be that we have some limitations in our thought of this type (Kahneman, 1994). No obvious evolutionary argument implies that this is not so, as it is unclear how our reproductive success under primitive conditions depended on our longer-term feelings of well-being. Normative decision theory on its own does not condemn as irrational a weakness for immediate gratification, and in this respect also, it can be criticised for being too weak.

We do not begin by defining $rationality_1$ in a way that makes it too strong or too weak. We see this personal rationality as a property that comes in degrees: it is something that be improved on. Sometimes impersonal principles from logic and decision theory are appropriate, and advice can be given on when and how to apply them (Evans, 1989). Further research on well-being may lead to discoveries that can be applied in particular cases to increase feelings of well-being, for those who want to do this (Strack, Argyle, & Schwarz, 1990). What we wish to point out is how often people display $rationality_1$ in attaining fundamental goals in ordinary affairs. We are not thinking of grand ends that embody lifelong ambitions, nor even of longer-term goals, such as getting a university degree, that are part of these. We are thinking of the "modest" steps necessary for any of the higher level ends. We have already given examples of these lower level, but vitally important sub-goals: the ones accomplished by looking at and classifying objects, performing actions that modify the objects in some way, working together in co-operative groups, and communicating with each other.

We often attain these goals without following any general rules, and sometimes without being conscious of the options before us, our preferences, or our probability judgements. Of course, we are sometimes aware, even for such simple goals, of choosing between a few options, but these can be immediately presented to our conscious minds as the relevant ones. The preconscious and almost automatic processes responsible for all this, perhaps after a period of learning, can be highly efficient as we have already pointed out. This is understandable from a biological point of view, as achieving such goals was clearly necessary for reproductive success in early hominids, apes, primates, and before. It is much harder to argue that the explicit application of many impersonal rules would have facilitated reproductive success in human beings under primitive conditions (see Reber, 1993, for an evolutionary argument for what he calls the primacy of the implicit).

EPISTEMIC GOALS AND UTILITY

At this point we need to expand our notion of the goals that people seek, to deal with the requirements of theoretical as well as practical reasoning. Although acquiring a belief is not the same as performing an action, people often have goals to do with the acquisition of knowledge or at least well supported beliefs, i.e. they have epistemic goals. They try to attain these goals through many sub-goals that directly require actions. Some of these are basic actions that can be performed even by simple animals, such as looking around to gather visual information, while others are aimed at gathering data about explicitly formulated hypotheses. All these actions can be led by conscious principles, but also depend on many automatic, implicit, and preconscious processes. Observation clearly requires such processes, but so does inference. To infer whether a hypothesis is probably true, for example, people try to gather evidence that is relevant to and informative about it (some of the psychological evidence concerning the way in which people do this is discussed in Chapters 4 and 5). When they are performing an inference to answer some question, they try to use all their relevant beliefs as premises. Many judgements about what is relevant and informative take place preconsciously and automatically (see Chapter 3). Sometimes we do make a conscious decision to try to remember beliefs that have these epistemic values of relevance and informativeness for some inference we want to perform, but even then we have little conscious awareness of how we bring these beliefs to mind. All we are conscious of is trying to remember such beliefs and then, if we are lucky, succeeding.

Reasoning from uncertain belief
As we pointed out in Chapter 1, people's ordinary inferences are almost always based on beliefs they take to be relevant, or what they are told by other people, and not on arbitrary assumptions. They also have to

take account in their reasoning of how confident they are in any beliefs they use as premises, or in what they are told. Logic is of limited help to them because its valid inference forms begin with arbitrary premises that are to be assumed to be true. Rejecting a narrow Popperian philosophy of science, as we did in Chapter 1, we could consider what is called a Bayesian view as a normative alternative (Howson & Urbach, 1993). This allows us to speak of confirming or disconfirming hypotheses—i.e. of giving them higher subjective probability, or lower, depending on the available evidence. More generally, the decision theory we have already described is Bayesian, at least to the extent of ascribing subjective probabilities to propositions. This extended normative theory can be of more help in everyday affairs. People do need to know how confident they can be in any conclusion they draw from premises that are probably and not certainly true—i.e. from beliefs or other premises that are uncertain to some degree.

As also discussed in Chapter 1, the uncertainty of the conclusion of a valid inference should not exceed the sum of the uncertainties of the premises. This can be a helpful principle to use explicitly at times, and although ordinary people can hardly be expected to do that, there is evidence that they implicitly adjust the confidence they have in conclusions of valid arguments to any uncertainty in the premises (George, 1995—see Chapter 5; Stevenson & Over, 1995).

The following principle from probability theory can sometimes be used to find the exact confidence one should have in one's conclusion:

2.2 $Prob(C) = Prob(P).Prob(C/P) + Prob(not\text{-}P).Prob(C/not\text{-}P)$

Here, Prob(C) is the subjective probability one should judge the conclusion of an inference to have, Prob(P) and Prob(not-P) are the subjective probabilities of the conjunction of the premises and of the negation of that conjunction, and Prob(C/P) and Prob(C/not-P) are conditional subjective probabilities. Using a valid inference, we know that Prob(C/P) = 1, but, in daily life, we can rarely make precise judgements about all the other probabilities. Ordinary people do not explicitly use or follow 2.2 in their reasoning, but they might effectively comply with it in cases where they have learned the relevant probabilities. As an example, suppose that you are in Plymouth expecting two visitors each travelling from Exeter, and that you hold the following premises:

1.   It is quicker to travel from Exeter to Plymouth by car than by train.
2.   Mr Jones is travelling by car.

3.   Mr Smith is travelling by train.
4.   Mr Smith and Mr Jones left Exeter at the same time.

A justified inference would be that Mr Jones will arrive before Mr Smith. However, no one would draw such a conclusion with certainty. Even supposing you were sure of premises 2–4 you could never be sure of 1. It is true in general, as you may know from personal experience, but of course cars can break down, have accidents, or be held up in traffic jams. In this case your degree of belief in the conclusion would be directly affected by your confidence in premise 1. Of course, things get more complex if other premises are questioned as well. Here we have to consider also the probability of the conclusion if the premises are *not* true. Suppose you are unsure of premise 3, and think it is possible that Smith may drive. However, your personal knowledge is that Jones is the faster driver so perhaps your confidence in the conclusion does not drop.

A very special case is where Prob(P) = 1 as well; then Prob(not-P) = 0 and the principle tells us a conclusion is certain if it follows validly from certain premises. Most psychological experiments on deductive reasoning are, in effect, about this special case. Subjects in these experiments are in actual fact almost never certain of the premises. But they are asked to assume the truth of the premises, and to ignore anything else, which would include a belief they had about the negation of the premises. Because people rarely have use for this kind of imaginary procedure in the real world, we should not be too surprised if subjects find it hard to follow such instructions, especially when on independent grounds they do have reason to disbelieve the premises (see Chapter 5 on "Prior belief" for discussion of "belief bias" effects in reasoning).

Diagnosticity and pseudo-diagnosticity

Bayes' theorem is another principle from probability theory, related to 2.2, and whether people conform to it has been far more extensively investigated. We shall explain aspects of this theorem informally here, leaving a more formal presentation to Chapter 5 where evidence for Bayesian reasoning in the psychological literature is also discussed in some detail. Informally, Bayes' theorem can be taken to prescribe how much confidence one should have in a hypothesis, after getting some evidence about it, given one's earlier confidence in this hypothesis and the diagnosticity of the evidence. Evidence is diagnostic to the extent that it is informative in distinguishing the hypothesis from its negation.

Suppose we are asked to find out whether a coin is fair or biased. We are initially given no reason to expect it to be the one or the other; we are to gather evidence ourselves for reaching a conclusion. We spin the coin five times and get heads all five times. Bayes' theorem tells us to consider the following:

2.3
$$\frac{Prob \ (E \mid H)}{Prob \ (E \mid not\text{-}H)}$$

H is the hypothesis that the coin is fair and not-H the alternative that it is biased; E is the evidence that the coin has been spun five times and come up heads each time. The principal principle tells us to make Prob(E/H), i.e. the probability, which is also called the likelihood, that the coin comes up all heads in this sequence of spins given that it is fair, equal to approximately 0.03. We might well be puzzled about Prob(E/not-H), the probability, or likelihood, that there is this sequence given that the coin is biased, because there are infinitely many ways in which it could be biased. However, context could tell us that this probability is at least relatively high, by suggesting, for example, that the coin may be so far biased towards heads that it could be used to cheat people effectively. On this basis, Bayes' theorem tells us to conclude that the probability is relatively high that the coin is biased given this evidence.

This appears quite intuitive and a conclusion that most people could come to, without doing all the calculations asked for by Bayes' theorem. That may indeed be so, but research suggests that people do not always ask for information about Prob(E/not-H), to add to what they are told about Prob(E/H), in order to evaluate the probability of some hypothesis H (Doherty, Mynatt, Tweney, & Schiavo, 1979). Instead subjects are observed to ask for more information about the same hypothesis, an effect which Doherty et al. refer to as "pseudo-diagnostic" reasoning and relate to the notion that people have a general confirmation bias in their reasoning.

In the Doherty et al. (1979) study, subjects were told to imagine that they were undersea explorers who had discovered a pot that they wished to return to its homeland—one of two islands. They were given a list of characteristics of the pot, such as that it had a curved handle, and permitted to seek six pieces of information, each in the form of the likelihood of a specified characteristic E being found on a pot from either island. That is, the subjects could ask about Prob(E/H) and Prob(E/not-H), where E is that a pot has a curved handle and H is the hypothesis that the pot comes from one of the islands and not-H that it comes from the other. In order to obtain diagnostic information, subjects should seek evidence about half of the characteristics with respect to both islands: they should find out about both Prob(E/H) and

Prob(E/not-H) so that they can get some idea of the ratio 2.3. However, subjects tended to form an early hypothesis favouring one island or the other and then mostly asked about that island—i.e. they tended to ask only about Prob(E/H) and not about Prob(E/not-H) as well. In a paper that replicates and extends these findings in a different domain, Mynatt, Doherty, and Dragan (1993) make the surprising and profound claim that "people can only think about one hypothesis at a time". We discuss the Mynatt et al. study in depth in Chapter 3 where we interpret its findings in the context of relevance theory.

Let us accept for the sake of argument that people do indeed consider only one hypothesis at a time and often reason in a pseudo-diagnostic manner. Clearly this is irrational$_2$ as judged by the standard of Bayes' theorem. Why might this occur? One possibility is that in real life people may normally hold prior, background beliefs about Prob(E/not-H), and for that reason not think to ask about this in an experiment. There may also be limitations on working memory that make it difficult for people to think about both Prob(E/H) and Prob(E/not-H), or what is relevant to each, at the same time (as Mynatt et al. suggest). There is also evidence for a general positivity bias in reasoning (Evans, 1989), which can be given a rational$_1$ interpretation, as we shall see in later chapters. In general, people focus on what is syntactically or semantically positive rather than negative, and upon what is probably true rather than probably false. This often makes sense, though it can lead to error and may form the basis of both "matching bias" in conditional reasoning (see Chapter 3) and confirmation biases (see Chapter 5). It would certainly make psychologically difficult the Bayesian requirement to consider the likelihood of the evidence given that the hypothesis under consideration is false.

Epistemic utility

When people seek to fulfil their epistemic goals, they must be motivated by some kind of pay-off. We refer to this as epistemic utility. (For a philosophical discussion of epistemic utility, see Levi, 1984.) Now if an epistemic goal is to check the accuracy of one's beliefs, then actions and evidence that satisfy this goal must have epistemic utility. Two questions immediately arise—a normative one and a descriptive one. What is the best measure of epistemic utility? What do people actually tend to place epistemic value on? The former question is obviously the normative one, while the latter is about people's subjective epistemic utility.

For discriminating a hypothesis from its negation, one answer to the normative question is information yield defined as the absolute log likelihood ratio:

2.4

$$ABS\left[LOG\left\{\frac{Prob\,(E\,/\,H)}{Prob\,(E\,/\,not\text{-}H)}\right\}\right]$$

The above is the result of taking the logarithm (say to the base 2) of 2.3, which is called the likelihood ratio, and then the absolute value of that, which ensures that the final result is a positive number. This number is a technical way of measuring how diagnostic the evidence E is here—i.e. how informative E is in discriminating between the hypothesis H and its negation not-H. Return to our example about the coin. Intuitively, it is far more probable that the coin will come up heads every time in five spins given that it is strongly biased to heads than given that it is fair. If that is so, actually spinning the coin five times and getting all heads should be highly diagnostic or informative—i.e. give us much greater reason to believe that the coin is strongly biased than that it is fair. This intuitive judgement will be reflected in the relatively high number that comes out of 2.4. Recall that, in this example, H is the hypothesis that the coin is fair and not-H that it is strongly biased, and let E be the evidence that there have been five heads in five spins of the coin. A relatively low probability for Prob(E/H) and a relatively high one for Prob(E/not-H) gives a relatively high number for the diagnosticity or informativeness of E from 2.4. (See Kullback, 1959, and Klayman & Ha, 1987, for how to use the log likelihood ratio to measure information or diagnosticity.)

So by the measure 2.4, evidence is more informative for you, the greater the extent to which it would lead you to revise your belief. Evidence is least informative when the likelihood ratio is one and the logarithmic transformation assigns zero in this case. The absolute transformation ensures that informativeness is symmetrical—i.e. that it matters not whether the diagnosticity favours H or not-H. The information will increase as the probabilities move away from 0.5 and towards 1 or 0 where this measure becomes, somewhat inconveniently, infinite. But that is not really a problem if one holds, as do many Bayesians, that the only propositions that should be assigned 1 or 0 are logical truths and logical falsehoods, respectively. We adopt this view, and so think that no apparent observations should give an empirical hypothesis a probability of 1 or of 0, because our eyes or any equipment we use can never be absolutely reliable. By saying that an empirical proposition has been verified or falsified (refuted), we mean only that it has a *probability* close to 1 or to 0.

If rationality$_1$ requires that people are motivated by epistemic utility, and if this in turn is defined by 2.4, then does not the evidence of pseudo-diagnosticity described above immediately prove that people are irrational$_1$? No. First of all, it is rational$_1$ for people to seek to fulfil all goals, not just epistemic goals. It may often be the case that other non-epistemic goals will conflict with epistemic ones. For example, as we have suggested above, it may be more important for some people, in some circumstances, to maintain self-confidence or self-esteem than to satisfy any epistemic principle. A necessary goal is to minimise processing effort, and seeking evidence on the alternative to our hypothesis can be difficult to combine with this, for reasons we discussed earlier. We may, however, be skilled at seeking those forms of evidence that are unlikely to occur unless our hypothesis is true. There is also evidence from Mynatt et al. (1993) themselves, that when subjects are asked to gather evidence on which to choose an action, rather than to evaluate a hypothesis, then they are much more likely to choose diagnostic information (although an alternative interpretation of this finding is offered in Chapter 3). This trend supports our general argument that people are better, by the highest normative standards, at practical rather than theoretical reasoning not directed at a practical goal.

We must also be careful not to assume that people are invariably pseudo-diagnostic simply on the basis of experiments such as those reported by Mynatt, Doherty, and colleagues. We shall see several examples in this book where experiments using quantitative word problems do not produce generalisable results, as already discussed in the case of probability learning calibration. It may be that tacit processing of evidence takes more account of diagnosticity than suggested by responses to explicit decision tasks. We return to the problem of belief revision, confirmation bias, and the like in Chapter 5.

As a matter of fact, our concept of subjective epistemic utility is much richer psychologically than can be captured by 2.4. That can only be laid down as an impersonal normative standard, though as we have seen, it has some basis in intuitive judgement, like all the best standards. People's subjective probabilities are generally too vague to be placed in an equation like 2.4. The value of information for them is also too vague, variable, and broad for any such fixed measure. People's subjective epistemic utility is affected by their whole set of relevant beliefs, and not just by a particular hypothesis that they may be considering. For example, discarding or updating a belief could be too costly if its consequence was to introduce a damaging inconsistency into some complex theory that was useful for attaining goals. It might even be best, as Harman (1986, pp. 15–16) has argued, for people to tolerate an inconsistency in such a theory if they cannot decide how to modify it to avoid this. People's non-epistemic goals affect how much value they place on any given amount of diagnosticity or information. Some evidence of fixed diagnosticity, by 2.4, may have high subjective utility for people in one context, where it confirms a hypothesis telling them how to get what they want, but not in another, when their epistemic or non-epistemic goals have changed. Of course, people do sometimes have the goal of discriminating a hypothesis from its negation without any other conflicting goals, and then subjective epistemic value for them may roughly correspond to that given by 2.4.

CONCLUSIONS

In this chapter we have discussed in some detail the relation between normative decision theory and rationality$_1$. Our view is that Bayesian decision theory provides a rational$_2$ framework that does not do much better at describing rational$_1$ decision making than formal logic does for rational$_1$ reasoning (see Chapter 1). As we have shown, this decision theory is both too strong and too weak to give an adequate account of personal rationality, and it is often impossible to apply in ordinary affairs.

Impersonal normative systems, which make no reference to individual goals, are laid down by abstract thinkers who themselves have goals in mind. Thus logic as a formal system can be seen as a way of specifying inference forms that will preserve truth from arbitrary assumptions. But the goals of ordinary people may be such that they have little use for inferences from a restricted set of premises thought of as, in effect, certainly true. Sometimes the explicit use of formal logic and of decision theory can help to achieve ordinary goals, and so we are not saying that these impersonal normative systems have no use outside abstract academic subjects. But as we have illustrated in this chapter, the development of normative theories of rationality is not at an end: there are still problems about how to do the best for ourselves in achieving some of our goals. Reflecting on people's successful practical thought and reasoning is itself a way of extending normative theories of how we ought to do these things (Over & Manktelow, 1993).

Of course, ordinary people do often engage in theoretical reasoning with the object of expanding their true beliefs, and so we have introduced the concept of epistemic utility. It is debatable what normative system should define this concept for scientific purposes, let alone what people's subjective epistemic values are really like. Now that we have introduced the complication of belief systems, as opposed to individual hypotheses, it should be apparent that a major difficulty ensues. How can we know which of our vast stores of beliefs are actually needed to deal with the problem at hand? How can we retrieve and consider a sufficiently small number that it becomes feasible to reason and make decisions in a manner that is both tractable and appropriate? This is the problem of relevance, to which the next chapter is devoted.

CHAPTER THREE

Relevance, rationality, and tacit processing

In the previous chapters, we have introduced our basic thesis that people's reasoning and decision making help them to achieve their basic goals within cognitive constraints. Rationality$_1$ is not an all or nothing matter: it comes in degrees. People will tend to be more rational in this sense in their practical thought about basic goals and sub-goals, than in their theoretical reasoning that is not directly related to practical goals. They will tend to be better at achieving their goals when they are relying on basic, preconscious processes, such as those that process visual information, than when relying on the explicit use of representations in their conscious reasoning, where their cognitive constraints can be serious. This view of rationality is the first of two basic theoretical foundations for the arguments advanced in this book. The second is that all human thought is highly subject to what we term relevance effects. For us this means that people reason only about a highly selective representation of problem information and prior knowledge, and that this selection is determined preconsciously. This idea connects with what some other authors in the field are describing as "focusing", as we shall see.

The purpose of this chapter is to explore this notion of relevance and associated issues. In particular we consider the extent to which reasoning and decision making are determined by conscious and unconscious processes. We also begin to explore the relationship between relevance and rationality.

RELEVANCE AND RATIONALITY

Relevance and pragmatics

There is a difference between relevance and what has been called "the principle of relevance". Both concepts have origins in the study of pragmatics—the study of how people use their background beliefs and their understanding of each other to communicate successfully. Grice (1975, 1989) pointed out that it is only possible to understand discourse by going beyond what can be logically derived from it, and that communication is generally a goal-directed activity in which those taking part co-operate to achieve common ends. For instance, an underlying reason for a group to communicate might be the building of a house, and to do that, ideas about the design would have to be shared and orders for materials issued before the necessary sub-goals could be achieved (cf. Wittgenstein, 1953). In our terms, Grice held that people display a high degree of rationality$_1$ when they communicate with each other. He argued that speakers and hearers could understand each other well because each presumed the other to be acting in line with a set of informal pragmatic maxims or principles. For example, a hearer expects a speaker to be as informative as is required to attain their presupposed goal but no more so.

One of Grice's maxims is "be relevant". This idea was developed into the principle of relevance by Sperber and Wilson (1986) and ceased to be a maxim in Grice's sense. Sperber and Wilson argued that all acts of communication, whether by speech, gesture, or other means, carry a guarantee of relevance from the communicator to the audience. It is fairly easy to show that we would have little chance of communicating with one another without this principle. Let us consider some example utterances:

3.1   I am going out now. The cakes will be ready in half an hour.

3.2   A: I don't think I will bother to take my raincoat.
      B: They're forecasting rain for this afternoon.

The speaker of 3.1 produces two utterances which, in purely linguistic terms, are entirely unconnected. However, the speaker would be violating relevance if the two sentences were indeed unrelated. An utterance such as 3.1 would probably occur in a context where the speaker had cakes baking in an oven and would be out at the time they were due to finish. So the communication to the listener is really to the effect that he/she should take the cake out of the oven in half and hour's time.

Sperber and Wilson reinforce Grice's view that understanding communication goes way beyond what people could logically extract from the content of statements made. In particular, they develop the notion of "mutual manifestness". The cognitive environment for an individual consists of facts that are manifest. A fact is manifest if the individual is capable of representing it mentally. In the case of utterance 3.1, manifest facts might include (a) that the listener was present when the cakes were put in the oven, (b) the smell of cooking cakes, or (c) an earlier conversation in which the speaker has told the listener that he/she will need to take the cakes out. A relevant discourse takes account of what is mutually manifest in the cognitive environment. In this case it may be mutually manifest that there was a similar previous occasion on which the listener forgot the cakes and they burnt. This would permit the speaker to add some additional comment such as "Remember what happened last time" whilst maintaining relevance.

In example 3.2, the relevance of weather is established by the utterance of A, even though no explicit reference to weather is made. This is because A has raised the issue of whether to take a raincoat and it is mutually manifest that such decisions are normally based on judgements about the weather. The reply of B which relays the weather forecast is not only therefore relevant in the context established but also communicates an implicature of advice to A that A should in fact take the raincoat. Again, it is perfectly clear that without these pragmatic principles the discourse in 3.2 makes no sense. There is no purely semantic analysis that can connect the two sentences.

The distinction between language comprehension and explicit deductive inference is hazy indeed. As our examples indicate, all discourse comprehension calls for inferences, often of an implicit nature. In a deductive reasoning task, of course, subjects are instructed explicitly to draw inferences. However, they are presented with sentences that have to be understood. These will be subject to the same kinds of influence of pragmatic factors as we have already discussed. Then there is the question of whether instructions for explicit reasoning do indeed elicit a conscious deductive process of a different nature from that of implicit inference. This may be the case (we return to this problem in Chapter 6) but we would argue that the cognitive representations to which such processes are applied are both highly selective and preconsciously determined.

Sperber and Wilson's theory is intended not simply as a pragmatic theory of communication but as a general theory of cognitive processing. This is made clearer by the recent reformulation of the theory (see, for example, Sperber, Cara, & Girotto, 1995) in which two principles of relevance are distinguished as follows:

The first (cognitive) principle of relevance:
Human cognitive processes are aimed at processing the most relevant information in the most relevant way.
The second (communicative) principle of relevance:
Every utterance conveys a presumption of its own relevance.

Note that the second principle corresponds to what was previously described as *the* principle of relevance. Sperber et al. also provide the following definition of relevance:

- The greater the cognitive *effect* resulting from processing the information, the greater the relevance.
- The greater the processing *effort* required for processing the information, the lesser the relevance.

In support of this cognitive theory of relevance, Sperber et al. (1995) present a new interpretation of work on the Wason selection task, which is discussed in Chapter 4. We agree broadly with their approach and in particular the emphasis upon processing effort, which is one of the bounding conditions on rational thought. However, following Evans (1989), our use of the term "relevance"—unless otherwise indicated—refers to more generally what determines the focus of subjects' attention or the content of thought. Our basic idea is that explicit or conscious thinking is focused on highly selected representations which appear "relevant" but that this relevance is determined mostly by preconscious and tacit processes. This notion of relevance is related to, but subtly different from, that of availability in reasoning.

The availability heuristic was introduced by Tversky and Kahneman (1973) in order to account for judgements of frequency and probability. It was argued that people judge frequency by the ease with which examples can be "brought to mind" and that psychological factors influencing availability result in a number of cognitive biases. This idea of availability has also been applied to reasoning, for example by Pollard (1982) who argued that both the salience of presented information and the retrieval of associated knowledge could influence response on reasoning tasks. However, there are a number of examples in the reasoning literature that show that the availability of information does not necessarily influence responding. A good example is the so-called base rate fallacy, which we discuss in detail in Chapter 5. In this case the base rate statistic is presented in tasks requiring posterior probability judgement, but not seen as relevant in the standard versions of the problem, and thus disregarded by most subjects. Thus availability is necessary but not sufficient for relevance. Note that the concept of availability is broadly equivalent to manifestness in Sperber and Wilson's system.

Relevance and tacit processing

Evans (1989) presented a discussion of preconsciously cued relevance in order to account for biases in reasoning. By "bias" we mean systematic errors relative to some impersonal normative standard, such as that of formal logic or probability theory. This work, presented prior to the analysis of Evans (1993a), made little reference to the issue of rationality. In our present terminology, biases—by definition—limit rationality$_2$. Whether they limit rationality$_1$ also, however, is a moot question and one to which we will devote much attention in this book. In general, we shall argue that many biases reflect processes that are adaptive in the real world if not in the laboratory—a good example being the belief bias effect discussed in Chapter 5. Where biases do not appear to be goal-serving in a natural setting, they may reflect some basic cognitive constraints on human information-processing ability.

The Evans (1989) work was based upon application of the "heuristic-analytic" (H-A) theory of reasoning. This theory was originally presented by Evans (1984) but is a development of an earlier "dual process" theory (Wason & Evans, 1975; Evans & Wason, 1976). The major development in the H-A theory is the explication of the concept of relevance. Unconscious heuristic processes are proposed to produce a representation of relevant information, which is a combination both of that selected from the present information and that retrieved from memory. Analytic processes are assumed to introduce some form of explicit reasoning that operates upon the relevant information in a second stage.

The current book builds upon the heuristic-analytic theory, extending and revising it in important respects. The H-A theory, as presented by Evans (1989), had two notable weaknesses that failed to elude several critics of the theory. One problem was that the issue of rationality was insufficiently addressed. We have already indicated that this is to be a central concern in the present work. The second problem is that the nature of the analytic stage was entirely unspecified, and hence the issue of how deductive competence is achieved was not addressed. This problem will not be avoided in the present volume, although its discussion is largely deferred until Chapters 6 and 7. For the time being we will content ourselves with the assumption that explicit reasoning does occur in an analytic stage, but only in application to information selected as relevant.

The word "heuristic" in the H-A theory is open to misinterpretation. The term is often applied to short-cut rules that may be applied in a conscious strategy in order to produce an output of some kind, such as the solution to a problem, or a decision taken. In the H-A theory, heuristic processes refer only to preconscious processes whose output is the explicit representation of relevant information. In the Evans (1989) theory, further, analytic processing is required before a behavioural outcome is observed. We now take a somewhat different view, which is explicated in detail in Chapter 7 of this book. Although tacit processes are certainly responsible for relevance and focusing, we believe that they may also lead directly to judgements and actions. Our position now is that explicit reasoning processes may determine decisions but need not. The central idea of the Evans (1989) theory, however, remains. Such explicit thinking as we engage in is mostly directed and focused by tacit, preconscious processes. These processes strongly constrain our ability to be rational$_2$. For example, our understanding of logical principles will avail us little if our attention is focused on the wrong part of the problem information.

Although we are not concerned in this book with the mechanisms of "heuristic" or tacit cognitive processes, we would like to note the similarity between our view of such processes and the characterisation of cognition by connectionist or neural network theorists (see Smolensky, 1988, on connectionist approaches to cognition). In network models, there are many units that have multiple interconnections, rather like neurons in the human brain—hence the term "neural net". Activity in the network consists of excitatory and inhibitory links between units. Learning occurs by modification to the set of mathematical weights that determine these connections. Hence, knowledge in a network is tacit or implicit. There is no need to postulate propositions or rules, just a set of weightings. The knowledge contained in a network—like the tacit knowledge contained in a human being—can only be inferred by observation of its behaviour.[1]

We are attracted to the neural network characterisation of heuristic processes for several reasons. We believe that what is relevant often "pops out" into consciousness very rapidly, despite great complexity in the nature of pragmatic processes and the very large amount of stored knowledge that has to be searched. For those who would argue that this is an implausible model of thinking, consider that we already know that much cognitive processing is of this kind—rapid, preconscious, and computationally very powerful. Visual perception provides an astonishing example in which our conscious percepts are immediately "given" in real time, despite the incredible amount of information processing required. Similarly, we (or rather our brains) effortlessly and immediately apply a combination of linguistic and pragmatic knowledge to derive, without any apparent conscious effort of thought, the meaning of everyday discourse. Such processes are almost unimaginably complex to model by sequential, propositional means but significant progress in both of these domains is being made by use of computer simulations based on neural networks.

Hence, our characterisation of the processes responsible for relevance in reasoning and decision making is entirely consistent with the nature of cognition in general and is plausibly modelled by the connectionist approach. We are not precluding the possibility of sequential and conscious reasoning at the analytic stage (see Chapter 6), but we are arguing that much important processing has been completed prior to or independently of conscious thought. We also see links between our proposals and those of researchers in the implicit learning tradition (see Berry & Dienes, 1993; Evans, 1995a; Reber, 1993). Research in this area suggests that there are separate explicit and implicit cognitive systems: people may hold knowledge at a tacit but not explicit level or vice versa. Tacit knowledge may reflect innate modules or compilation of once conscious knowledge but it may also be acquired implicitly without ever being in the explicit system. The defining characteristic of tacit knowledge is that people can demonstrate it in their behaviour—i.e. they have procedural knowledge of how to do something, but cannot verbalise it. We take this to mean that they are not conscious of the truth of some explicit propositional representation of this knowledge. (Ryle, 1949, provides the philosophical background to much contemporary discussion of the difference between *knowing how* and *knowing that* or propositional knowledge.) With tacit knowledge, there can also be a lack of meta-knowledge—people may not be aware that they possess knowledge held tacitly.

The rational function of relevance

Why is it adaptive, or rational$_1$, for relevant representations to pop up from preconscious processes and for our explicit reasoning to be limited by such representations? Reber (1993) presents an evolutionary argument for the "primacy of the implicit" in which he suggests that the implicit system is highly adaptive, and that much of it evolved first in our early human and pre-human ancestors, and is shared with other animals. But whether our tacit abilities are old in evolutionary terms, as aspects of our visual system must be, or relatively young in these terms, as some of our tacit linguistic abilities must be, the evidence shows that these abilities are far more robust in the face of neurological insult than are explicit processes (see also Berry & Dienes, 1993). This is evidence not simply for their primacy but also for their distributed, connectionist nature. The reason that implicit processes serve rationality$_1$, however, is that they are so enormously computationally powerful, allowing extremely rapid real time processing of vision, language, and memory. The explicit system, by contrast, is an inherently sequential processing system of highly limited channel capacity. For example, the amount of information that can be held in verbal working memory and thus reported (see Ericsson & Simon, 1980) is the merest fraction of that which the brain must process in order to allow us to execute the simplest of behaviours.

Although almost all cognitive psychologists accept that tacit processing underlies much cognition, there is still a widespread identification of reasoning and decision making with conscious explicit processes. We hold that this is mistaken, though we do agree that explicit processes have an important part to play in intelligent thought. The principal problem for consciousness is the vast overload of information both in the environment and in memory that is potentially available. Without very rapid and effective selection of relevant information, intelligent thought would be virtually impossible. The network approach manifests rationality$_1$ in that networks essentially acquire their knowledge through interaction with the environment. For example, a network classifying patterns is doing so by implicit learning of previous exemplars, and not by the application of explicit rules or principles.

We do not take the epiphenomenalist position of arguing that conscious thought serves no purpose. On the contrary, we believe that explicit processes can produce logical reasoning and influence decision making (see Chapters 6 and 7). Our point is that explicit reasoning can only be effectively applied to a very limited amount of information, the representation of which must derive from preconscious, implicit relevance processes.[2] Otherwise, as Oaksford and Chater (1993, 1995) have indicated, real life reasoning based on a large set of beliefs would be hopelessly intractable.

In previous chapters we have stated that effectively pursuing goals makes for rationality$_1$. We have stressed the fundamental importance of practical thought, motivated by the need to solve problems and make decisions in order to achieve everyday objectives. Also of importance is the basic theoretical reasoning closely tied to such practical thought. When effective, this reasoning is motivated by an epistemic goal, such as inferring whether some tree has apples on it, that will help to attain some practical objective, such as getting an apple to eat. As indicated earlier, Sperber and Wilson argue that relevant information is that which will have the most cognitive effects for the smallest processing effort. We would stress that not just any cognitive effects, for however little effort, determine relevance. What is subjectively relevant is what is taken to further the currently active goals, be they epistemic, practical, or a combination of both. With the practical goal of getting an apple to eat, we have the epistemic sub-goal of inferring whether a tree we are looking at in the distance has apples on it. Anything we can remember that will help us infer whether it does or it does not will be relevant to us in this context. Anything anyone else can say to help us perform either inference will also be relevant.

Thus relevance is partly to be explained in terms of what has epistemic utility, but there is more to it than that, except in the case of pure, *academic* theoretical reasoning, not aimed at any practical goal. The defining characteristic of relevance processes, as we understand them, is that they selectively retrieve information from memory, or extract it from a linguistic context, with the object of advancing some further goal. Nor would we wish to restrict our notion of what is retrieved to verbal as opposed to procedural knowledge. Previously learned rules and heuristics, for example, may be retrieved as relevant in the given context.

As noted in the previous chapter, Anderson's (1990) rational analysis of cognition has similarities with our own approach, and we would regard him essentially as a theorist of personal rationality. He has recently revised his earlier ACT* model into ACT-R, which is a theory of adaptive cognition based upon production systems (see Anderson, 1993). Such systems are programmed with a set of production rules of the form "if <condition> then <action>". Like ourselves, Anderson relies on an extension of the distinction between knowing how and knowing that. He distinguishes *procedural knowledge*, which he tries to account for using production rules, and *declarative knowledge*. People can only display the former in their behaviour, but can give a verbal report of the latter. Clearly his distinction is close to the one we have made between tacit or implicit states or processes, and explicit ones that can be reported. Sometimes explicit, conscious representations can be difficult to describe, as Anderson points out. For example, some people are good at forming mental images that they find hard to describe fully. We discuss the problem of introspective report and explicit processes in Chapter 7. In general, we believe that explicit processes are identifiable through verbalisations, but not necessarily by self-describing intro-spective reports.

We are then in agreement with Anderson about the importance of a number of issues. We usually prefer to speak of implicit or explicit states and processes, rather than of knowledge, because these states or processes can go wrong, and then they do not embody or yield knowledge. This can happen in unrealistic psychological experiments, because of general cognitive limitations, or quite simply because people make mistakes. Anderson's main interests are in memory, skill acquisition, and other cognition that for the most part is not directly related to reasoning and decision making. The tacit, implicit, or procedural is of widely recognised importance in these other areas of cognition, but our argument is that it is of equal importance in reasoning and decision making. These states and processes are essential, we argue, for selecting relevant information for explicit representation and processing in explicit inference.

RELEVANCE IN REASONING

Conditional reasoning is the study of how people make inferences using "if" and other ways of expressing conditionality. In the deductive reasoning literature, relevance effects have been most clearly demonstrated on conditional reasoning tasks. We will give a brief historical survey in this section of how such effects were discovered, as well as pointing to some of the most recent evidence concerning relevance and reasoning.

The conditional truth table and selection tasks

In textbooks on propositional logic, the sentence "if p then q" is treated as an extensional conditional, with the truth table:

Case	Truth of rule
p, q	true
p, not-q	false
not-p, q	true
not-p, not-q	true

Thus this conditional is considered to be true whenever its antecedent condition is false. For example, "If that animal is a dog then it has four legs" is true both of a cat (which has four legs) and a goldfish (which does not). Wason (1966) suggested that this is psychologically implausible and that people actually think that conditionals are irrelevant when the antecedent condition is false. For example, the above conditional only applies to dogs. He called this hypothesis the "defective truth table".

The first experiment to test Wason's hypothesis was conducted by Johnson-Laird and Tagart (1969) who gave subjects a pack of cards with a letter-number pair printed on them. They were then given a conditional such as "If the letter is a B then the number is a 7" and asked to sort the cards into three piles, "true", "false", and "irrelevant". As Wason predicted, most false antecedent cards (ones with a letter which was not a B) were classified as irrelevant to the truth of the conditional.

Evans (1972) ran a variant on this experiment in which subjects were asked to construct in turn cases that made the conditional statement true or made it false. His materials were different from those of Johnson-Laird and Tagart, but if we imagine that the same kind of conditional was tested, the task of the subject was effectively to construct a letter-number pair to verify or to falsify a conditional. The key point of this experiment, however, was that subjects were instructed to perform these tasks exhaustively—i.e. to construct all logically possible ways of verifying and of falsifying the statement. Thus any case that was not selected was inferred by the experimenter to be irrelevant. The idea was to avoid demand characteristics that cue the subject to think that some cards are irrelevant.

The method of Johnson-Laird and Tagart has become known as the truth table evaluation task and that of Evans as the truth table construction task. Not only did Evans (1972) replicate the basic findings of Johnson-Laird et al., but in a later study (Evans, 1975) demonstrated that the results of using the construction and evaluation forms of the truth table task are effectively identical. In other words, subjects omit on the construction task precisely the same cases that they judge to be irrelevant on the evaluation task. This quite surprising task independence was an early indication of the power of relevance effects in conditional reasoning.

A more significant feature of the Evans (1972) study was the introduction of the "negations paradigm" into the truth table task. In this method, four types of conditionals of the following kind are compared:

Form	Example
If p then q	If the letter is A then the number is 3
If p then not q	If the letter is D then the number is not 7
If not p then q	If the letter is not N then the number is 1
If not p then not q	If the letter is not G then number is not 5

This task led to the accidental discovery of a second relevance effect in conditional reasoning, which Evans termed "matching bias". In addition to being more likely to regard any of these statements as irrelevant when the antecedent condition was irrelevant, subjects were also more likely to regard as irrelevant cases in which their was a mismatch between the elements referred to in the statements and those on the cards. For example, consider the case where the antecedent is false and the consequent true (the FT case). For the conditional "If the letter is A then the number is not 4" such a case is created by an instance such as G6, i.e. by a pairing a letter that is not an A with a number that is not a 4 (a double mismatch). On the other hand, for the conditional "If the letter is not A then the number is 4" the FT case is produced by A4, a double match. In the former case, the great majority of subjects failed to construct the FT case (and in later evaluation tasks reported in the literature, rated it as irrelevant). However, the dominant response in the second case is to construct the case as a falsifier of the statement (or to rate such a case as false). It was subsequently discovered that the same two causes of relevance apply on the better known and much more investigated problem known as the Wason selection task (Wason, 1966). There are many published experiments on the selection task which have most recently been reviewed by Evans et al. (1993a, Chapter 4). In what is known as the standard abstract form of the task, subjects are shown four cards displaying values such as:

T   J   4   8

together with a statement such as:

If there is a T on one side of the card then there is a 4 on the other side of the card.

Subjects are instructed that each card has a letter on one side and a number on the other. They are then asked which cards need to be turned over in order to discover whether the statement is true or false. Wason's original findings, which have been replicated many times, were that few intelligent adult subjects (typically less than 10%) find the logically correct answer which is the T and the 8 (p and not-q). Most choose either T alone (p) or T and 4 (p and q). T and 8 are the logically necessary choices, because only a card which has a T on one side and does not have a 4 on the other could falsify the conditional. Wason's original interpretation was that subjects were exhibiting a confirmation bias by looking for the case T and 4. However, from a strictly logical point of view, turning the 4 to find a T does not constitute confirmation because the conditional is consistent with this card no matter what is on the back.

Application of the negations paradigm to the selection task (first done by Evans & Lynch, 1973) shows that matching bias provides a much better account of the data than does confirmation bias. Consider, for example, the case of the conditional with a negated consequent: "If there is a B on one side of the card, then there is not a 7 on the other side". If subjects have a confirmation bias, then they should choose the B and the card that is not a 7, in order find the confirming TT case (true-antecedent and true-consequent). If they have a matching bias, however, they should choose the B and 7, which are the logically correct choices. The latter is what the great majority of subjects actually do. In fact, on all four logical cases, subjects choose cards that match the lexical content of the conditional far more often than cards that do not (see Evans et al., 1993a, for a review of the experiments).

When selection task choices are averaged over the four conditionals, so that matching bias is controlled, what is found is that the true-antecedent is the most popular and the false-antecedent the least popular choice. This, of course, links with Wason's defective truth table hypothesis and the findings on the truth table task. In summary, the two tasks provide evidence of two (independent) sources of relevance:

- Cases appear more relevant when the antecedent condition is fulfilled.
- Cases appear more relevant when their features match those named in the conditional.

Evans (1989) attributes these two findings to the *if-* and *not*-heuristics respectively, which determine relevance in the preconscious manner discussed earlier. The linguistic function of "if" is to direct the listener's attention to the possible state of affairs in which the antecedent condition applies, hence enhancing relevance for true antecedent cases. The linguistic function of "not" is to direct attention to (i.e. heighten the relevance of) the proposition it denies. We do not normally use negation in natural language to assert new information; rather we use it to deny presuppositions. If we say "We are going to choir practice tonight" or "We are not going to choir practice tonight", the topic of the discourse is the same in either case. In the latter case, the listener will be thinking about us going to choir practice, not any of the many things we may be doing instead. The statement will also only be relevant in a context where we can presume that the listener did think that we were going and needed to know that we were not—a fellow member of the choir, perhaps, who could give apologies.

Experimental evidence of relevance in conditional reasoning

Some critics complain that the relevance account of the selection task and matching bias does little more than describe the phenomena. However, several types of evidence have now been produced in support of the relevance explanation of the truth table and selection task data. First, let us consider the role of explicit and implicit negation.

Evans (1983) suggested that the use of explicit negations in truth table cases should reduce or eliminate the matching bias effect. He slightly modified the task by using conjunctive sentences to describe the cases. For example, for the statement "If the letter is A then the number is not 4" the control group received a description of a letter-number pair using implicit negation as is used in the standard task—i.e. "The letter is B and the number is 7" was used to convey the FT case, instead of just "B7". In the experimental group, however, explicit negations were used, so that this case became "The letter is not A and the number is not 4".

Note that with the explicit negation form, all cases now match the statements in terms of the letters and numbers. Evans (1983) found a substantial and significant reduction of the matching bias in this condition and a corresponding increase in correct responding. We should, of course, expect that the use of explicitly negative cases on the cards would similarly inhibit matching bias on the selection task. Several recent studies have shown that explicit negatives do not by themselves facilitate correct choices on the affirmative abstract selection task (see Girotto, Mazzocco, & Cherubini, 1992; Griggs & Cox, 1993; Jackson & Griggs, 1990; Kroger, Cheng, & Holyoak, 1993). However, none of these studies used the negations paradigm to allow a proper measure of matching.

A relevant recent study was conducted by Evans, Clibbens, and Rood (in press a) in which the negations paradigm was employed throughout. In the first experiment they attempted to replicate the findings of Evans (1983) using the truth table task, and also to extend the effect from the usual *if then* to other forms of conditionals—namely *only* if conditionals, i.e. "(Not) p only if (not) q" and reverse conditionals, i.e. "(Not) q if (not) p". With all three forms of conditionals, very substantial matching bias was found with implicit negations. With explicit negations, however, the effect was all but eliminated. Thus the findings both very strongly replicated and extended the findings of Evans (1983). In two further experiments, Evans et al. (in press a) generalised this finding to the selection task where explicit negative cases completely removed the matching bias effect.

The latter results do not conflict with those of other recent studies quoted earlier, however, because this reduced matching bias was *not* accompanied by a facilitation in correct responding. The previously mismatching cards were selected more frequently regardless of their logical status. Moreover, it is consistent with the H-A theory that release from matching should facilitate logically correct responses on the truth table task but not the selection task. This is because the truth table task is proposed to elicit analytic as well as heuristic processes, whereas the selection task generally reflects only relevance judgements (Evans, 1989). The issue of whether analytic reasoning can affect selection task choices, however, is dealt with in Chapter 6.

A different approach to providing evidence for relevance on the selection task is to try to show directly that subjects attend specifically to the cards they select. As noted above, Evans (1989) has argued that on the selection task (but not the truth table task) the data can be accounted for by relevance or heuristic processes alone. The argument is that the cards that are not selected are simply not thought about, rather than thought about and rejected after analysis of the consequence of turning them over. In this account, in fact, there is no reason to suppose that any analytic reasoning about the backs of the cards occurs at all. The first evidence of attentional bias was presented by Evans, Ball, and Brooks (1987) who used a computer version of the task in which subjects had to signal a decision for every card—Yes to select, No to reject—by pressing a key. They found a correlation between decision order and choice. Matching cards, for example, were not only chosen more often but decided about earlier.

A much stronger method was devised recently by Evans (1995b and in press). This also used a computer presented version of the selection task. In this case subjects had to choose cards by pointing with a mouse at the card on the screen and then clicking the mouse button. The innovation was an instruction to subjects to point at the card they were considering selecting, but not to press the button until they were sure. The time spent pointing before selecting was recorded by the computer as the card inspection time. Evans reported several experiments that used this method and that permitted the testing of two predictions:

P1   Those cards that have a higher mean selection frequency will also have a higher mean inspection time.

P2   On any given card, those subjects who choose the card will have higher inspection times than those who do not.

Prediction P1 is at the usual theoretical level of overall performance. P2, however, is stronger because it attempts to differentiate the subjects who choose a given card from those who do not. No current theory of reasoning attempts to account for these kinds of individual differences. In the experiments, a variety of abstract and thematic versions of the selection task were employed and in all cases strong support was found for both predictions. To illustrate P2, the predicted difference between choosers and non-choosers, we present the data from one of the experiments in Fig. 3.1. The results, as can be seen, are quite dramatic. Subjects scarcely inspect at all the cards that they do not choose.

A commonly asked question about these findings is: Why do subjects spend 15 or 20 seconds looking at a card that they will choose anyway? What are they thinking about? The answer to this was provided by an

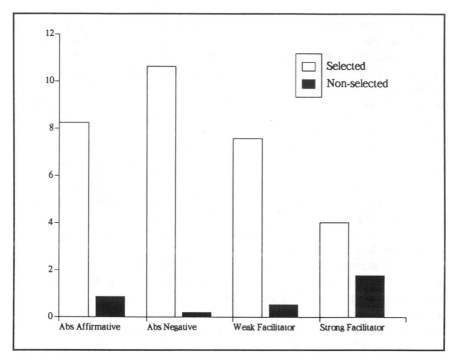

FIG. 3.1. Mean inspection times for selected and non-selected cards on each conditional in the study of Evans (in press, Experiment 1).

experiment of Evans (1995b) in which concurrent verbal protocols were recorded. First, it was found—in confirmation of the inspection time data—that people tended only to refer to the cards that they ended up selecting. (A similar finding is reported by Beattie & Baron, 1988.) More interestingly, when subjects chose a card they also referred quite frequently to the value on the *back* of the card. This finding suggests that subjects do engage in analytic reasoning on the selection task but that *this does not affect the choices they make*. First, cards that are not selected are not attended to. Hence, analytic reasoning is not used to reject cards. Secondly, when subjects do think about a card, they generally convince themselves to select it. This may be a peculiarity of the selection task and its instructions. For example, Evans and Wason (1976) presented four groups of subjects with alternative purported "solutions" to the problem and found that subjects would happily justify the answer they were given. In fact, none complained they had been given the wrong answer!

Relevance, focusing and rationality

Recently, Sperber, Cara, and Girotto (1995) have presented a new relevance theory of conditional reasoning, based on the Sperber and Wilson (1986) theory and different in some significant ways from the Evans (1989) account. For example, they do not accept the distinction between heuristic and analytic processes, arguing instead that all levels of representation and process in human cognition are guided by relevance. What the results of their experiments and those of other recent researchers (Green & Larking, 1995; Love & Kessler, 1995) show is that manipulations that cause people to focus on the counter-example case of p and not-q facilitate correct responding on the selection task.

What other authors refer to as "focusing" is also closely related to what we call relevance effects. Legrenzi, Girotto, and Johnson-Laird (1993), for example, suggest that subjects focus on what is explicitly represented in mental models. Other psychologists are using the term focusing without necessarily linking it with mental model theory (e.g. Love & Kessler, 1995). A useful terminological approach here might be to use the term focusing to refer to the phenomenon of selective attention in reasoning in a theoretical neutral manner. In this spirit we are happy to use the term ourselves, but will argue theoretically that relevance is the main cause of focusing. The further theoretical argument that focusing reflects what is explicitly represented in mental models is not incompatible with this position, because pragmatic considerations such as relevance are required in any case to explain what people represent in their mental models.[3] We will discuss the relation between relevance and model theory further in Chapter 6, but suffice it to say that Evans (e.g. 1991, 1993b) has already suggested that what is subjectively relevant might be that which has explicit representation in a mental model.

A final point to consider before moving on is this: How can relevance effects be rational if they lead to biases such as matching bias? As well as being irrational$_2$, matching bias may appear to be irrational$_1$—it certainly does not serve the subjects' goal of getting the right answer in the reasoning experiments. However, the notion of rationality$_1$ is embedded in the concept that we have evolved in an adaptive manner that allows us to achieve real world goals, not to solve laboratory problems. Indeed, central to our theoretical view is the argument that subjects cannot consciously adjust their tacit or procedural mechanisms for the sake of an experiment. Matching bias is, in fact, a consequence of generally useful mechanisms that lead us to direct attention appropriately when understanding natural language. The *if*-heuristic enables us to expand our beliefs efficiently, or the information we extract from discourse, when we believe, or have been told, that a conditional is true. The *not*-heuristic helps us to co-operate on a topic for discourse and to determine how much confidence we should have in what we are told.

Suppose someone says to us that we are not looking at an apple tree. To understand this and how believable it is, we are better off thinking about apple trees and engaging our, largely tacit, recognition ability for them. We could not have such an ability for the unlimited set of completely heterogeneous things that are not apple trees.

RELEVANCE IN DECISION MAKING AND JUDGEMENT

We now turn to consideration of some recent studies in the psychology of decision making, which in our view provide evidence of relevance effects, even though they are not presented in these terms by their authors. We start by consideration of some of the very interesting experiments summarised by Shafir, Simonson, and Tversky (1993).

Relevance and reason-based choice

The theoretical emphasis of Shafir et al. is on reason-based choice, although they wisely avoid a mentalistic definition of "reasons", which would imply that these are found in propositions that people explicitly represent and can report. Shafir et al. recognise the evidence in the literature of the unreliability of introspective accounts of the reasons for decision making (see Chapter 6). They define "reasons" as the "factors or motives that affect decision, whether or not they can be articulated or recognised by the decision maker" (p.13). When we examine the phenomena they discuss, we find that this analysis of reason-based choice is closely related to what we hold to affect relevance. That is, factors that induce selective attention or focusing on certain aspects of the available information, and that explain why people make particular choices.

Perhaps the best example discussed by Shafir et al. is a study of "reasons pro and con" (Shafir, 1993). In this experiment subjects consider two choices that have a number of attributes. One choice is fairly average on all dimensions; the other is positive on some and negative on others. One group of subjects are asked to decide which option to choose and the other which option to reject: logically, but not psychologically equivalent tasks. For example, here are the positive and negative versions of one of Shafir's problems:

Prefer
Imagine that you are planning a vacation in a warm spot over spring break. You currently have two options that are reasonably priced. The travel brochure gives only a limited amount of information about the two options. Given the information available, which vacation spot would you prefer?

Cancel
Imagine that you are planning a vacation in a warm spot over spring break. You currently have two options that are reasonably priced, but you can no longer retain your reservations on both. The travel brochure gives only a limited amount of information about the two options. Given the information available which would you decide to cancel?

The subjects of either group are then shown the following information:

Spot A	*Spot B*
average weather	lots of sunshine
average beaches	gorgeous beaches and coral reefs
medium-quality hotel	ultra-modern hotel
medium-temperature water	very cold water
average nightlife	very strong winds
	no nightlife

Subjects who were asked which they would prefer, showed a clear preference for Spot B (67%). However, this dropped sharply in the cancel condition where only 48% chose B (by cancelling A). The difference seems to imply a violation of impersonal principles for rationality$_2$, but strikes us as a clear example of a relevance effect on a decision-making task. Note first that the subjects do not make a choice arising from their own desires in a case of actual decision making. They are asked to make a hypothetical choice, and pragmatic factors affecting relevance should have an effect. When asked for a preference, the relevance of the positive aspects of the options is highlighted. There are more positive reasons to choose B (more sunshine, better beaches and hotels). When asked to make a decision to cancel, however, the negative aspects of the options come into focus. B is now less attractive because it has some clear negative features (cold water, no nightlife, etc.), which could justify a decision to cancel.

Another phenomenon of interest to us discussed by Shafir et al. is the "disjunction effect" (see also Shafir & Tversky, 1992; Tversky & Shafir, 1992). A set of experiments show a further violation of an impersonal standard, as captured by Savage's (1954) sure-thing principle, which informally states the following: If you would prefer A to B when you know that C has occurred, and if you would prefer A to B when you know that C has not occurred, then you should prefer A to B when you do not know whether C has occurred or not. One experiment providing evidence of violation was also about a possible holiday, this time at the Christmas break and in Hawaii (Tversky & Shafir, 1992). All groups were told that they had just taken a tough qualifying examination and had three choices: to buy, not buy or (at a small cost) to defer their decision. The result was that 54% of the subjects told they had passed the examination chose to buy and 30% to defer. For the group told that they had failed the exam, the figures were very similar: 57% buy and 31% defer. However, of the group who were told that they did not know the result, but would know it after the period of deferral, only 32% chose to buy with deferral being the most popular option (61%). The interpretation of this finding offered by Shafir et al. is that the reasons for taking the holiday are different in the case of passing (celebration) and failing (consolation) but uncertain in the case of the group with the unknown result. Lacking a clear reason, they suggest, subjects prefer to defer the decision until they know the result of the examination.

Notice again that the subjects are asked to make a hypothetical choice. One reason why people might opt to defer a decision like this in real life until they know all the relevant facts, is difficulty in predicting how they will feel. That is, they may think it only fairly probable that they will want a consolation holiday if they hear of failure in the examination, and wonder as well if they will then be too depressed to enjoy a holiday. That would give them a good reason, as Shafir et al. are aware, to put off their decision until they do hear the result and know exactly how they feel. Many more factors can be relevant in real life than should strictly be taken into account in a controlled experiment. Even the way one hears whether one passed or failed—e.g. from a sympathetic or an unsympathetic lecturer—could affect how one feels about the holiday.

The general psychological significance of the disjunction effect, we believe, is that subjects' choices are determined more by past experience and available experience than by calculation of future, uncertain possibilities. This is the aspect stressed by Shafir and Tversky (1992) who themselves discuss a possible connection between the disjunction effect and the characteristic failure of subjects on the Wason selection task. The selection task also requires subjects to cope with an uncertain disjunction of hidden values on the back of cards. Recall our argument (in Chapter 2) that no one could make most ordinary decisions by considering all the possible states of affairs that might result from alternative actions, and by combining computations of probability and utility in order to choose optimally. Our view is that actual decision making is affected more by past experience and learning, e.g. about one's feelings in similar cases, than by reasoning about uncertain possibilities. In many real world situations, it would be hard to distinguish these hypotheses, because past experience would also form the basis of any reasoning and calculation of outcomes. However, on novel experimental problems, such as the selection task or the disjunction problems of Shafir and Tversky, the absence of decision making based on forward reasoning becomes apparent.

Relevance in data selection tasks

Due to the fame of the Wason selection task, it has perhaps been overlooked in the literature that there is a class of experimental problems that might be defined as selection tasks, of which Wason's famous problem is just one. A generic selection task, we suggest, is one on which subjects are required actively to seek or choose information in order to make a decision. A task that fits this description is that associated with the pseudo-diagnosticity effect (Doherty, Mynatt, Tweney, & Schiavo, 1979), which we discussed briefly in Chapter 2. In this task, subjects are trying to decide between two hypotheses (H1 and H2) with respect to two alternative pieces of evidence (D1, D2). To illustrate with one of the problems used in a recent paper by Mynatt, Doherty, and Dragan (1993), subjects are trying to decide whether a car is type X or Y. Two types of information that are potentially available concern whether the car does better than 25 miles per gallon and whether it has major mechanical problems within the first two years of ownership. The two types of information about the two hypotheses can be described in the form of a 2×2 table with cells A, B, C, and D (see Fig. 3.2).

In the standard experiment subjects are given information A, Prob(D1/H1), and asked which of B, C, or D they would choose to know in order to decide if the car is X or Y. Note the close structural similarity to the Wason selection task in which subjects have to choose which card to turn over (to reveal information) in order to decide whether the statement is true or false. The main difference is that on Mynatt et al.'s problem subjects are restricted to one choice, whereas subjects on the Wason selection task can choose all or any cards. The correct choice would appear to be cell B because information can only be diagnostic, in a Bayesian approach, if it gives the likelihood ratio of two hypotheses— i.e. Prob(D1/H1)/Prob(D1/H2). However, the classic finding is that subjects reason pseudo-diagnostically, by seeking more information about the hypothesis under consideration—in this case from cell C, giving Prob(D2/H1). For example, in Experiment 1 of the Mynatt et al. paper, choices were: B 28%, C 59%, and D 13%.

Information	Alternatives	
	Car X (H1)	Car Y (H2)
% over 25 mpg	Cell A	Cell B
(D1)	Prob(D1/H1)	Prob(D1/H2)
% no problems in two years	Cell C	Cell D
(D2)	Prob(D2/H1)	Prob(D2/H2)

FIG. 3.2. Pseudo-diagnosticity problem from Mynatt et al. (1993).

In discussing this effect, Mynatt et al. put forward an important psychological hypothesis. They argue that subjects can only think about one hypothesis at a time, or, putting it more generally, only entertain one mental model of a possible state of affairs at once. This notion of highly selective focus of thinking is of course compatible with our general theoretical approach. In support of their claim, Mynatt et al. compare the above problem with a similar one in which subjects have to decide instead on which car they would choose to buy: an action as opposed to inference version of the problem. This task does not require hypothetical reasoning about alternative states of the world, and so the authors suggest will be less susceptible to pseudo-diagnostic reasoning. (There is an analogy here to the distinction between the indicative and deontic versions of the Wason selection task, to be discussed in Chapter 4.) Choices in the action version were B 51%, C 40%, and D 9%.

Taking the effect of relevance into account, we would say that, in the inference problem, hypothesis 1 (car X) is foregrounded by presentation of information A. This relates to hypothesis 1, directing attention to it and so leading to choice C. A slightly different interpretation of the shift of responding in the action version—and one more in line with relevance effects—is that in this version the attribute of fuel consumption becomes foregrounded, leading to the great frequency of B choices. The preamble to this problem reads:

> You are thinking of buying a new car. You've narrowed it down to either car X or car Y. Two of the things you are concerned about are petrol consumption and mechanical reliability.

The wording here indicates the concern with the attributes. When the information A is presented, petrol consumption is given pragmatic prominence, and attention is focused on it rather than mechanical reliability. Mynatt et al. assume that the proportion choosing B on this task is simply a function of their different utility judgements for the two dimensions. Because they did not have a condition in which A described reliability information, we cannot tell whether this is right. It is plausible, however, that a significant difference in utility between the two attributes could cause people to focus on the one with the greater value, whichever attribute was given in A. In any case, consider now the preamble to the inference version:

> Your sister bought a car a couple of years ago. It's either a car X or a car Y, but you can't remember which. You do remember that her car does over 25 miles per gallon and has not had any major mechanical problems in the two years since she owned it.

This is quite different psychologically, because instead of stressing the dimensions of fuel consumption and reliability, specific information about the car is given. This encourages subjects to form a concrete mental model of the sister's car. When information A is then presented it is actually the following: 65% of X cars do over 25 miles per gallon.

Because the majority of X cars are like the sister's, the subject will tend to attach X to the mental model to form the hypothesis that this car is an X, leading to the characteristic choice of C, with more information about X cars. Suppose that the evidence in A disconfirms that the car is an X. This should then lead to subjects attaching Y to the model, forming the hypothesis that the car is a Y, and so choosing predominantly choice B. However, because attention is focused on the attribute of fuel consumption in the action problem, this manipulation should not affect this version. This way of looking at the findings is supported by Experiment 2 of Mynatt et al. in which the information A was: 35% of X cars do over 25 miles per gallon. Choices for the inference version were now: B 46%, C 43%, and D 10%—a big shift from C to B compared with Experiment 1, whereas the action choices were B 52%, C 38%, and D 10%—very similar to those of Experiment 1.[4]

A recent experiment reported by Legrenzi et al. (1993) in their study of focusing effects also required subjects to seek information relevant to a decision. Subjects were asked to imagine themselves as tourists in one of several capital cities and asked to decide in turn whether or not to attend a particular event (sporting event, film, etc.). Subjects were then instructed to request information from the experimenter before making a decision. What happened was that most subjects asked several questions about the event itself, but hardly any about alternative actions that might be available to them. For example, if deciding whether or not to view a film on a one day visit to Rome, subjects asked about the director of the film, price of admission, and so on, but rarely asked about other ways they could spend their day in Rome. This fits with the claims of Mynatt et al. that, due to limitations on working memory, people can only have a representation of one object at a time—or a single mental model. This may not be a severe limitation in practical thought about action if people can focus on what has reasonable utility for them, or on what has been pragmatically given utility by someone else in a piece of discourse. It may, however, be more of a problem when the object is to infer, in theoretical reasoning, which one of two or more hypotheses is most likely to be true. Certainly, accurate deductive reasoning usually requires consideration of multiple mental models, although subjects are known to find this very difficult (see Johnson-Laird & Bara, 1984).

CONCLUSIONS

In this chapter, we have started to develop our psychological theory of how people reason and make decisions, building on our preference for a personal, rather than an impersonal, view of rationality. In the previous chapters this was principally an argument concerning the appropriate normative methods for assessing rationality, but the discussion of relevance and selective thinking in the present chapter has added psychological distinctions to the argument. In both the study of reasoning and decision making, psychologists who presuppose an impersonal view of rationality expect people to be rational by virtue of conscious, explicit reasoning. For example, the classic "rational man" of behavioural decision theory makes choices by constructing decision trees in which future events are analysed with utilities and probabilities, and by consciously calculating the action most likely to maximise utility.

What is significant is that people are reasonably good at achieving many of their basic goals, thus appearing to be sensitive, to some extent, to the probabilities and utilities of outcomes. However, this results more from experience, learning, and the application of preconscious heuristics than from conscious reasoning about hypothetical alternatives, and almost never from the explicit representation of probabilities and utilities as numbers. We have discussed a number of sources of evidence in this chapter showing that people have rather little ability to reason in this way. On the Wason selection task, subjects appear to think only about certain cards, and to be influenced not at all by hypothetical reasoning about hidden values; the disjunction effect of Shafir and Tversky shows that people can hesitate to make a decision to perform an action that they may have different reasons for; and the pseudo-diagnosticity effect also suggests that people are only able to think about one hypothesis—or mental model—at a time. It appears that people tend to build a single mental model in their working memories and have little capacity for the consideration of alternative, hypothetical possibilities there.

The reasons that we believe these tight constraints on conscious reasoning to be compatible with rationality$_1$ lie in the power and adaptiveness of what we term relevance processes. These are the essentially preconscious processes responsible for building our mental representations or directing the focus of our attention. We have discussed our general conception of such processes as reflecting computationally powerful and parallel processes of the kind envisaged in neural network or connectionist theories of cognition. We have also emphasised the crucial role of pragmatic principles and mechanisms in the determination of relevance.

We are not dismayed by the experimental evidence of reasoning biases shown in experiments described in this chapter and elsewhere in the literature. Most of these experiments require people to engage in conscious hypothetical reasoning in order to find the correct answers—precisely the weakest area of human cognition in our view. The fallacy is to infer that this will necessarily lead to highly irrational decision making in the everyday world. Many ordinary decisions derive from highly efficient processes that, in effect, conform to the pragmatic and relevance principles discussed in this chapter. In the following two chapters (4 and 5), we will consider the experimental literature on reasoning and decision making from the complementary perspectives of rationality$_1$ and relevance theory. We will show that much behaviour in the laboratory, including that which is normally described as biased, can be viewed as rational$_1$, especially when we assume that normally effective processes are carried over, sometimes inappropriately, into the laboratory setting. We will also continue to emphasise the largely preconscious nature of human thinking and the importance of pragmatically determined relevance. We then address the issues of deductive competence and explicit reasoning in Chapter 6.

NOTES

1. For an argument that tacit learning in networks is rational in a sense similar to our use of the term rationality$_1$ see Shanks (1995).
2. Jonathan Lowe (personal communication) suggests that we overstate the problem of information overload because the system need only respond to significant *changes* in the background state. However, to our understanding, the ability to detect and respond to potentially many such changes implies a highly developed, pre-attentive mechanism.
3. We are grateful to Paolo Legrenzi for a useful discussion with us about the connection between the terms "focusing" and "relevance".
4. Preliminary results from some current research in collaboration between Legrenzi, Evans, & Girotto are indicating support for the relevance interpretation of the Mynatt et al. results advanced here.

CHAPTER FOUR

Reasoning as decision making: The case of the selection task

We introduced the Wason selection task in Chapter 3, together with arguments and evidence that subjects choose cards that appear relevant. In particular, the evidence from the inspection time experiments of Evans (1995b and in press) is that subjects focus their attention only on the cards they choose, even when thematic and deontic versions of the task are presented. Because the logical analysis of the selection task requires consequential reasoning about the hidden sides of each card, it is not surprising therefore that behaviour on this task often appears illogical or irrational$_2$. However, as we have repeatedly argued, the tacit processes that underlie relevance typically produce behaviour that is rational$_1$—serving the personal goals of the individual. Our purpose in this chapter is first to argue that subjects' choices on various forms of the selection task are often rational$_1$, provided that the task is viewed as one of decision making rather than deductive reasoning. Secondly, we will suggest a mechanism by which such rational$_1$ choices come about—via the cueing of relevance that causes subjects to focus on particular mental models. Relevance serves rationality$_1$ because it is closely linked to the current goal that the subject is pursuing.

Only in the past few years has it been recognised that there are two distinct forms of the Wason selection task: indicative and deontic, depending on which kind of conditional and instruction is employed. We use conditionals of an indicative form to codify both common sense and scientific knowledge, and of a deontic form to express laws, regulations, social agreements, and moral rules. The Wason selection task has been extensively used in the experimental study of these two forms, and for very good reasons, as we shall see in this chapter. We will explore the possibilities of a decision theoretic analysis of the task: one that sees it as a decision problem requiring judgements of subjective probability and utility.

In the selection task people are presented with cards and asked to make a decision to achieve some goal. At the most general level, there are two kinds of goal in selection tasks so far studied, corresponding to the two general forms of the conditionals used. Indicative conditionals, such as "if it is a car then it has an engine" state factual relationships that may be true or false, whereas deontic conditionals, such as "if a car is three years old then it must pass a roadworthiness test" express rules that may be obeyed or disobeyed. The standard abstract version of the Wason selection task (introduced by Wason, 1966) uses an indicative conditional statement so that the goal is to discover whether or not the conditional is true. Most, but not all, thematic selection tasks, however, employ deontic rules, so that the task becomes that of deciding whether or not the rule has been obeyed. Now, people often have goals of both types in ordinary affairs, but such general goals are very rarely just ends in themselves. Not even scientists have the sole goal of discovering whether a scientific hypothesis is true or false. They usually want to achieve as well some further ends beyond this, such as helping humanity with a practical application, gaining a promotion, or winning a Nobel prize. Most of us want to uncover violations of laws, regulations, agreements, and moral rules in order to take corrective action, immediately or at some time in the future, to protect specific things we value.

People pursue certain outcomes of action as goals, ends, or purposes because they value these in some way. In other, more technical words, these outcomes have high expected subjective utility for the people who think of them as goals. That is, a goal is an outcome that is preferred to other outcomes and is sufficiently probable as to be worth pursuing. From people's preferences, we get their subjective utilities in the technical sense. In decision theory, we need the concept of subjective probability as well as that of subjective utility to describe people's behaviour (see Chapter 2). If people think that they are very unlikely to attain an outcome of high value, they do not necessarily try to get it. They may well concentrate their energies on a less valuable outcome that they are more likely to succeed in reaching.

A decision theoretic analysis of the selection task does not necessarily imply that people themselves represent their preferences or their probability judgements with numbers, nor of course that they use the formal machinery of decision theory to calculate what they should do. Even if successful, such an analysis is far from a complete explanation of people's responses in the task. It presupposes that people have preferences and make probability judgements; it does not provide cognitive mechanisms that could account for these. In Chapter 2, we rejected the idea that people could explicitly *follow* the rules or axioms of normative decision theory in everyday affairs. However, we believe that they could *comply* with these principles, in relatively simple tasks, because of what they have learned about benefits and costs in ordinary life. We shall try to assess in this chapter the extent to which this is so before considering the mechanism that underlies such rational₁ behaviour.

THE DEONTIC SELECTION TASK

Johnson-Laird, Legrenzi, and Legrenzi (1972) were the first to study a clearly deontic selection task. Their task was modified and studied further by Cheng and Holyoak (1985), who used the following deontic conditional:

4.1   If a letter is sealed, then it must carry a 20 cent stamp on it.

Cheng and Holyoak gave selection tasks based on this conditional to different populations of subjects, who were presented with four envelopes: one showing that it was sealed, one that it was unsealed, one that it had a 20 cent stamp on it, and one showing a lower value stamp. By turning over an envelope, one could tell whether it was sealed or not, or whether it had a correct stamp or not. All the subjects were asked to turn over just those envelopes needed to check whether 4.1 was being followed. One population of subjects had experience of postal regulations like 4.1 and they performed well on this selection task, tending to choose just the sealed and the incorrectly stamped envelopes (the p and not-q cards). Another population had no experience of any such regulation and performed badly if they were given no rationale for it. However, subjects from the latter population performed much better if they were told that the rationale was "to increase profit from personal mail". Cheng and Holyoak were the first researchers to recognise the deontic nature of rules like 4.1 and to bring out the importance of practical goals for understanding them.

By calling 4.1 a rule or regulation, we mean to stress that it is an attempt to guide or govern action or behaviour. By setting up this as a rule, the Post Office is not trying to describe the world but rather to change it. The Post Office is not a scientific institution that is attempting to state what is true of some natural phenomenon. It is, at least in part, a business that is trying to change the world in a way that brings it more money. Rules and regulations do not have to contain a strong deontic operator, like "must", "should", and "ought to", or a weak one, like "may". Although the use of these deontic terms in a conditional indicates that it does not have the same logical form as an indicative conditional, sometimes the deontic nature of a conditional can be understood from context alone. (For a detailed discussion of deontic conditionals see Manktelow & Over, 1995.)

Having laid down 4.1 as a rule, the Post Office would have an interest in finding violations of it. A violation would be the action performed by someone who sealed a letter without placing a 20 cent stamp on it. Of course, the Post Office would be mainly, if not exclusively, interested in cases in which a stamp of *less* value less 20 cents was used, or no stamp at all was placed on the letter. Finding such a case, the Post Office could take a number of steps to save itself the full cost of delivering the letter normally, and to deter future violations. It could destroy the letter, deliver it very slowly in a second class service, or return it to its sender.

Deontic selection tasks with "logical" solutions

Long before the deontic/indicative distinction was recognised, researchers were claiming that thematic or realistic materials "facilitated" solution of the Wason selection task—i.e. induced subjects to make the logically correct choices of p and not-q. This claim originated with Wason and Johnson-Laird's (1972) famous monograph on reasoning, and the history of the thematic facilitation effect is discussed by Griggs (1983) and by Evans et al. (1993a, Chapter 4). With hindsight, we now know the thematic facilitation hypothesis to be wrong on several counts. Indicative and deontic conditionals have different logical forms, and therefore propositional logic is not the appropriate normative theory to apply to deontic selection tasks. The correct solution to a deontic task is not a logical one, but rather one in line with what we have called here personal rationality (Manktelow & Over, 1991, and Over & Manktelow, 1993). However, it is true that a number of the deontic tasks studied have a correct solution of p and not-q that corresponds to that analysed as logically correct on the indicative selection task. Typically, subjects succeed in finding such a solution far more often than they do on the indicative task. We consider such tasks in this section. A second reason why we should not think of this research as showing facilitation of logical reasoning, however, is that other deontic selection tasks, considered in the following section, have solutions that do not correspond to the p and not-q pattern analysed as correct for the indicative task.

Almost all "facilitatory" forms of the selection task are not only thematic but deontic. Also they require use of an appropriate scenario, however brief. For example, one of the most reliable and best known facilitators is the drinking age problem introduced by Griggs and Cox (1982). The rule concerns people drinking at a bar and is made congruent with the actual law where subjects are tested. For example, in the State of Florida, the rule is "If a person is drinking beer then that person must be over 19 years of age". In this version the cards represent drinkers with beverages shown on one side and ages on the other. Given a choice of "beer", "coke", "16 years of age" and "22 years of age" most subjects chose correctly: "beer" (p) and "16 years of age" (not-q). The problem is preceded by a short paragraph in which subjects are told to imagine that they are police officers checking whether people drinking in a bar are conforming with a rule. If this paragraph is omitted, then the facilitation effect disappears (Pollard & Evans, 1987).

By use of scenarios, subjects can be encouraged, in selection tasks with a rationale, to take the point of view of an authority that wants to check whether violations have occurred. They may identify with the Post Office itself in the postal task and choose cards that could reveal violations, in order to take steps to prevent a loss or to deter future losses, as we have just explained. They may also identify with Post Office workers who would lose their jobs if they do not catch violations and prevent the Post Office from losing money. Either way we can now describe the decision they make in somewhat more technical terms. Faced with one of the envelopes—say, the one with a low value stamp on it—they obviously have two options. They can decide to turn over this envelope or not to do so. If they turn it over, they spend a small amount of time and energy, but they have a chance of finding a violation and taking corrective action. If they do not turn it over, they run the risk of overlooking a violation and suffering a loss. The latter alternative seems inferior to the former, and for that reason, they opt for the former and turn over the envelope. (See Manktelow & Over, 1991, and Over & Manktelow, 1993, for this kind of analysis of deontic selection tasks.)

Kirby (1994a) shows us how to describe this decision more technically but still intuitively using the terminology of signal detection theory. He points out that it is natural to call turning over an envelope and finding a violation a HIT, and turning it over and not finding a violation a FALSE ALARM, or FA for short. Then not turning over the envelope and overlooking a violation is a MISS, and not turning it over when it would reveal no violation is a CORRECT REJECTION, or CR for short. Now consider the following for any given envelope:

4.2   *Prob(HIT).Util(HIT) + Prob(FA).Util(FA)*

In the above, let Prob(HIT) and Prob(FA) represent respectively our judgement (a) about the probability that we will find a violation given that we turn over the envelope, and (b) about the probability that we will not find a violation given that we turn it over. The quantities Util(HIT) and Util(FA) are to represent respectively the utility we get from turning over an envelope and finding a violation, and the utility we get from turning it over and not finding a violation. Util(HIT) would be relatively high in a standard postal task if we identified with the Post Office. It represents the benefit we would get from finding a violation and being able to take corrective action. Util(FA) would be relatively small. It represents the cost in energy and time of turning over an envelope and finding no violation, and we could think of it informally, though not necessarily formally, as being a negative number standing for a small cost.

Altogether 4.2 represents the subjective expected utility of turning over an envelope. The total sum will be relatively high for us if we think there is a reasonable probability that a violation will be revealed by turning over the envelope. In order to decide what to do, we should compare 4.2 with the following for the same envelope:

4.3   *Prob(MISS).Util(MISS) + Prob(CR).Util(CR)*

Here Prob(MISS) and Prob(CR) are respectively our subjective probabilities that there will be a violation on the other side of the envelope given that we do not turn it over, and that there will not be a violation there given that we do not turn it over. Of course, Util(MISS) is the utility we would get by not turning over the envelope when there is a violation there, and Util(CR) is the utility we would get by not turning it over when there is no violation there. The latter represents a small saving in time and energy, but the former stands for relatively serious cost of letting someone get away with paying too little for a sealed letter. Overall 4.3 represents our subjective expected utility for *not* turning over the envelope. If 4.2 is high and 4.3 low, we should turn over the envelope: this is the way to maximise our subjective expected utility when we are faced with this decision.

People faced with a choice between options should, according to strict normative decision theory, pick the one with the highest subjective expected utility and so maximise this quantity. In the postal selection task we have described, there is no chance that any violators will be revealed by turning over the unsealed envelope and the one with the 20 cent stamp on it. If we believe this, then 4.3 for these envelopes will seem greater to us than 4.2, as turning over either envelope would be a cost, however small, in time and energy without any potential benefit.

The matter is different, however, when we consider 4.2 and 4.3 for the other two envelopes. There is some chance that these will reveal violations, and if we believe this, 4.2 for them will be seem greater to us than 4.3. People do tend to choose these cards in this deontic selection task, and thus they make the best decision about it.

Deontic selection tasks with "non-logical" solutions

In the postal task the best decision is to choose the card showing that the antecedent of the deontic conditional is true and the one showing the consequent false (p and not-q)—corresponding to the logically correct choices on the indicative task. This decision is not, however, the best one in *all* deontic selection tasks. Consider the following deontic conditional from the "shop task" in Manktelow and Over (1991):

4.4   If you spend more than £100 then you may take a free gift.

We should note that 4.4 is a conditional permission, indicated by the use of "may", and not a conditional obligation like 4.1, which is expressed using "must". The rationale for this task essentially stated that a shop had laid down this rule, which gives its customers permission to take a gift under a certain condition, in order to improve business. In the context of its use, it is natural to infer pragmatically that the only way the customers can get permission to take the gift is to spend £100. That being so, there are four ways in which the rule, or what is understood pragmatically by its utterance, could be violated. These are ways in which the shop could fail to satisfy its goal (that of increasing sales) in giving this conditional permission:

- The shop could take the right money but not issue the gift.
- The shop might not take the right money but still issue the gift.
- The customers could spend the right money but not take the gift.
- The customers could take the gift but not spend the right money.

Manktelow and Over asked subjects to imagine that they had been brought in because a shop supposedly applying this rule was in difficulty. By introducing variants into the scenario, different groups of subjects were cued to one of the four perspectives that we have just listed. For example, one group of subjects was, in effect, told to suspect that the shop might have been issuing gifts that the customers were not entitled to: this is the second difficulty in the above list. Now, in this task, a HIT would be finding that someone either had spent the right amount of money but had not received a gift or had received a gift but not spent the right amount of money. In the example we are using, the subjects were encouraged to suspect the latter possibility, and this should have affected their probability judgements.

Table 4.1 summarises the design of this study, showing the cards with high HIT probabilities according to the suspected violation cued by the scenario in each of the four groups. These were also the card combinations that most subjects chose: in two of the four cases this means that the non-logical selection of not-p and q was the pattern of choice preferred on the deontic selection task. This experiment thus clearly provides evidence that subjects choices on the deontic selection task are rational$_1$ but not rational$_2$, and that thematic facilitation effects—when they occur—do not do so by facilitating logical reasoning. Similar effects of what are called perspective shifts in deontic selection tasks have been shown in other recent studies. (See Politzer & Nguyen-Xuan, 1992, and Gigerenzer & Hug, 1992, for these. For a schema account of perspective shifts, see Holyoak & Cheng, 1995, with comments and a reply.)

Cosmides (1989) claimed that when people choose the right cards in selection tasks they are looking for cheaters—i.e. those who take benefits without paying an appropriate cost. An example of a cheater is a customer who takes a free gift without paying at least £100 in the scenario of the shop task. Cosmides held that an innate tendency exists, which she called a "Darwinian algorithm", to look for cheaters because it was adaptive under primitive conditions to discover those who took benefits from others without ever paying anything in return. Dennett (1995, p. 489) has repeated that all cases in which subjects get the right answer in selection tasks are ones where they are trying to detect

TABLE 4.1
Probabilities of HITS in the study of Manktelow and Over (1991)

	Card			
Suspicion cued to subject	More than £100 spent (p)	Less than £100 spent (not-p)	Gift taken (q)	Gift not taken (not-q)
Shop takes the money but does not issue gift	HIGH			HIGH
Shop does not take money, but issues gift		HIGH	HIGH	
Customer spends money but does not receive gift	HIGH			HIGH
Customer does not spend money, but receives gift		HIGH	HIGH	

cheaters. But this is not so (Manktelow & Over, 1990a, 1990b). There is no cheating, for example, when the shop itself gives customers more than that to which they are entitled. People who violate the rule studied by Manktelow and Over (1990b), "If you clean up spilt blood then you must wear rubber gloves", are not cheaters. Subjects solve correctly a selection task based on this prudential rule, which has the point of preventing diseases caused by infected blood. Its violators are not cheating but rather endangering their own lives.

Judgements about benefits and costs are to do with much more than cheating. This has been recognised by Cosmides and Tooby (1992), who propose that the mind consists of a number of innate mechanisms or Darwinian algorithms for dealing with specific problems: one for detecting cheaters, one for avoiding what is life threatening, and others. All these algorithms are supposed to have developed because they were adaptive under primitive conditions, but whether or not they exist, it does not follow that people can only think about very specific problems. Dennett (1995, pp. 490–491) points out that people might begin with particular innate structures, but still acquire wider abilities through learning. They might indeed learn general ways of avoiding costly outcomes. There is even evidence from abstract indicative selection tasks that people grasp some formal logical principles. If the not-q card is turned over in these tasks and a p revealed on the other side, people will respond that the abstract conditional "if p then q" is false, though few of them chose the not-q card in the first place. (See Chapter 6 for more evidence that people do have some general logical competence.)

Recent work has also shown how subjective probability judgements affect deontic selection tasks (Kirby, 1994a; Manktelow, Sutherland, & Over, 1995). Consider someone working as an official at an airport who has the job of checking people's immigration cards for violations of this rule:

> If a person has ENTERING on one side of their immigration
> card then they must have CHOLERA on the reverse side.

Cheng and Holyoak (1985) used essentially this rule in a selection task. One side of a card stated whether a person was entering the country or was in transit, and the other side gave information about inoculations the person had had. The point of the rule was said to be to protect those entering the country from disease. Manktelow et al. (1995) modified this task mainly by giving information on the country of origin of the person on the side of the card that had ENTERING or TRANSIT on it, and by using an enlarged array of cards. Some of these cards showed that the person was from a tropical country (e.g. Thailand) and others that the person was from a European country (e.g. Germany). The rationale stated that the official was concerned that people with cholera should not be allowed in the country, and also that cholera is common in tropical countries.

Manktelow et al. predicted that more tropical cards than European ones would be selected in this extended task, and this is what they found in their results. The cost of allowing someone with cholera to enter from a European country would be as great as that of allowing someone to enter with this disease from a tropical country. But the latter would be more probable than the former, and thus the expected cost of the latter would be greater than the former. Notice that what is relevant here is the probability that someone entering from a tropical country, or from a European one, will have cholera, and not the probability of a tropical or European violation *per se*.

People clearly display rationality$_1$ in the simple deontic selection tasks we have examined so far. They tend to select cards that seem relatively likely to reveal serious costs when turned over. If corrective steps are not taken, these outcomes could prevent a goal from being achieved. There are indeed some deontic selection tasks people do less well in by strict normative standards. It seems to be characteristic of these tasks that people are not at risk of suffering a cost, but have the chance of getting a small benefit. This would be consistent with other evidence that people tend to be more sensitive to possible costs than to possible benefits (see Kirby, 1994a; Manktelow & Over, 1990b; and Over & Evans, 1994). It could be rational$_1$, to some extent, to have some loss aversion, as this would be called. If one is reasonably satisfied, it may be an efficient use of cognitive resources to look out more for what will lower this satisfaction rather than raise it. (See Kahneman & Varey, 1991, on loss aversion, and Kahneman & Tversky, 1979, for a descriptive decision theory that covers loss aversion.) The extent of any loss aversion in deontic selection tasks will have to be investigated more fully in the future, but in any case, the evidence is that people can generally use their practical thought to make the right decisions in deontic selection tasks. Rules, regulations, laws, and social agreements could hardly be more important to us in all aspects of our lives, and it is certainly interesting that an experimental study of these should show that we have such good understanding of them.

Relevance in the deontic selection task

So far we have used only normative decision theory to specify what the right choices in these deontic tasks should be. The unbounded nature of this theory, which we complained about in Chapter 2, does not preclude its application as a normative standard for these very simple tasks, where the options are so limited. It may then appear that subjects are rational$_2$ on these tasks, but that would require the further assumption that they make decisions by explicitly following decision theory rules, computing SEUs for all the cards, and so on. In fact, we have already presented evidence in Chapter 3 that contradicts this view. On deontic as well as indicative selection tasks, subjects appear to focus straight away on the cards that they end up choosing (Evans, 1995b and in press). It is important now that we consider *how* people actually make their choices. It is not sufficient to show that people make adaptively rational decisions: we need to provide a psychological mechanism by which this can be achieved.

In attempting to understand deontic reasoning, it is important to recall that relevance is related to the current goal that is being pursued. Information will be more relevant, the greater extent to which it bears upon the chances of achieving the current goal. Relevance should also be increased by the salience of the goal—in particular the extent of any costs and benefits associated with it. Say, for example, you subscribe to a local newspaper that routinely carries advertisements for second-hand car sales. Most days you probably never look at these ads at all. However, if you are currently pursuing a goal of buying or selling a car, then this information will temporarily acquire high relevance and be scrutinised carefully. Like the relevance effects discussed in Chapter 3, goals may cue relevance by tacit processes acting at a preconscious level. For example, if you are in a crowded room in which two people are discussing the price of second-hand cars, your attention may switch to this conversation that would otherwise have gone unnoticed.

Now, it is clear in the deontic selection task that cards which could reveal an outcome costing the subjects something, such as the extra money for a sealed letter or the spread of a disease, have high goal relevance for the individual. How is it that subjects are able to detect this relevance and choose accordingly? Consider first, subjective probability. Tversky and Kahneman (1973) have argued that the main method by which we judge probability of events is by their availability, or the ease with which examples of the event "come to mind". Thus to say that a particular event is subjectively probable in a given context, is also to say that a mental model of that possibility is available—i.e. likely to be formed and considered. Availability is not sufficient for relevance, however, which is where utility of outcomes plays a role. An available model will become relevant and thus the focus of attention provided that it has high goal relevance, which is effectively the same thing as a high expected cost or benefit.

We do not conceive of probability and utility as exerting their influence in a strictly sequential manner. In so far as we have characterised the implicit cognitive system as connectionist (see Chapter 3), it is perfectly reasonable to suppose that both likelihood and significance can exert parallel influence through a network in the determination of relevance. High probability, whether or not determined by high availability, is not a necessary condition for relevance, because we know that improbable outcomes with high utility may sometimes become the focus for decision making. People may know that it is objectively improbable that their houses will burn down, but still buy insurance because this misfortune would be so very costly. Again, what makes the outcome relevant for them is its high expected cost. Sometimes, of course, the availability, vividness, and apparent cost of the unlikely outcome can be enhanced by emotive coverage of disasters in the media and the sales pitch of insurance agents.

In the case of deontic selection tasks, we propose that an integrated mental model, including a combination of two card values, becomes the focus of attention. For example, in the shop task discussed earlier, the overall goal of the subjects is to help the shop improve its business. A variant of the scenario makes one costly outcome relatively probable, say, where the company is giving gifts to customers who are not spending the required amount of money. A model of this outcome becomes the one the subjects take as relevant and focus on, and they consequently choose cards that could reveal whether it holds or not . Further variants of the scenario make relatively probable other costly outcomes, where the shop's business is not improving because of different mistakes. Other models then become relevant and become the focus of attention, leading to different card choices.

In the abstract selection tasks discussed in Chapter 3, there is no relevant experience of the problem domain that can help to cue models of possible combinations of values on the cards. With an arbitrary conditional such as "If there is an A on one side of the card, then there is a 3 on the other side of the card", the subjects will have no pragmatic influences which will remind them, for example, that As are usually paired with 4s, let alone have some sense of value or pay-off associated with such a model. This is why we have argued that relevance of the facing sides of the cards alone determines decisions, and that this relevance is itself a function of linguistic cues such as the *if* and *not* heuristics. However, recently authors have begun to apply decision theoretic approaches to selection tasks that are abstract and indicative, as well as to those that are thematic and deontic. It is to this issue that we now turn.

INDICATIVE SELECTION TASKS

An indicative selection task is one based on an indicative rather than a deontic conditional. Indicative conditionals are not used to guide or regulate behaviour. These conditionals are not rules for correct action, but are rather used to express beliefs and to try to state truths or make justified assertions about the world. (Edgington, 1995, is a major survey of views on the semantics and assertibility of indicative conditionals.) Consider the following form of an example often used in the philosophy of science:

4.5   If it is a raven then it is black.

This is not an attempt to get ravens to be black, like a rule for the correct dress at funerals. What scientists who utter 4.5 seriously are trying to do is to state a truth or a fact about ravens, but that does not mean they would use only theoretical reasons, and not any practical thought, to help them achieve the epistemic goal of finding out how well supported 4.5 is.

Scientific research requires many decisions about which actions to perform in gathering data and in experiments. Consider how we should collect empirical data to confirm or to disconfirm 4.5 to some degree—i.e. to find out how probable or how improbable 4.5 is. It matters little how probable or improbable 4.5 seems to us initially, as long as we do not think it certainly true or certainly false. Independent of that, we must make a decision about which actions to perform to collect relevant data. There is an underlying similarity between this decision and the one subjects face in an indicative selection task, which should make this task of interest to philosophers of science as well as to cognitive psychologists. Which of the following should we do, individually or in combination?

   (i) Look for ravens.
   (ii) Look for non-ravens.
   (iii) Look for black things.
   (iv) Look for non-black things.

One option can be eliminated immediately as the worst if we want to be at all scientific. This is the "null" option: to do none of the above and so collect no empirical data at all. On the other hand, the best option in this case seems to be (i) alone. If we examine a number of ravens and find that they are all black, then 4.5 has a fair amount of confirmation. If one of these ravens appears to be white, then 4.5 is strongly disconfirmed. The other options alone or in combination with (i) seem far less attractive here. For example, doing (iv) on its own or in combination with (i) appears inefficient. The set of non-black things is huge, "scattered", and heterogeneous, and finding a non-black non-raven, like a white cloud, would do almost nothing to confirm 4.5. We might get lucky and find an apparently non-black raven, and that would disconfirm 4.5. Even if such a raven exists, however, we would have to be very lucky indeed to find it efficiently by looking among the non-black things. For the set of ravens is quite small relative to the non-ravens, and thus any non-black thing we examine is most probably a non-raven in any case. (See Howson & Urbach, 1993, for more on this example in the philosophy of science; and also Wetherick, 1993, and Over & Evans, 1994, for its relevance to the selection task.)

Let us apply these points to an indicative selection task based on the following conditional:

4.6   If a card has a vowel on one side then it has an even number on the other.

The subjects are presented with the usual four cards in this task, and can do any of the following individually or in any combination:

(i′) Turn over the card showing a vowel.
(ii′) Turn over the card showing a consonant.
(iii′) Turn over the card showing an even number.
(iv′) Turn over the card showing an odd number.

The subjects are asked, in an indicative task like this one, to decide which cards should be turned over to see whether the conditional is true or false. For a long time, the vast majority of researchers on the task held that the correct choices for subjects are (i′) and (iv′) (i.e. p and not-q). These are the choices that might reveal a case that would falsify 4.6, with its antecedent true and its consequent false. They are the logically correct choices if the conditional is interpreted as one about only the four cards, as subjects in most selection tasks are told that it should be. But the subjects tend to select just (i′) alone, or (i′) and (iii′) together (see Evans et al., 1993a, Chapter 4).

Until recently, most researchers would have said that the subjects make a bad mistake in not selecting (iv′) (the not-q case). However, Kirby (1994a) points out that the set of vowels is small relative to that of consonants, and so the subjects might think it improbable that they would find a vowel on the back of a card with an odd number on it. They may, in effect, ask themselves why should they turn over this card if it is almost bound to have a consonant on it. For them, selecting (iv′) may seem inefficient, a bit like going out and looking for non-black things to see if 4.5 is true or false. We would add that it is unusual to assert a realistic general conditional like 4.5 about only four objects, and no matter what subjects are told in the instructions, they may interpret 4.6 as referring to a large number of cards.

This way of looking at this particular selection task is too simple, as individual vowels are more common in normal text than individual consonants. We shall merely use this task for the moment as an example of what might be going on generally in indicative selection tasks. Suppose we write out 4.2 and 4.3 for the card with the odd number on it, as a strict way of deciding whether we should turn it over, i.e. opt for (iv'). Following Kirby, we would call an apparently falsifying case a HIT. If we think it improbable that there is such a HIT on the back of this card, because there are so few vowels relative to the consonants, then 4.2 for us will be relatively low. At the same time, 4.3 will be relatively high for us, as the probability of a CORRECT REJECTION is fairly high, and not turning over the card saves us time and energy. If 4.3 is higher than 4.2, we should reject turning over this card—i.e. not opt for (iv')—in order to avoid the expected cost.

Effects of subjective probability in indicative selection tasks

The general point under consideration here is whether subjective probability judgements affect choices in indicative selection tasks. We have already seen that these judgements not only should, but actually do affect decisions in deontic selection tasks. Kirby (1994a) tries to show that subjective probability judgements really do affect decisions in indicative tasks as well. We can bring out some important points by examining his Experiment 2 in some detail. All the subjects in this experiment were told the following:

> A computer was given the task of printing out cards with an integer from one to 100 on one side, and one of two arithmetic symbols (+ or –) on the other side of those cards.

Subjects were then divided into three groups for three different "p set" conditions, and according to their group, they were given one of the following statements:

Small p set   If a card has a 1 on one side then it has a + on the other side.

Medium p set   If a card has a number from 1 to 50 on one side then it has a + on the other side.

Large p set   If a card has a number from 1 to 90 on one side then it has a + on the other side.

Here we have three conditionals of the form "If p then q". The set referred to by the antecedent, the p set, expands from the small to the medium to the large in these conditionals. As this happens, the subjects in the different groups should find it more and more probable that a falsifying case will be revealed by turning over the not-q card. Using 4.2 and 4.3 in his analysis, Kirby predicted, and actually found, that more subjects selected the not-q card as the size of the p set increased. Here it is important to note that Kirby did not tell his subjects that the three conditionals were just about the four cards they could see. It would seem natural for them to take the conditionals to be about all the cards the computer has printed out.

We can perhaps make Kirby's point clearer by using 4.5 as the more intuitive example. Suppose this conditional was used successively to make a statement about just 3 flocks of 100 birds, and we knew that there were 2 or 3 ravens in the first flock, about 50 in the second, and about 90 in the third. Imagine also that we get our first view of these flocks at some distance, from which we can tell that there is a small set of black birds in the first, a medium set of black birds in the second, and a large set of black birds in the third. We have no idea whether 4.5 is true of any of these flocks, and want to get some evidence to help settle the question. To see if 4.5 is true of the first flock, we simply look for a raven in it. We do not go to the trouble of getting a closer look at any of the non-black birds in this flock; it is just too improbable, in any case, that any given one of these is a raven. Certainly by the time we get to the third flock, our attitude is different, and we have started to look closely at the non-black birds. There are a small number of these in this flock, and it is much more probable that any one of these is a raven.

Kirby's position is well argued, but unfortunately there is a possible problem with the design of the experiments he uses to support it (Kirby 1994b; Over & Evans, 1994). There is, however, an older set of experiments in the literature providing strong support for his position. Pollard and Evans (1981) tested a hypothesis of Van Duyne (1976) with improved methodology in selection tasks, and found evidence that subjects choose more false consequent cards for conditionals they believe to be false than for those they believe to be true. Their interpretation of this finding was that, when a conditional is believed to be false, the falsifying case, with the antecedent true and the consequent false, is available from memory. The more strongly the conditional is believed to be false by people, the more confident they should be that the antecedent will be found to be true on the back of a false consequent card. This hypothesis is then similar to Kirby's.

In a second study, Pollard and Evans (1983) demonstrated facilitation of false consequent cards across a whole set of abstract conditionals with and without negative components. These conditionals concerned values on cards the probabilities of which were established in a probability learning task prior to the selection task. Pollard and Evans trained subjects with a set of cards that were red on one side and blue on the other. The red side, for example, might have a triangle or be blank, while the blue side might have a star or be blank. A selection task could be based on a conditional like:

If there is a triangle on one side then there is a star on the other.

Such a conditional could be established as "usually true" in the probability learning task with this set:

seven cards with a triangle on one side and a star on the other;
one card with a triangle on one side and a blank on the other;
seven cards with a blank on one side and a star on the other;
seven cards with a blank on one side and a blank on the other.

The subjects were also trained to think of other conditionals as "usually false". For the "usually true" conditionals, the probability of a false consequent given a true antecedent was low, as was the probability of a true antecedent given a false consequent. But for "usually false" conditionals, the consequent values were reversed in the training phase, so that the probability of a false consequent given a true antecedent, and of a true antecedent given a false consequent, were both relatively high. The subjects themselves picked the four cards, without of course seeing what was on the other side of them, for the selection task. They were told that the given conditional was only about these four cards. In other selection tasks, subjects might well not take proper notice of an attempt to restrict their attention to just the four cards, and might act as if they were dealing with a more general conditional like 4.5. But in this task their training had taught them that all the conditionals were false of the packs of cards as a whole, and the only question could be about the four cards they had chosen. As predicted, substantially more false consequent cards were chosen in selection tasks based on "usually false" conditionals than in ones based on "usually true" conditionals.

This work of Pollard and Evans provides good support for the hypothesis that probability judgements generally can affect decisions in indicative selection tasks. Kirby's method with improved methodology might do this as well, but it might not be as successful. In his task, subjects were given information that probabilities could be computed or inferred from, whereas in Pollard and Evans' studies, subjects either knew contingencies from real world experience (Pollard & Evans, 1981) or learned them for abstract conditionals (Pollard & Evans, 1983). Thus it is likely in the Pollard and Evans procedure that the contingencies were learned at a tacit level, while Kirby relies on explicit verbal presentation of information. The weakness of such explicit presentation of probability or statistics will be a feature of our commentary on the literature on the base rate fallacy in Chapter 5. We generally expect the implicit learning of frequencies to have a more profound influence on judgements than explicitly given propositional representations. The specific point here is that the training or prior belief is acting at the heuristic level to focus the attention of subjects either on to the combination p and q for the usually true conditional, or p and not-q for the usually false one. We can thus account for the card choices in terms of the extended relevance theory presented earlier in discussion of the deontic selection task.

Oaksford and Chater's rational analysis model
Oaksford and Chater (1994) have proposed an analysis of the selection task that makes use of information theory. They independently present in technical detail what was originally stated by Dorling (1983), who claimed that the expected information gain, in the sense of Shannon-Wiener, from the q card is greater than that from the not-q card in a standard indicative selection task. Dorling supported his view with points about set size similar to Kirby's, and assumed that the subjects would tend not to restrict the conditional to what was presented on the four cards—e.g. they would take it to be about an entire pack of cards. It is necessary to consider this view in some detail, as what is informative or uninformative certainly does affect reasoning and decision making. (See also Over & Evans, 1994.)

Oaksford and Chater's most fundamental presupposition is that subjects in an indicative selection task ought to, and actually do, have the epistemic goal of reducing their uncertainty about whether the conditional is true. But there are clear normative and experimental reasons for rejecting both the idea that they should have this goal and that they do in fact have it. To measure the uncertainty of a hypothesis H, Oaksford and Chater use the following Shannon-Wiener formula from information theory:

4.7 $Information = -p(H)log_2 p(H) - p(not\text{-}H)log_2 p(not\text{-}H)$

Oaksford and Chater argue that people should think about the probable gains in information, in the above sense, from possible card selections. This leads them to a computation of Expected Information Gain (EIG), where information gain is defined as uncertainty reduction. They hold that cards with the highest EIGs should be the most frequently chosen. Their analysis is based on some debatable assumptions, e.g. that the subjects never restrict the conditional to what is represented on the four cards, and that a number of parameters take certain values. Given these assumptions, Oaksford and Chater find evidence that EIGs correlate with subjects' choices in various selection task experiments. However, theirs is also a controversial way of defining information in hypothesis testing. In Bayesian analysis, information is more commonly defined in terms of the the log likelihood ratio, as in 2.4—a normative measure that is much closer to our notion of subjective epistemic utility than is EIG (Evans & Over, in press; Laming, in press).

In order to see why information gain, in the sense of Oaksford and Chater, should not be a normative measure of epistemic utility, let us examine exactly how 4.7 works. Anyone who thought Prob(H) = 0.5 and Prob(not-H) = 0.5 would by 4.7 be in the state of greatest uncertainty. From this point of indifference between the hypothesis and its negation, people would reduce their uncertainty by gathering some evidence showing one of the two as more probable than the other. As the probability of the hypothesis approached 1 or 0, the people's state of uncertainty would approach 0 by 4.7. This seems right as far as it goes, but Oaksford and Chater's position implies something much stronger: that reducing one's uncertainty and getting an epistemic benefit are always the same thing, which is clearly false. Suppose we are at a point of doubting one of our hypotheses, H: we think Prob(H) = 0.4 and Prob(not-H) = 0.6. Now we get some evidence and find that Prob(H) has risen to 0.6 and of course Prob(not-H) has fallen to 0.4. It follows that our uncertainty, as measured by 4.7, has not been reduced, and we have had no epistemic benefit. There may be some people whose only goal is to reduce their uncertainty, but scientists and most ordinary people care much more about finding out how probable or improbable a hypothesis of importance to them is. Even if our hypothesis was not-H in this case, we would still think of ourselves as getting an epistemic benefit, though we might feel disappointed.

Even more serious problems for Oaksford and Chater can be illustrated by supposing that the evidence we get only raises Prob(H) from 0.4 to 0.5, dropping Prob(not-H) from 0.6 to 0.5. Now we have increased our uncertainty and consequently suffered an epistemic cost, according to Oaksford and Chater's position. This cannot be right if our epistemic goal is not merely to reduce uncertainty, but to make a better judgement about how probable or improbable the hypothesis is. Compare a conditional that is probably true in one selection task with one that is probably false in another. By the Oaksford and Chater measure, there is less reason to investigate the latter than the former. Confirming the conditional that is probably false can increase our uncertainty, by taking its probability closer to 0.5, and this can be reflected in a relatively low expected value for, say, the p card in this task. This problem does not arise for the task with the probably true conditional, and the expected value of the p card there can be relatively high. But there are no good normative grounds for thinking that there should be less reason to investigate such a probably false conditional than a probably true one.

Moreover, Evans and Over (in press) point out that the Pollard and Evans (1983) experiment described earlier produces an empirical disconfirmation of Oaksford and Chater's model: this follows from the fact that their analysis gives less reason to investigate a probably false conditional than a probably true one. Oaksford and Chater's calculations all depend on assumptions about parameter values such as the "rarity assumption" which assigns low values to $P(p)$ and $P(q)$. However, the Pollard and Evans procedure fully specifies not only the probability of the conditional statement being true or false, but the precise probabilities of finding any particular value on the back of each card. We believe also that it is clear to the subjects that these probabilities—not default ones—apply to the selection task they are given, because they themselves select the four cards from the training pack. Thus in our view, this experiment is the best available in which to test the EIG model. Evans and Over computed EIGs for this experiment and showed them to predict the opposite to what actually happens. For example, EIG was considerably higher for the not-q card when the conditional was probably true than when it was probably false, although choices of this card in the experiment were actually higher in the latter case than in the former.

There are also respects in which Oaksford and Chater's analysis is not general enough. They always compare a model in which the conditional is true (the dependence model) with an alternative one in which the conditional is false (the independence model). As its name suggests, the latter is a model in which the consequent of the conditional is independent of the antecedent. But this should not always be the alternative model. Consider yet again 4.5. The model in which this is false should be one in which no ravens are black, or at least in which no male or no female ravens are black. The point is that ravens as a biological species of bird form a highly homogeneous set: all its members are the same colour or at most males and females differ. The experimental evidence is that ordinary people grasp such facts about such sets (Nisbett, Krantz, Jepson, & Kunda, 1983). They would tend to become highly confident in 4.5 after the observation of just a few black ravens. This evidence would disconfirm relatively quickly an alternative model of the sort we have described.

Oaksford and Chater's work is very stimulating and rightly draws attention to the importance of information in reasoning and decision making. But we do not think that they characterise information in the right way, nor that they have a sufficiently decision theoretic analysis of the selection task. It would be better to use the expected value of the absolute log likelihood ratio, 2.4, as an impersonal normative measure, and the descriptive results would be at least as good as using Oaksford and Chater's EIG. However, there are no grounds for assuming that people always place the same overall subjective utility on getting optimal information in any sense. Like so many coins, so many bits of information will sometimes have more utility for people and sometimes less, depending on their other epistemic and non-epistemic goals. Both 2.4 and 4.7 make use of subjective probabilities, but neither takes account of the different personal goals individuals have, nor their cognitive limitations. Future research on the selection task will have to investigate what individual people find informative there and the subjective preference they have for it, and how that is related to what they find relevant and focus on.

Cueing of counter-examples in the indicative selection task

One interpretation of the Pollard and Evans experiments is that subjects were induced to focus on the counter-example case p and not-q. This is not dissimilar to the explanation offered at the time by Pollard and Evans (1981, 1983) who referred to the *availability* of this case from memory. It is hard to see how a conditional is perceived to be false except by the availability of its counter-example. For example, if you rate the statement "If it is a swan then it is white" as false, this is presumably because you have seen or read about the existence of black swans which readily come to mind.

Several recent studies have shown the importance of cueing counter-examples in the indicative selection task. Green (1995; Green & Larking, 1995) has shown, for example, that if subjects are asked to write down a case where the conditional could be false before performing the standard letters and numbers selection task, then the number of p and not-q selections is greatly facilitated, especially for subjects who succeed in identifying this counter-example in the pre-task. Of particular interest here are the experiments reported by Love and Kessler (1995) who used scenarios with both indicative and deontic selection tasks in which the probability and utility of counter-example cases was manipulated. The authors interpret their findings in terms of "focusing" on the counter-example case. We will cite examples here of indicative tasks, although results with deontic ones were similar.

In Experiment 1a, Love and Kessler presented a science-fiction scenario in which creatures called Xow flourish in force fields. As a visiting starship captain, the subject has to test whether the following statement, held in the folklore of the local culture, is true:

If there are Xow, then there must be a force field.

This selection task is clearly indicative. Two versions of the problem were presented, one of which indicated high probability and significance of counter-examples by reference to the possibility of mutant Xows that can survive in the absence of a force field and that were scientifically important to discover. The p and not-q selections were 47% in this enhanced Xow problem compared with 23% on the standard problem. Experiment 1b separated the effects of probability and significance (utility) of the counter-examples and found that both significantly influenced responding. Further support for this was found in Experiment 2.

The recent series of experiments presented by Sperber et al. (1995) in support of their own relevance theory of the selection task also involve the use of scenarios that focus subjects on to counter-example cases. They argue that conditionals can be used in several ways in natural discourse, one of which is to rule out the case p and not-q. They show that use of conditionals of this type is associated with high correct selection rates on the selection task. In one of their scenarios, for example, an opinionated woman named Mrs Bianchi utters a conditional in a way that rules out the possibility of so much as a single exception. This should make the possibility of counter-examples more relevant and raise the combined selection of p and not-q cards alone, and this is what Sperber et al. found.

A general conditional like "If it is a swan then it is white" is strictly false, but specific instances of it, such as "If you saw a swan in the river today then it was white", can be used with some confidence because counter-examples to the general case are so infrequent. Recent experiments by Evans, Ellis, and Newstead (in press b) are relevant here. In their Experiment 1, subjects were asked to rate the truth of conditionals with respect to arrays that contained either no, few, or many counter-examples. Those with a few counter-examples were rated as intermediate in truth value. In other experiments, subjects were asked to construct their own arrays to represent situations in which conditionals were true, and frequently included a small number of counter-example, p and not-q cases. Evans et al. (in press b) also found that when constructing arrays to represent false conditionals, *many* such counter-examples were included, so that falsifying "if p then q" was similar to verifying "if p then not q".

In view of the above, it is perhaps not surprising that searching for falsifying cases occurs only when there are strong cues to the relevance of counter-examples. For example, in the Sperber et al. study, the conditionals that "facilitated" selection task responses were those strongly claimed to have no counter-examples at all. In the case of the Pollard and Evans experiments, subjects chose p and not-q for conditionals where many counter-examples had been encountered, and in the Love and Kessler study, such cases were cued as being either very frequent or very important.

The findings discussed here fit very well to the extended relevance model of the selection task that we presented earlier in order to account for rational$_1$ choices on the deontic selection task. Although card selections on abstract indicative tasks are usually cued simply by the relevance of the facing sides of the cards (Chapter 3), this need not be the case when experimental procedures are introduced to cue counter-example cases. In our discussion of the deontic selection task we argued that both subjective probability and subjective utility contribute to the perceived relevance of mental models. Although indicative conditionals may be asserted despite knowledge of occasional counter-examples, the studies reviewed here show that either frequency or significance (utility) of such cases causes subjects to focus on the counter-example model and choose cards accordingly. Moreover, procedures that simply draw attention to counter-examples, as in Green's experiments, will cause subjects to focus on such a model. The reason that the mere availability of counter-example cases is sufficient for their perceived relevance in indicative selection tasks is that subjects are there pursuing only the epistemic goal of discovering whether the statement is true or false. Hence, the possibility of a falsifying case, once considered, inevitably becomes relevant.

CONCLUSION

The selection task has been the main technique employed in the psychological literature for investigating people's understanding of deontic and indicative conditionals. It is unrivalled as a controlled way of raising deep questions about how we use conditionals to achieve goals from the moral to the epistemic. It has been treated in the past as a reasoning problem, but is primarily a decision task calling for judgements of subjective probability and utility. People's choices in deontic tasks show a high level of rationality$_1$. In indicative selection tasks, they are frequently illogical or irrational$_2$ when they are supposed to think about the four cards and nothing else. But they generally display more rationality$_1$ when they view the task as a wider one in decision making about more realistic cases. We have presented an extended relevance theory account of the selection task that shows how manipulations affecting probability and utility come to affect card choices. We believe not that subjects perform mental calculations of expected utility, but rather that their degrees of belief and subjective preferences together cause them to focus on particular mental models.

CHAPTER FIVE

Prior belief

The influence of prior belief on reasoning and decision making has perhaps produced more experimental investigations, more claims of bias, and more arguments about human rationality than any other single issue. There are three substantial cognitive literatures concerned with this issue, which we will examine in some detail in this chapter, namely:

- *The use or neglect of prior probabilities in tasks designed as tests of Bayesian decision making.* Most famously, this literature includes a claim that information about base rates is grossly neglected when subjects make posterior probability judgements in the light of specific evidence.
- *Confirmation bias*—which is defined as a tendency to seek information that will confirm rather than falsify existing beliefs, theories, and hypotheses. Evidence for confirmation bias is adduced from work within several different paradigms and traditions.
- *Belief bias*—which is an effect studied in the deductive reasoning literature and consists of a tendency for people to judge the validity of an argument on the basis of the prior believability of its conclusion.

In addition to these cognitive literatures, there is substantive evidence from research in cognitive social psychology that appears to show irrational influence of prior beliefs that is analogous to confirmation and belief bias effects. In particular, people appear (a) to be overly influenced by information they receive first, (b) to seek evidence likely to support their beliefs, and (c) to assess evidence for or against a favoured position in a biased manner (for a review and discussion of such evidence see Nisbett & Ross, 1980, Chapter 8; Baron, 1988, Chapter 15).

In this chapter, we examine the effects of prior belief with our distinction between rationality$_1$ and rationality$_2$ firmly in mind. Where claims of bias and irrationality are rampant, as in the literatures discussed here, the first essential is to decide whether people are being irrational$_1$ as opposed to irrational$_2$. Where this is established we seek an explanation at the level of the cognitive mechanisms that may fail for one of two main reasons: (a) inherent limitations in information-processing capacity; and (b) the possession of inappropriate training and experience linked with an inability to adapt to the demands of a novel situation, such as maybe provided by a psychological experiment. As we have repeatedly argued, the nature of the cognitive system underlying rational$_1$ behaviour is primarily tacit, shaped by past experience and beyond the control of consciousness. This implies that the ability of people to modify habitual and normally effective methods of thinking in order to comply with experimental instructions should be limited. As we shall see, this is broadly true, but people can respond to instructions to a sufficient extent to have interesting implications for the discussion of deductive competence and rationality$_2$ that follows in Chapter 6.

It is clear that the persistence of prior belief is frequently the cause of behaviour that is irrational$_2$. From an impersonal viewpoint, there is little doubt that undue influence of prior beliefs, preconceptions, and prejudice is the cause of much poor decision making in the real world. Politicians, for example, are notorious for disregarding the reports of enquiries that provide answers inconsistent with their political dogma, even when they themselves have commissioned the reports. But then such behaviour may serve their private and selfish goals and thus be rational$_1$. As another example, consider Dixon's (1976) chilling analysis of incompetence in military leadership. One of the strongest of the many psychological factors that he identifies is the tendency to persevere with preconceived beliefs despite evidence to the contrary. He cites numerous examples of military disasters which resulted from generals dismissing or ignoring critical field intelligence that disconfirmed their prior belief about the situation. He also points out that this tendency can be a way of trying to preserve self-esteem. Changing one's prior belief may force one to admit a mistake, and generals who do that may have to accept that they have sent men to their deaths for nothing. In Chapter 2 we referred to evidence (Ackerman & DeRubeis, 1991; Taylor & Brown, 1988) that some unrealistic optimism may promote mental well-being, but clearly in extreme cases it can lead to disaster.

Whether belief persistence is irrational$_1$ can be a complex matter to decide. First, it has to be shown that the behaviour concerned is ineffective in achieving the personal goals of the individual. Even where the action in a particular experiment clearly fails to support the individual's goals, we still cannot describe such action as irrational$_1$ if it reflects inappropriate training and experience. In these literatures it is not even straightforward to assess rationality$_2$ because of the inconsistent and controversial use of normative systems. For example, the literature on base neglect assumes a Bayesian model of rational inference, whereas that on confirmation bias has assumed a Popperian falsificationist approach rather than a Bayesian model for the testing of theories and hypotheses. The literature on belief bias, forming part of the deductive reasoning field, adopts yet another normative framework. Here, it is assumed that subjects are in error when they fail to comply with the instructions and endorse conclusions in violation of the principles of formal logic. Let us now consider each of the relevant literatures in turn.

USE AND NEGLECT OF BAYESIAN PRIORS

Bayesian decision theory is a well-established normative system for reasoning about hypotheses in the light of evidence. As we have already indicated, we are sympathetic to the views of some contemporary philosophers of science (such as Howson & Urbach, 1993) that the Bayesian approach to science should be preferred to that of Popper (see Chapter 1). Recall that Popperian philosophy rests everything on the logical deduction of predictions from hypotheses, which are then absolutely falsified if the predictions turn out to be false. It sees no legitimate place for confirming hypotheses, i.e. making them more probable. The Bayesian approach, by contrast, is one of confirmation or disconfirmation—it specifies how belief should be revised in the light of evidence discovered for or against a hypothesis. The other crucial difference, as far as this chapter is concerned, is that to the Bayesian, all evidence should be related to the prior belief held about the hypothesis. This is formalised in Bayes' theorem, which in one of its simpler forms can be shown as:

5.1
$$\frac{P(H/D)}{P(\overline{H}/D)} = \frac{P(H).P(D/H)}{P(\overline{H}).P(D/\overline{H})}$$

where H and $\overline{H}$ (not-H) are complementary and mutually exclusive hypotheses about some state of affairs. From left to right, the equation can be read verbally as:

Posterior Odds = Prior Odds * Likelihood Ratio

In the Bayesian approach, probabilities are subjective and represent nothing more nor less than degrees of belief. Hence, the effect of this equation is to weight prior belief—as expressed by the ratio of probabilities between two hypotheses—by some specific evidence in order to form a revised, posterior belief. Bayesian revision is often applied recursively to sequential sampling and decision-making problems. In this application the posterior odds at trial n become the prior odds at trial n+1. Under conditions of ignorance, the prior odds will typically be set to evens at the start but will gradually move towards the "correct" hypothesis as the evidence mounts.

Bayesian decision theory is of course a formal and impersonal normative system, and we do not suggest that ordinary people *follow* Bayesian rules, by having mental representations of numbers for probabilities and performing calculations with them. The extent to which people *conform* with Bayesian rules is more difficult to determine, as we shall see. We do feel that the essence of the Bayesian approach captures our intuitions about epistemic utility and rational$_1$ decision making far more closely than the Popperian approach. The epistemic utility that some evidence holds will always be relevant to prior beliefs, expectations, and goals held by the individual at the time. It is therefore of interest to view the psychological literatures that have tested Bayesian decision theory as a descriptive model. Do people actually take account of prior belief and revise hypotheses in the way that Bayes' theorem prescribes?

As several authors have noted (e.g. Fischhoff & Beyth-Marom, 1983; Gigerenzer & Murray, 1987), the two main paradigms that have addressed this question have produced paradoxical claims. The earlier literature, reviewed by Peterson and Beach (1967), used the "book bag and poker chip task" in which formal sampling situations with bags or urns containing coloured chips are described with hypotheses and base rates clearly specified. Research with this task led to the conclusion that people are highly conservative Bayesians. That is, they do revise opinions as evidence is collected, but more slowly than Bayes' theorem would predict. They need more evidence to revise beliefs than is required. In other words, the Bayesian prior exerts more influence than it should from a normative point of view. The death of this literature coincided with the birth of another, inspired by the paper of Kahneman and Tversky (1973) who claimed evidence of quite the contrary effect: systematic neglect of base rate information that should constitute the Bayesian prior.

In the "engineers and lawyers problem", one group of subjects was told that a group of 30 engineers and 70 lawyers had been interviewed by psychologists who had prepared thumb-nail descriptions of each. They were asked to read each description and rate the probability that the person described was an engineer. Another group was given a similar task except that the base rate was reversed so that there were 70 engineers and 30 lawyers. An example of a thumb-nail sketch was the following:

> Jack is a 45-year-old man. He is married and has four children. He is generally conservative, careful, and ambitious. He shows no interest in political and social issues and spends most of his free time on his many hobbies, which include home carpentry, sailing, and mathematical puzzles. (Kahneman & Tversky, 1973, p.241.)

Now clearly, it is allowable that subjects will view this description as more typical of an engineer than a lawyer. But according to the standard Bayesian analysis of this task, this should affect only their judgement of the likelihood ratio, whereas the answer they have been required to give corresponds to the posterior odds. Hence, this should be moderated by the prior odds which are vastly different between the two groups: 70/30 in favour of engineers or 70/30 in favour of lawyers. In fact, Kahneman and Tversky found that probability judgements were quite similar in the two groups and concluded that base rate information was largely ignored.

Another well-known problem designed to demonstrate the base rate fallacy is the cabs problem first published by Kahneman and Tversky (1972a):

> 85% of the cabs in a particular city are green and the remainder blue. A witness identifies a cab involved in an accident as blue. Under tests, the witness correctly identifies both blue and green cabs on 80% of occasions. What is the probability that the cab was in fact blue?

This is clearly a problem to which Bayes' rule is applicable. Given the datum (D) of the witness' testimony, the posterior odds between the blue (B) and green (G) hypothesis are the product of the prior odds and the likelihood ratio [P(D/B) divided by P(D/G)]. Hence, the odds are still in favour of the cab being green in spite of the witness' statement. However, many subjects give the probability of blue at 80%, ignoring the base rate information entirely. If the witness' information is omitted, however, subjects will give the probability at 15% in line with the base rate. This is very interesting as not only is the base rate data available in the standard problem, but it appears that it should be taken into account by the principle of relevance discussed in Chapter 3: why present information if it is not needed?

The interpretation of the literature on base rate neglect has in fact proved highly controversial, especially with regard to the question of whether or not it means that people are bad Bayesians. An interesting argument from our perspective is that of Bar-Hillel (1980) that subjects neglect base rate data because it does not appear relevant. Relevance can, however, be enhanced by various manipulations. Hence, when scenarios are used that induce the perception of a causal link between the base rate and the individual case, subjects' responses change dramatically and approach the prescriptions of the Bayes' theorem (Ajzen, 1977; Bar-Hillel, 1980; Tversky & Kahneman, 1980). For example, people take account of base rate in the cabs problem if they are told that there are an equal number of cabs in the city, but that 85% of the cabs involved in accidents are green. It would seem that the critical psychological factor is that in this version people perceived the green cab drivers as reckless and therefore causing more than their share of accidents.

The three major rationalist arguments against bias research identified by Evans (1993a—see Chapter 1) have all been applied to research on the base rate fallacy. First, authors have questioned whether Bayes' theorem is the appropriate normative system (Cohen, 1981; Gigerenzer & Murray, 1987). Second, there have been arguments about interpretation, especially whether subjects may think they are judging the likelihood of the evidence rather than the posterior probabilities (e.g. Braine, Connell, Freitag, & O'Brien, 1990) and whether pragmatic factors in the wording of the questions may enhance or inhibit perceived relevance of the base rate data (Maachi, 1995). Finally, there have been numerous doubts expressed about the external validity of the experimental tasks, especially in their standard form. For example, Gigerenzer and Murray (1987) claim that the relevant base rates assumed by the experimenter are poorly defined to the subject in standard versions of the experimental problems. They also claim that the tasks are psychologically impoverished in that they present specified information, preselected by the experimenter:

> The main point is that by reducing thinking to calculation on specified probabilities, a broad range of thought processes are eliminated from consideration, which concern information search and evaluation ... In real world situations the subjects must themselves search for the relevant information and decide for themselves. (Gigerenzer & Murray, 1987, p.164.)

How should we view the literature on base rate neglect in terms of our own framework? Here we have much sympathy with the views expressed by Gigerenzer and Murray. In fact, we have already seen in Chapter 4 that subjects may not think about just the four cards in most indicative selection tasks, but treat these as problems where they have to search for information as they do in the real world. In experiments on base rates, it is wrong to assume that quantitative statements will be processed by subjects in conformity with the normative views of the experimenters. Note that the introduction of pragmatic content (causal scenarios), or the use of experimental training (Christensen-Szalanski & Beach, 1982) that induces subjects to perceive a connection between base rate and evidence, has a marked effect on performance. Although these interpretations of the effect have been recently challenged by Maachi (1995), her own experiments point only to an alternative relevance effect surrounding pragmatic factors in the text. All the studies lead to the conclusion that subjects can moderate their judgements with the use of base rate data, but only if it is perceived as relevant.

The basic problem in the base rate literature that we would like to stress is that the Bayesian priors used in the normative analyses are not prior beliefs. Subjects do not arrive at the experiment with established beliefs about the numbers of lawyers and engineers in a psychological study or the frequency of green and blue cabs in an imaginary city. This raises issues of external validity. If the purpose of the research is simply to test a kind of statistical problem solving, then there is no problem. The research can probably be generalised to the conclusion that people do not make good use of statistical statements about base rate data in their everyday judgements. However, to infer from this literature that people are poor Bayesians who habitually neglect prior probabilities is not justifiable in our view. The mere presentation of these pieces of information in the wording of the instructions will not produce an internalised belief of the kind common to much real world reasoning, and so it is not surprising to us that the information is ignored in the absence of pragmatic cues as to its relevance.

The practice in this literature contrasts sharply with that in the study of belief bias in reasoning, reviewed later in this chapter. In belief bias studies, the normal practice is to use statements about which people hold prior beliefs, established by rating studies on separate subject groups drawn from the same population. We know of only one study of the use of Bayesian priors that has taken this approach. Evans, Brooks, and Pollard (1985) made use of prior ratings about the likelihood of undergraduate students having particular hobbies as a function of their major subject of study. For example, in one problem subjects were told that 20 business study students had been interviewed and asked to give a forced choice preference between "going to discos" and "meditation" as a leisure activity. Some subjects were told that 70% preferred discos, which was congruent with prior belief as established in the prior rating study. Other subjects were told that 70% preferred meditation, which was incongruent with belief. The question put to the subjects required a judgement of posterior probability:

> Having seen the results of this survey, how likely do you think it is that business studies students do, in fact, have a preference in the direction observed in the sample?

Now if subjects reasoned in analogous fashion to those presented with the engineers/lawyers problem, they should have based their judgement solely on the sample evidence. In fact, judgements were massively influenced by prior belief, with subjects generally rating their posterior probability in the direction of prior belief even when this conflicted with the evidence of the survey. These results stand in very sharp contrast with reports of base rate neglect in the standard paradigms.

We are not claiming that people will always make a rational use of prior probabilities and base rates in real world reasoning to achieve their ordinary goals. First, we have denied, of course, that people have unbounded rationality$_1$. Of particular relevance here is our view that people have a much lower capacity to be rational$_2$. People's ability to achieve high-level and long-term goals, described only in language, can be seriously limited, as we all know only too well. The conditions that produce base rate neglect in the laboratory will also produce it in analogous real world situations. We have in mind particularly the low impact of statistical information presented only by verbal communication and on matters that do not correspond directly to people's own experience. It is notoriously difficult, for example, to modify people's behaviour where there are long-term risks, the consequences of which will appear when it is too late. One good example is cigarette smoking, which persists in the light of statistical evidence so pervasive that the most defensive smoker finds it hard to avoid or deny. However, to take account of such stated statistical evidence (as opposed to probabilities learned by experience) requires rationality$_2$—conscious reasoning about explicit knowledge based on understanding of normative principles. Whereas rational$_2$ thinking requires anticipation of future consequences, rationality$_1$ responds to past experience and the fulfilment of immediate goals such as the craving for nicotine.

In summary, our view of the literature on base rate neglect is that it shows significant limitations in statistically untrained subjects' ability to reason in a rational$_2$ manner about probabilities. This will limit rational actions in real world situations where statistical evidence is relevant to the beliefs we should form about particular situations. However, this is not incompatible with our views that *prior beliefs*—internalised from our actual experiences—will modify our interpretation of evidence in a broadly Bayesian manner, in line with our conception of rationality$_1$. Even within the standard paradigm, we have seen that the manipulations that cue the causal relevance of the base rate data cause it to influence people's judgements.

When the conditions are right, prior belief will undoubtedly exert a strong influence on our judgements and actions. The question then becomes whether such beliefs exert *too much* influence. This takes us on to consideration of confirmation and belief bias effects.

CONFIRMATION BIAS

Confirmation bias is the alleged tendency in people to seek information that confirms, and to avoid that which disconfirms, their current beliefs or favoured hypotheses. If such a bias exists, it stands in marked contrast to the still influential (at least in psychology) philosophy of science of Popper (1959, 1962), who advocated quite the opposite practice for scientists. It is clear that much of the literature on confirmation bias is inspired by subscription to the Popperian view and consequently that claims of irrationality have arisen as a result.

A number of different research paradigms in cognitive and social psychology have been used as evidence for confirmation bias. Some authors view these literatures as providing evidence of rather different effects that have been lumped together under one label. For example:

> Confirmation bias ... has proven to be a catch-all phrase incorporating biases in both information search and interpretations. Because of its excess and conflicting meanings the term might best be retired. (Fischhoff & Beyth-Marom, 1983, p.257.)

Although we have considerable sympathy with this view, we note that the term has not in fact been retired from the psychological literature. Indeed, it is often claimed as one of the best demonstrated and most pervasive biases in human cognition (e.g. Baron, 1985, 1988). However, as we shall see, the specific evidence for this bias is far from undisputed.

Within the psychology of reasoning, evidence for confirmation bias is most clearly associated with the reasoning tasks invented by Peter Wason, who originally preferred the term "verification bias". The existence of this bias was the preferred explanation of results in early studies of the selection task (see Wason & Johnson-Laird, 1972), which employed abstract and affirmative conditionals of the form "if p then q". The view was that subjects chose the p and q cards in order to seek the verifying combination of a card with a p on one side and a q on the other. They failed to select the not-q because they were not looking for the falsifying combination of p and not-q. This explanation was abandoned by Wason and others, however, following the demonstration of matching bias on the selection task by Evans and Lynch (1973, see Chapter 3). In particular, the finding that subjects select the falsifying cards p and q when the rule is changed to "if p then not q", rather than the verifying p and not-q cards, was indisputable. As a good Popperian, Wason abandoned his own hypothesis in the face of such clear falsifying evidence!

Curiously enough, however, both Wason and a number of other psychologists maintained the confirmation bias interpretation of the "2 4 6" problem (Wason, 1960, 1968) for many years. It was not effectively challenged until the late 1980s (Klayman & Ha, 1987; Evans, 1989), although the essential problem with the task had been pointed out almost immediately by Wetherick (1962). On this task subjects are told that the experimenter has in mind a rule for classifying triples—groups of three integer numbers—and that an example that belongs to the rule is "2 4 6". The subjects are then asked to generate their own triples and are told by the experimenter whether each belongs or not. The subjects are normally encouraged to record a reason or hypothesis for each triple tested, but are only allowed to announce the rule when sure that they know it.

What happens on this task—which has been replicated many times in the psychological literature—is that subjects test hypotheses such as "increasing with equal intervals" and do so by generating almost exclusively positive examples such as:

10	12	14
20	30	40
1	50	99

and so on. However, because the experimenter has adopted the rule "any increasing sequence", the subject invariably gets positive reinforcement for every triple. They all belong. Subjects then become convinced that their hypothesis must be correct and baffled when told that they have announced a wrong rule. Some even announce new rules that are the same ones in different words—for example, "add a number always the same, to form the next number".

There is no doubt that the behaviour of subjects on this task is confirmatory. Nor is there any dispute about the basic phenomenon of persisting with positive testing that has been many times replicated. Current interest in the task continues, with several experimental studies based on the task appearing in the recent literature (Kareev & Avrahami, 1995; Kareev & Halberstadt, 1993; Kareev, Halberstadt, & Shafir, 1993; Wharton, Cheng, & Wickens, 1993). The effect has been generalised to non-numerical tasks of analogous structure, and its robustness demonstrated by resistance to instructions that exhort subjects to adopt a falsification strategy (see Evans, 1989, Chapter 3 for a full review). The mystery is why—until very recently—researchers persisted in interpreting and labelling the effect as a "confirmation bias".

The difficulty with the 2 4 6 problem, as Wetherick was the first to point out, is that the behaviour cannot be judged to be motivated by confirmation from the subjects' perspective. Subjects do not know that they have been induced to form a hypothesis that is a subset of the experimenter's rule and that all positive tests will therefore confirm. In most situations, positive testing of hypotheses may well lead to disconfirmation. In science, positive testing is the norm: we predict how the world should be if our theories are true. But of course such tests frequently fail. For example, the first author (Evans) predicted that matching bias would occur in disjunctive reasoning, only to discover that it did not (Evans & Newstead, 1980). As the phenomenon of matching bias was understood at the time, it should have applied equally to disjunctive as to conditional reasoning. The fact that it did not was a key stimulus to later theoretical revisions. Actually Evans was well aware of the likelihood that falsification would occur when designing this experiment, due to existing but incomplete evidence in the literature on disjunctive inference. So how could this positive test be construed as exhibiting confirmation bias?

The question to be explained, then, is why people test hypotheses in predominantly positive ways. The answer is because it is generally more effective. Klayman & Ha (1987) presented an analysis of a range of situations under which hypotheses may be tested and showed that the conditions of testing created by the 2 4 6 task are unusual and that under most circumstances a positive test strategy is the most effective way to discover whether a hypothesis is true or false. One reason is that positive terms in our language tend to refer to smaller or more homogeneous sets than negative terms (see Over & Evans, 1994 and Chapter 4 of the present volume). To return to the standard example in the philosophy of science, we can hardly test the claim that "All ravens are black" effectively by searching the world for non-black objects in case they turn out to be ravens.

Evans (1989) presented a slightly different argument that is not incompatible with the theory of Klayman and Ha. Instead of talking of strategies—a term that has connotations of conscious control—Evans proposes that there is a general positivity bias. This links with matching bias and relevance and comprises a tendency to think about positively rather than negatively defined information. In support of this he shows that the difficulty of the 2 4 6 and another Wason problem, the THOG (Wason & Brooks, 1979), can be offset when attributes of the problem that are normally negatively defined are given positive labels.

Even if Popperian falsification is accepted as the appropriate normative model, the argument that the 2 4 6 problem constitutes evidence of irrationality retreats in the face of the Klayman and Ha analysis, which appeals, in effect, to rationality$_1$. They suggest that people have learned a method of reasoning that is generally effective and only err because an experiment has contrived a situation in which it will not work. (We will make a very similar argument about the belief bias literature in the next section.) Because we believe that the processes underlying rationality$_1$ are primarily tacit and learned, then the connection between their argument and the positivity bias of Evans (1989) is easily made. Positive information is preconsciously selected as relevant because it is effective to do so given the limitations on human information processing, working memory capacity, and the time available for searching the world for evidence.

Despite the problems with interpretation of the Wason tasks, discussed earlier, we wish to draw a less sharp distinction between positivity bias and confirmation bias than that implied by the discussion of Evans (1989). Focusing on what is true rather than false is itself a positivity effect and we consider that believability or plausibility of hypotheses is a major determinant of relevance in reasoning and decision making. In fact, there is evidence of genuine confirmation biases to be found elsewhere in the psychological literature that is rather more convincing than the studies of the Wason 2 4 6 task. We have encountered one example earlier, in the pseudo-diagnosticity task (Chapter 3) where there is good evidence that people focus on only one hypothesis at a time (see Mynatt et al., 1993) and are apparently insensitive to the normative diagnosticity of information. We have also given an argument, analogous to that of positive testing, as to why this may be a rational$_1$ strategy (Chapter 3).

Even on the abstract Wason selection task, where matching bias—another form of positivity bias—has been demonstrated as the major cause of perceived relevance and card selections (see Chapter 3), there is evidence that orientation towards falsification, or more strictly disconfirmation, can facilitate the choice of p and not-q cards. First, there is the case of the Pollard and Evans (1981, 1983) experiments discussed in Chapter 4. When subjects are trained to believe that the conditional in the selection task is false, they start to choose the cards that could falsify it—the p and not-q ones. One interpretation of this is that subjects' attention switches from a focus on the hypothesis that the rule is true, to the hypothesis that it is false. Such a switch foregrounds, or makes relevant, the counter-examples case of p and not-q. Hence, the falsifying behaviour observed is, at a higher level, confirming current belief. We have already given our psychological account of these experiments in Chapter 4. The available mental model has high epistemic utility—and therefore relevance—whether it verifies or falsifies, because the epistemic goal is to discover whether the rule is true or false. However, because subjects then choose cards to see whether the model in focus is true, this could be regarded as a form of confirmation bias. We have seen that manipulations that focus subjects on counter-examples facilitate correct choices (Green, 1995; Green & Larking, 1995; Love & Kessler, 1995) and in some circumstances instructions that emphasise the need to detect violations of the rule can encourage p and not-q choices (see Chapter 6).

In commenting on the literature on the base rate fallacy earlier, we pointed out that presented statistics did not constitute genuine prior belief. We could similarly argue that the cognitive literature on hypothesis testing and reasoning gives a rather weak test of confirmation bias, because the subjects hold a relatively small stake in the hypotheses adopted for an experiment compared with real world beliefs. Though it is beyond the scope of this book to examine the social psychological literature in any detail, we are aware of a mass of evidence that people seek information that will confirm their current beliefs and tend to avoid or discredit evidence that conflicts with them (for reviews see Baron, 1988; Nisbett & Ross, 1980). However, we have already indicated that we accept that in general people do tend to focus on particular hypotheses that are believable, and indeed suggest that belief itself is a major determinant of relevance. The *bias* towards positive representation includes thinking about what we expect to be true rather than false—a feature intrinsic, for example, to the mental model theory of deduction (Johnson-Laird & Byrne, 1991).

Where we differ from authors such as Baron (1985, 1988) is that we do not see this as necessary evidence of irrationality. Apart from the cognitive constraints already discussed, there is a further consideration. We do not hold our beliefs in isolation but as part of a complex belief system. This system enables people to construct a model of the world without which they would literally be unable to function. Certainly it is often rational$_1$ for their model to be accurate, but it is essential that the system helps them to achieve their most important goals. As we indicated at the end of Chapter 4, people even find it useful to assert and accept conditionals to which they know there are counter-examples. But they will look out for possible counter-examples if these would be too costly for them.

A more critical issue for rationality, perhaps, is what we do when disconfirming evidence is encountered—whether we were looking for it or not. In the cognitive literature on concept learning and inductive reasoning the answer is generally simple—subjects do infer that hypotheses are false when this occurs. If a not-q card in a selection task is turned over and a p revealed, subjects will generally say that this shows the conditional to be false. Some subjects will continue to insist, however, that they were right not to choose the not-q card in the first place (see Wason, 1969). This has been used as a striking example of irrationality, but that is not so clear. If someone presented us with a non-black raven for free, as it were, we would conclude that it is false that all ravens are black. Still, we would have good grounds for continuing to hold that we were right not to search ourselves among the non-black things for a counter-example.

In the 2 4 6 literature, subjects tend to abandon their hypotheses with little resistance once a disconfirmatory result is discovered—itself evidence that the testing strategies reflect cognitive constraints rather than a confirmatory motive (see Evans, 1989). However, in these kinds of experiments subjects again have no real stake in the arbitrary hypotheses about letters and numbers. It is in the social psychological literature where real beliefs are involved, that evidence for the "irrational persistence of belief" (Baron, 1988) is strongest. The claim here is that prior belief can bias not simply the search for evidence but also its evaluation. People apparently seek to discredit and disregard evidence incompatible with their beliefs by a variety of devices. The cognitive reasoning literature that most closely investigates this kind of process is the study of belief biases, to which we now turn.

BELIEF BIAS

Belief bias and confirmation bias are two related but distinct phenomena. Whereas confirmation bias refers to a tendency to seek evidence that supports a prior belief—and avoid evidence that conflicts—belief bias refers to biased evaluation of the evidence that is encountered. There is a long established literature on belief bias in syllogistic reasoning, although many of the earlier studies were methodologically dubious (see Evans, 1982, pp.107–111 for a review and critique of such studies). The major finding is that subjects instructed to engage in deductive reasoning—i.e. to draw conclusions that follow from necessarily and only from the premises given—are influenced by the *a priori* believability of the conclusion. They are apparently unable to distinguish the judgements of validity from judgements of real world truth value. The analogy with Bayesian inference is that the subject is being asked to judge the likelihood (in fact deductive certainty) of a conclusion in the light of given evidence (the premises) and is quite specifically instructed to disregard prior belief. In apparent contrast to the base rate fallacy literature, subjects are apparently unable to disregard such prior beliefs. As we have already indicated, however, in the belief bias literature the convention is to use statements about which subjects hold genuine beliefs, and not ones that give only arbitrary statistics.

Drawing believable and unbelievable conclusions

Standard research on belief bias is focused on the effect of asking people to evaluate arguments whose conclusions are either believable or unbelievable. Recent studies of the phenomenon have used principally one of two methods. In the conclusion evaluation task, subjects are given two premises and a single conclusion and asked whether the conclusion follows logically from the premises—yes or no. We will take the study of Evans et al. (1983) as a basis for the main findings to be explained. Although the gist of this study was described in Chapter 1, we need to give it a more detailed examination here. First, we quote the typical form of deductive reasoning instructions:

This is an experiment to test people's reasoning ability. You will be given four problems. In each case you will be given a prose passage to read and asked if a certain conclusion may be logically deduced from it. You should answer this question on the assumption that all the information given ... is in fact true. If you judge that the conclusion necessarily follows from the statements in the passage, you should answer "yes", otherwise "no".

The key to these instructions—as in other experiments—is that subjects are told to assume the premises. Evans et al. conducted three experiments and found that intelligent adults were unable fully to follow or comply with such instructions. Although their acceptance of conclusions was strongly influenced by logic, it was equally strongly influenced by believability (see Fig. 5.1). Moreover, there was an interaction between the two factors, such that the belief bias effect was most marked on invalid arguments. The major influence was the

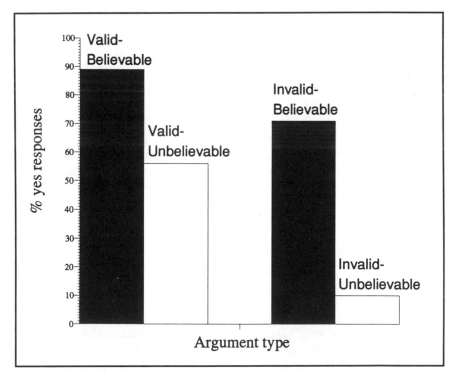

FIG. 5.1. Conclusions accepted (%) as a function of argument type in the three experiments reported by Evans, Barston, and Pollard (1983).

tendency to endorse invalid but believable conclusions, as in the following example.

5.1   No addictive things are inexpensive
       Some cigarettes are inexpensive
       Therefore, some addictive things are not cigarettes

Such arguments were accepted as valid by 71% of subjects, whereas the identical syllogistic form with an unbelievable conclusion, for example:

5.2   No police dogs are vicious
       Some highly trained dogs are vicious
       Therefore, some police dogs are not highly trained

was accepted by only 10%.

Note that the invalid conclusions are ones that are compatible with the premises but not necessarily true. If invalid arguments are used having conclusions that are incompatible with premises (i.e. they are determinately false given the premises) then the interaction disappears completely and the belief bias itself is only weakly observed (see Newstead, Pollard, Evans, & Allen, 1992, Experiments 1 and 2). This result indicates—as with other reasoning biases discussed in this book—that belief bias cannot simply be a response bias external to the reasoning process. What it does seem to suggest is that subjects have a weak understanding of the concept of necessity, so that when a conclusion is logically indeterminate they allow belief disproportionately to influence their response. (For a review and discussion of rival theoretical accounts of the belief bias effect see Evans, 1989, Chapter 4; Evans et al., 1993a, Chapter 8). However, it is important to note that belief bias effects are not restricted to the conclusion evaluation task, but are also observed when subjects are asked to generate their own conclusions from some premises (Markovits & Nantel, 1989; Oakhill & Johnson-Laird, 1985; Oakhill, Johnson-Laird, & Garnham, 1989). In this case subjects are more likely to generate a conclusion that conforms to prior belief.

We pointed out in Chapter 2, in the section on "Reasoning from uncertain belief", that people are usually concerned in their real world reasoning to infer conclusions from all their relevant beliefs. Provided that their beliefs are justified, it would indeed be irrational₁ for them not to do this, and not to take account of how confident they are in their beliefs. The unrealistic feature of most deductive reasoning experiments, especially in the work on belief bias, is the requirement that subjects take the premises they are given as, in effect, certain and add nothing, however relevant, to them. Some recent evidence shows that people's willingness to draw inference is influenced directly by their confidence in premises (George, 1995; Stevenson & Over, 1995). These findings bear directly on the question of why subjects will sometimes show a belief bias on valid arguments—i.e. withhold sound conclusions that are unbelievable, as happened in the study of Evans et al. (1983, see Fig. 5.1). Some researchers have found that on simple reasoning problems, obviously valid conclusions may be withheld when they are unbelievable.

The mental model theory of belief bias tested by Oakhill et al. (1989) tries to explain the acceptance of believable conclusions of invalid arguments by claiming that subjects fail to search for counter-examples in such cases. Where conclusions conflict with belief, on the other hand, subjects are motivated to look for counter-examples. If they do find a model in which the premises are true and the conclusion false, then they should accept that the conclusion follows. However, contrary to the predictions of the theory, Oakhill et al. found belief bias on valid arguments—even very easy "one-model" syllogisms (i.e. ones whose premises can represent only one situation), such as the following two examples of the same form:

5.3   Some of the communists are golfers
       All of the golfers are Marxists
       Therefore, some of the Marxists are communists

5.4   Some of the communists are golfers
       All of the golfers are capitalists
       Therefore, some of the communists are capitalists

In the first case (believable) 95% of subjects generated the correct conclusion, but in the second case (unbelievable) only 65% did so (Experiment 1). The authors were forced to propose an arbitrary mechanism of "post-conclusion filtering" to reject unbelievable conclusions of valid arguments. Apart from being *ad hoc*, this is also unparsimonious as it requires one mechanism to account for the acceptance of believable conclusions of invalid arguments, and another one to explain the rejection of unbelievable conclusions of valid arguments.

Reasoning from believable and unbelievable premises

In order to understand the belief bias effect better, we need to consider the effects of believability in the *premises* of the arguments, a factor generally ignored in standard research on belief bias. Let us think of what it is rational$_1$ to do, on the supposition that one has rational$_1$

beliefs. A good reason not to be persuaded by the unbelievable conclusion of a valid argument is that it has an unbelievable premise, or a set of premises that are unbelievable as a group. Notice that the two premises in 5.4 cannot be true together, given background beliefs about communists and capitalists, unless the communist golfers are rare exceptions like Engels. It will be relatively easy to see problems like this with valid one-model syllogisms. People do have some deductive competence (Chapter 6), but they may not always distinguish, in the experiments we have discussed, between saying that a conclusion does not necessarily follow because an argument is invalid, and saying this because it has unbelievable premises. One should remember as well that subjects can vary in their subjective judgements about how believable or unbelievable premises are.

That people are, in fact, reluctant to draw conclusions from unbelievable premises has been demonstrated in recent studies of conditional inference. A number of studies have shown that the easiest inference of all—*modus ponens*—can be suppressed with thematic content conditionals (see Evans et al., 1993a, pp.55–61 for a review of relevant studies). Consider the following argument:

If John goes fishing then he will have fish supper
John goes fishing
Therefore, John has a fish supper

This is the *modus ponens* inference that most subjects will endorse. However, if an extra premise is added:

If John goes fishing then he will have fish supper
If John catches a fish then he will have a fish supper
John goes fishing
Therefore, John has a fish supper

then far fewer subjects will make *modus ponens*. The example is from Stevenson and Over (1995) although the effect was first demonstrated by Byrne (1989). However, suppose we now add yet another premise:

If John goes fishing then he will have fish supper
If John catches a fish then he will have a fish supper
John is always lucky when he goes fishing
Therefore, John has a fish supper

Subjects are now inclined to make *modus ponens* again. Stevenson and Over argue that the crucial factor is the degree of belief in the major premise. They go on to show that with a series of different qualifying premises—John is usually/rarely/never lucky etc.—the rate of *modus ponens* moves up and down in proportion to the effect that this has on belief in the conditional. Their findings are supported by an independent and parallel study by George (1995) using a somewhat different methodology. George showed that subjects' willingness to draw *modus ponens* with thematic conditionals—in the absence of qualifying premises—was a direct function of the believability of the conditional, i.e. the extent to which subjects believed the connection between antecedent and consequent.

From a Bayesian perspective, it is even rational$_2$ to take account of one's prior degree of belief in the conclusion of an argument, and then of one's degree of belief in the premises. The former can be used in Bayes' theorem to help fix the probability of the conclusion given the premises, and the latter can be used in the following formula we gave in Chapter 2 as 2.2:

$$(2.2) \quad Prob(C) = Prob(P).Prob(C/P) + Prob(not\text{-}P).Prob(C/not\text{-}P)$$

This formula shows exactly how confident one should be in a conclusion, if one knows the probability of the conjunction of the premises, the probability of the negation of that conjunction, and the relevant conditional probabilities. One of the reasons that Popperian philosophy of science has been rejected by some Bayesians is that Popper did not provide an adequate account of the probability of evidence (Howson & Urbach, 1993, pp.125–6). Well-founded theories cannot be rejected out of hand on discovery of some apparently falsifying evidence, for that evidence itself may be suspect. Even the evidence of studies conducted by the most competent and honest of researchers, reported in the most stringently refereed journals may be in error. The results could reflect a statistical fluke, a malfunction of equipment, a human coding or transcription error and so on. The probability of the evidence must be properly considered along with the probability of the theory and its rivals. In an uncertain world, beliefs that have served us well are not lightly to be abandoned.

Actually, some versions of Bayesianism themselves allow evidence to be learned with certainty. Suppose we have worked out the conditional probability of the hypothesis given some evidence and think that we have learned the evidence with certainty. We would then use what is called strict conditionalisation to infer that the probability of the hypothesis equals its probability conditional on the evidence. Strict conditionalisation is basic for Bayesians who think that we can often learn that evidence is certainly true. Aside from the problems with this we have already referred to, these Bayesians have to hold that the order in which we learn pieces of evidence with certainty does not matter: no matter what the order in which the evidence is collected, the final probability of the hypothesis always comes out the same. The descriptive adequacy of this version is even more limited than that of Bayesianism in general, because there are order effects in ordinary reasoning (Hogarth & Einhorn, 1992).

However, 2.2 can be modified to tell us how to conditionalise on uncertain evidence and allow for the order in which we learn the evidence to have an effect. Suppose that P states the evidence that we have come to believe with degree Prob(P). Taking 1 − Prob(P) gives us, of course, our new degree of belief in the negation of that statement, not-P, and we leave the conditional probabilities the same. That is, by becoming more or less confident in some evidence we do not think that the conditional probability of C, the hypothesis, given this evidence changes, and we think that the same holds for the conditional probability of C given not-P. Now we use 2.2 to work out a new probability for the hypothesis C. Using this procedure is called Jeffrey conditionalisation (see Howson & Urbach, 1993, pp.105–108). It allows us to avoid imagining that we can come to believe evidence with certainty, and also allows for our confidence in the evidence to be affected by when we learn it. For example, if the first raven we see is apparently red, we may be highly confident that it is red and have correspondingly low confidence that all ravens are black. But we may have severe doubts that our eyes are giving us reliable information in this unusual case, if we come across the apparently red raven after observing many black ones, and becoming highly confident that all ravens are that colour. Such examples show that there can be good epistemological reasons for taking account of the order in which we learn evidence, and cognitive constraints can force us in ordinary affairs to focus on recent evidence that we easily remember.

CONCLUSION

The psychological literatures that we have considered in this chapter contain a confusing mixture of claims that people take both too much and insufficient account of prior belief, and accusations of irrationality have been made on both counts. This is a nice illustration of the problems created by concentrating only on rationality$_2$. If we look at what the subjects are actually doing and the psychological factors that influence them, a much more coherent and consistent picture emerges.

It is naïve to think that competence in reasoning can be assessed simply by presenting a task that by structure and instructions should conform to some normative system of the experimenter's preference and then checking whether subjects solve it or not. What subjects actually do in experiments is a complex function of their prior knowledge and belief, their habitual reasoning methods, and precise features of the experimental problems and instructions. In particular, pragmatic factors can exert strong influences. The literature on base rate neglect, for example, shows us that people have great difficulty in relating presented statistics to individual cases, although we have also seen that this difficulty can be largely offset by subtle pragmatic manipulations, such as the introduction of a causal scenario. However, as we have already indicated, this literature concerns itself with Bayesian prior probabilities in only a technical sense—it has little to do with prior belief. The literature on confirmation bias is somewhat better in this regard because subjects are at least induced to form a hypothesis of their own that they go about testing—albeit one formed for the sake of an experiment in which they have only a limited stake. What this literature shows is that people have a strong preference for thinking about positive rather than negative information which sometimes leads them into confirmatory behaviour, especially when an experiment such as Wason's 2 4 6 problem has been specifically designed to entrap them. We believe that focusing on positive cases is rational$_1$ in that (a) it provides economical use of limited processing capacity and (b) it leads to successful hypothesis testing in most real world situations.

Where real world beliefs are studied in the belief bias literature and similar literatures in social psychology, the general accusation is that they have too much effect on reasoning. But whether these beliefs prevent the achievement of real world goals is a question that should not be overlooked. In other words, to what extent are the beliefs rational$_1$? To repeat, we are not claiming that people have unbounded rationality$_1$. People can fail to achieve many long-term and high-level goals, for the reason that their high-level beliefs do not give them anything like an accurate view of the world. Thus politicians can fail to satisfy the goal of improving the economy because they are led astray by unjustified political dogma. But merely to carry on living from day to day, people have to achieve many essential goals in their reasoning and decision making. Beliefs based directly on their implicit visual processes, for example, will usually be reliable, and must often be employed in their reasoning and decision making to achieve goals.

Certainly it is the case in the belief bias literature that people cannot fully follow or comply with instructions to assume the premises and ignore prior beliefs. The unspoken idea that compliance with instructions is a fair test of rationality is, in our view, associated with another: that people's reasoning is a completely conscious thought process within their control. But suppose we instruct you to look around the room in which you are reading this book and not to see the colour blue. You will find it impossible to comply with this instruction (if your eyes are normal). Does that mean that you are irrational or that your visual system is somehow defective? Of course not. Your visual processes, you will argue, are automatic—tacit but highly adaptive. Our argument is that the same is true of the thought processes responsible for integrating relevant prior belief into reasoning. However, the two cases cannot be entirely parallel as subjects can to some extent ignore belief and reason from a limited number of assumptions when instructed to do so. We will return to this point in the following chapter.

CHAPTER SIX

Deductive competence

Throughout most of this book, we have argued our thesis that people are basically rational$_1$ to a reasonable degree—i.e. that they think, reason, and act in such a way as to achieve many basic personal goals. We have also shown that judgements of irrationality are typically made by authors who demand that people should have rationality$_2$—i.e. think or reason according to some impersonal normative system, such as some version of formal logic. These authors expect subjects to be rational$_2$ in abstract or unrealistic experiments, where they may not interpret the instructions in the way the experimenters intend. Against this, we have emphasised the importance of subjective relevance and the role of tacit processing in thinking and reasoning, and in interpreting verbal instructions. However, we have not claimed that there is no place for rationality$_2$. It is a necessary goal itself at times, to advance ordinary and scientific knowledge, and ordinary people do possess it up to a point. They follow logical rules to some degree in their reasoning, and there is an explicit as well as implicit cognitive system.

In this chapter we will ask to what extent subjects can follow logical rules, and whether this is linked to explicit thinking of the kind that is susceptible to verbal instruction and measurable through verbal protocol analysis. Traditional approaches to reasoning research presuppose certainly the first of these concepts—the possession of deductive competence—and in many cases the second also. However, this to confuse the study of reasoning processes with the study of reasoning experiments. We have already shown that much of the behaviour in the experiments cannot be attributed to the following of logical rules or to other explicit processes.

Although our broad objective is to address both reasoning and decision processes in one framework, we make no apology for focusing this chapter entirely on the fundamental case of logic and deductive reasoning—a complex issue in its own right. We do believe that the outcome of our analysis will have broader implications for thinking and decision making as a whole as we hope to show in Chapter 7. We start by considering the evidence for deductive competence, which is provided by experiments in the deductive reasoning literature, and then give critical consideration to the current theories of deductive competence in the literature.

COMPETENCE AND BIAS IN REASONING: THE EVIDENCE

Conditional reasoning

Let us return to the Wason selection task, which has been discussed extensively in earlier chapters. Of all the problems in the reasoning literature, in our view this task provides the least evidence of deductive competence. Perhaps we should not be surprised by this, because the task involves meta-inference, hypothesis testing, etc. and is not a direct test of people's ability to draw deductive inferences. We have provided detailed theoretical discussion of what we believe to be the causes of card choices on various versions of this task: subjects choose cards that appear relevant. Factors affecting relevance that we have discussed include linguistically based heuristics, probability judgements, epistemic utility, and concrete pay-offs or costs. We have suggested that realistic versions of the task that facilitate p and not-q choices alone, usually taken as the correct responses, do so through helpful pragmatic cues rather than by inducing logical rule-following. Above all, we have argued that the task should be viewed as a measure of thinking and decision making, and not as a problem that elicits deductive reasoning.

That some authors persists in viewing the selection task as a deductive reasoning problem has unfortunate consequences. For example, the study of Cheng, Holyoak, Nisbett, and Oliver (1986) addressed the question of whether training in logical principles and attendance at logic courses could facilitate ability for general deductive reasoning. In our view, the choice of the selection task was not the right one for this study. It surprises us not at all that the results were negative, because few people get past a relevance judgement on this task. In terms of the Evans (1984, 1989, Chapter 3) heuristic-analytic theory, people's card choices are entirely heuristic and the analytic processes do not get engaged.

Now the fact that people do not generally exhibit deductive competence on the Wason selection task does not mean that they do not possess it. In fact, one of the main theoretical challenges in considering this task is to explain why people do not apply the competence that is exhibited on other conditional reasoning problems. For example, in the studies reviewed by Evans et al. (1993a, Chapter 2) subjects are shown on average to endorse *modus tollens* more than 60% of the time with affirmative conditionals. In other words, given a conditional such as:

If there is an A on one side of a card, then there is a 3 on the other side of the card

and the information that the card does not have a 3, most subjects will correctly infer that the card cannot have an A. However, only around 10% will choose to select the number that is not the 3 on the selection task. Similarly, the experiments using the truth table task show that most subjects can correctly identify the falsifying case of such a conditional: a card that has an A on one side and does not have a 3 on the other. Subjects can follow *modus tollens* as a general inference rule, but they do not apply it to make their choices in the indicative selection task. Even if they are told that the conditional is about only the four cards, an implicit heuristic makes certain cards appear relevant, as we have already argued. These cards represent cases that would help them to investigate efficiently a realistic conditional about many more objects in the real world.

We have discussed in Chapter 5 what happens if the cards are turned over at the end of an indicative selection task. When the not-q card is turned over and a p revealed on the other side, subjects will state that this makes the conditional false. Here subjects are surely following a logical and semantic rule for determining when a conditional is false. This is an example of explicit thought, displaying deductive competence, in which the subjects have a good reason for what they say—they are rational$_2$. In our example about ravens, remember that it is inefficient to investigate the conditional by checking things in the unlimited and heterogeneous set of non-black to see if they are ravens. It is efficient for an if-heuristic to make ravens relevant. One then focuses on the homogeneous set of ravens and uses one's implicit recognition ability to pick these out and observe their properties. However, if one does happen without extra trouble to come across, or be told about, a non-black raven, then one benefits from awareness that this falsifies or strongly disconfirms the conditional. Consciousness can here fulfil its role of taking account of the unexpected, which cannot be done by a fixed heuristic. Good implicit heuristics and explicit thought can work together effectively.

Recall as well that looking for the false consequent case can become efficient when the consequent has a negative in it, such as "not a raven". The *not*-heuristic here makes ravens relevant, and so subjects again focus on a relatively small and homogeneous set. Actually it is wrong to say that subjects do not explicitly reason in the selection task, but rather we should say that this reasoning does not normally affect the choices made. In the studies of card inspection times described in Chapter 3 (Evans, 1995b and in press), subjects are shown to spend some time justifying decisions apparently already made, and an analysis of concurrent verbal protocols also indicates reasoning about the hidden values of cards focused on (see also Beattie & Baron, 1988). There is no necessary conflict between heuristics that determine choices, and lead to good search processes, and the later explicit justification of choices. In fact, when asked to justify their choices, subjects do explicitly refer to an attempt to establish the truth of a conditional of the form "if p then q" by picking the true antecedent card, and attempt to establish the falsity of one of the form "if p then not-q" by choosing the false consequent card (Wason & Evans, 1975). That is not inconsistent, as it is generally efficient to look for confirmation in the former case, and disconfirmation in the latter.

Subjects cannot be explicitly reasoning about each card in turn, to infer what is on the back or to work out expected epistemic values, if they do not attend to the cards they do not choose. This point has been made in criticism of the pragmatic reasoning schema theory of deontic selection tasks (Cheng & Holyoak, 1985) in a recent paper by Evans and Clibbens (1995). Recent work (Green & Larking, 1995; Love & Kessler, 1995; Platt & Griggs, 1993) does show that subjects will change their choices even in indicative tasks given certain verbal manipulations, which seem, at least in part, to draw attention to counter-examples and invoke analytical (explicit) rather than heuristic (implicit) thought. Thus it is possible that even on the selection task, explicit reasoning processes may sometimes determine choices, as opposed simply to providing justifications for them. However, exactly what is happening in these experiments will have to await future research.

With other conditional reasoning tasks, the evidence for deductive competence is much easier to locate. For example, we saw in Chapter 3 that the conditional truth table task is also strongly susceptible to matching bias. That is, mismatching cases are more likely to be classified as irrelevant. However, matching has nothing to do with how the relevant cases are sorted into true and false: these decisions are clearly influenced by logic. For example, the true-antecedent and false-consequent combination (TF)—when perceived as relevant—is nearly always classified (correctly) as falsifying the conditional. Interestingly, when explicit negative cases were used to release the matching bias effect (Evans, 1983; Evans et al., in press a), this led to an increase in logically correct responding that does not occur when matching bias is released by the same manipulation on the selection task (see Chapter 3). In the latter case, all mismatching cards—both logically right and logically wrong—are more often selected (Evans et al., in press a). This confirms our proposal that analytic reasoning occurs much more on the truth table task.

Conditional inference tasks test the following types of inference:

Modus ponens (MP)	If p then q, p, therefore q
Denial of the antecedent (DA)	If p then q, not-p, therefore not-q
Affirmation of the consequent (AC)	If p then q, q, therefore p
Modus tollens (MT)	If p then q, not-q, therefore not-p

Classically, MP and MT are described as valid inferences and DA and AC as "fallacies". However the latter are not fallacious if the conditional is read as the biconditional "p if and only if q", which is sometimes the natural pragmatic reading in context. With abstract affirmative conditionals, the data summarised by Evans et al. (1993a, Table 2.4) show consistent near 100% MP rates, but with considerable variability on all the others. The median values observed were DA 48%, AC 42%, and MT 63%. Apart from *modus ponens*, these figures are not very informative about the competence/analytic reasoning issue. Clearly MT is more difficult than MP, but how do we know if subjects are reasoning or mostly guessing with the former? Do the frequent endorsements of DA and AC indicate poor reasoning (fallacies), biconditional readings, or again just guessing?

Curiously enough, it is the evidence of bias in the conditional reasoning task that shows us that subjects are reasoning. It was discovered some while ago (Evans, 1977a) that when negations are introduced into the conditional statements, as on the selection and truth table tasks, they have a massive influence on the frequency of inferences drawn. In this case it is not matching bias but a separate effect called "negative conclusion bias" (Evans, 1982) that has been claimed. The early evidence suggested that on all inferences except *modus ponens*, subjects were more likely to endorse conclusions that were negative rather than affirmative. The effect appeared to be a response bias, external to any attempt at reasoning, and was discussed in these terms (for example, by Pollard & Evans, 1980). However, recent experimental evidence has provided a rather different perspective.

Evans, Clibbens, and Rood (1995) reported three experiments investigating the effect of negations on conditional inference. These experiments included both conclusion evaluation and conclusion production tasks, and extended the investigation to three forms of conditional statement:

If (not) p then (not) q
(Not) p only if (not) q
(Not) q if (not) p

The results were consistent. Subjects did indeed endorse or produce negative conclusions in preference to affirmative ones but only consistently did so on DA and MT inferences. There was no evidence of a bias on MP and little on AC. The two inferences affected are ones that Evans et al. call "denial inferences" because they lead from the denial of one component to denial of the other. Compare the following two *modus tollens* arguments:

6.1   If the letter is G then the number is 7
       The number is not 7
       Therefore, the letter is not G

6.2   If the letter is not T then the number is 4
       The number is not 4
       Therefore, the letter is T

Subjects consistently make more MT inferences with problems like 6.1 than with ones like 6.2.[1] The critical variable is a negation in the part of the conditional denied in the conclusion of the argument. Hence, DA inferences are less frequently made when the consequent of the conditional is negative. Evans et al. (1995) discuss in some detail how this might come about and consider ways of extending both the mental logic and mental model theories to account for it. In either case it seems that some kind of double negation effect is involved. Difficult forms always require the denial of a negative in order to infer an affirmative— for example, it cannot be the case that there is not a T, therefore it must be the case that there is a T.

These findings lead us to two very important conclusions. First, the bias cannot be a response bias—otherwise it would show on affirmation as well as denial inferences. Next, the bias must be a consequence of an effort at reasoning because otherwise the double negation difficulty would never be encountered. Hence, the picture that emerges is one of subjects attempting to reason according to the instruction, but whose ability to do so is subject to some problem connected with double negation.

There is more than this to explain for a theory of conditional reasoning, however. For example, on the affirmative conditional, MT is not inhibited by the double negation effect and yet is still only made around 60% of the time. Recall from Chapter 1 that one should sometimes reject the conditional rather than perform MT in ordinary reasoning from uncertain beliefs. One should sometimes be even more doubtful about applying MT when one would have an affirmative rather than a negative conclusion after the application of double negation. It is more risky to draw a conclusion about what is a raven (i.e. a member of a homogeneous and relatively small set) than one about what is not a raven (i.e. a member of a heterogeneous and unbounded set). Recall as well from Chapter 1 that one almost never has grounds for rejecting the conditional rather than performing MP in ordinary reasoning from uncertain beliefs. The same points can be made about DA and AC under a pragmatic interpretation of the conditional as a biconditional. It may be possible to combine these points with the hypothesis of a *caution* effect in reasoning (Pollard & Evans, 1980) to get some insight into negative conclusion bias, or why double negations are not always removed, with the result made explicit in mental representations.

It will also be important for later discussions to appreciate that matching bias (see Chapter 3) is not a response bias either. We now know that matching bias only occurs under certain specified conditions. First, there is evidence that the bias may be specific to the linguistic form of the connective (Evans & Newstead, 1980), although recent evidence calls some of the earlier conclusions into question on this point (Evans, Legrenzi, & Girotto, submitted). Next the effect disappears when thematic materials or scenarios are used, even when these do not facilitate correct choices (Evans, 1995b; Griggs & Cox, 1983; Reich & Ruth, 1982). Finally, the effect is critically dependent on the use of implicit rather than explicit negative cases (Evans, 1983; Evans et al., in press a). Before considering the implications of these findings for theories of competence, however, we examine some relevant evidence from other parts of the deductive reasoning literature.

Syllogistic reasoning and belief biases
Apart from the Wason selection task, the most intensively studied reasoning tasks in the psychological literature derive from the logic of syllogisms. This is a very restricted from of logic in which arguments consists of a major premise, minor premise, and conclusion. For a

conclusion of the form A–C, the major premise links a middle term B to C and the minor premise links the middle term B to A. For example:

6.3   No good researchers are good administrators
       Some teachers are good researchers
       Therefore, some teachers are not good administrators

There are four figures of syllogisms depending on the order of terms B,C in the minor premise and A,B in the major premise. There are also 64 moods as major premises, minor premises and conclusion can take one of four forms conventionally labelled by the letters A, E, I, and O:

A   All X are Y
E   No X are Y
I   Some X are Y
O   Some X are not Y

Of the 256 logically distinct syllogisms, only 25 have been reckoned to be valid by logicians. Psychologically speaking we can double these figures to include syllogisms in which the order of major and minor premises are reversed. Premise order is important as the conclusions favoured are subject to a "figural bias" (Dickstein, 1978; Johnson-Laird & Bara, 1984). Many psychological experiments have been reported in which subjects have been asked to assess the validity of such syllogisms, or to generate conclusions from pairs of major and minor premises. This research, together with numerous psychological theories of syllogistic inference, is reviewed in detail by Evans et al. (1993a, Chapter 7) and we will summarise here only the main points of relevance to our argument.

The most common method involves presenting subjects with a choice of four conclusions of the type A, E, I, and O, plus an option "no conclusion follows". This provides a chance rate of 20% for correct solution. Actual results show solution rates well above this chance rate: for example Dickstein (1978) using a wide range of syllogisms reports 52% correct responses. As with research on conditional inference, then, we have clear evidence of deductive competence on syllogistic reasoning problems. Because it is normal practice to exclude subjects with training in formal logic, we can also infer that such competence is exhibited with abstract and novel problems that are of a nature not previously encountered by the subjects of these experiments.

As with conditional reasoning also, logical error rates are high and are subject to systematic biases. With abstract syllogisms, people are influenced by the mood of the premises beyond their effect on the logic of the problems—an effect variously interpreted as an "atmosphere effect" or conversion errors. Similarly, the figure of the premises produces non-logical biases such that the order of terms in premises influences the preferred order in the conclusion. As we have already seen in Chapter 5, when pragmatically rich content is introduced, subjects are strongly influenced by a "belief bias" in which believable conclusions are judged to have greater validity than unbelievable ones.

Excluding a certain amount of random error, syllogistic reasoning performance—like conditional reasoning performance—is subject to two systematic influences that we may term the logical and non-logical component. In all these experiments subjects are significantly influenced by the logic of the problem—our inescapable evidence for deductive competence—but also influenced by a variety of non-logical "biases". The data of Evans et al. (1983) discussed in Chapter 5 and summarised in Fig. 5.1 are paradigmatic. When analysed by logic, 72% of subjects accepted valid conclusions compared with only 40% who accepted invalid conclusions. When analysed by the non-logical belief factor, however, 80% accepted believable conclusions and only 33% accepted unbelievable conclusions.

We have indicated that we are interested in this chapter not only in the question of whether subjects possess abstract deductive competence—which it seems they do—but also in whether such competence is linked to explicit, verbal reasoning. We have already seen some evidence for this linkage in our discussion of the selection task in the previous chapter. Research on belief biases provides further relevant evidence. An important question concerns the ability of subjects to respond to deductive reasoning instructions that tell them to disregard their prior beliefs and base their reasoning only on the premises given. Now in fact, some kind of instruction to this effect is included in all the standard belief bias literature including the study of Evans et al. (1983), so we might conclude that subjects' ability to take account of such instructions is very limited. However, recent studies have been reported in which the standard type of instructions have been both weakened and strengthened.

Newstead et al. (1992, Experiment 5) employed augmented instructions that gave added emphasis to the concept of logical necessity. Standard instructions, given also to the control group, included the following:

> You must assume that all the information that you are given is true; this is very important. If and only if you judge that the conclusion logically follows from the information given you should write "YES" in the space below the conclusion on that page.

Thus even for the control group, it is clear that deductive reasoning is required and prior belief irrelevant—without such instruction the claim that prior belief exerts a "bias" would be empty. However, augmented instruction groups additionally received this:

> Please note that according to the rules of deductive reasoning, you can only endorse a conclusion if it definitely follows from the information given. A conclusion that is merely possible but not necessitated by the premises is not acceptable. Thus, if you judge that the information given is insufficient and you are not absolutely sure that the conclusion follows you must reject it and answer "NO".

The emphasis on logical necessity is particularly relevant in the attempt to remove belief bias, because the effect principally reflects the acceptance of invalid but believable conclusions (see Fig. 5.1). The effect of these additional instructions in the Newstead et al. study was dramatic. Acceptance rates for invalid-believable arguments dropped from 50% under standard instructions to only 17% under augmented instructions, effectively removing the belief bias effect entirely. However, subsequent experiments reported by Evans, Allen, Newstead, and Pollard (1994) showed that belief bias could be maintained even in the presence of such augmented instructions. The conclusion of Evans et al. (1994) was that instructions reduce but do not eliminate the effects of belief.

Two recent studies of the influence of belief on reasoning have taken the opposite strategy of weakening the instructional requirements for deductive reasoning. Stevenson and Over (1995) were concerned with the suppression of *modus ponens* by use of auxiliary premises that served to weaken belief in the conditional premise (see Chapter 5). In Experiment 1 they used conventional deductive reasoning instructions in which subjects were told to assume that the premises were true and to indicate what conclusion followed. In Experiment 2, however, they were asked to imagine they were listening to a conversation and to indicate what they thought followed. The effect of this change on responses was very substantial. In Experiment 1, rates of *modus ponens* and *modus tollens* were 83% and 79% with an additional premise supporting the conditional, dropping to 40% and 40% with a premise undermining the conditional. Note that this is a substantial suppression effect despite the use of deductive reasoning instructions. However, in Experiment 2 the corresponding figures were 60% MP and 38% MT, dropping to 12% and 12%.

George (1995) also looked at suppression of valid conditional inferences based this time on *a priori* belief in the conditional premise. In his Experiment 3, one group was told to assume absolutely the truth of the premises and another to take into account the uncertainty in the premises. He concluded that belief-based reasoning was easier than premise-based reasoning because in the second group 96% of subjects conformed with instructions and took account of belief, whereas in the first group only 43% were able to comply with the instruction to assume the premises and ignore prior belief.

The evidence from these studies points to some conclusions about deductive competence. In discussing the belief bias effect in Chapter 5, we argued that it is rational$_1$ to reason in real life from all relevant and well-justified beliefs, and not just from some arbitrary set of assumptions. However, it is clearly irrational$_2$ not to restrict oneself to given assumptions in a logical reasoning task. All of the studies described show that the use of deductive reasoning instructions, however strongly worded, cannot totally suppress effects of belief on reasoning, thus supporting our argument that rational$_1$ reasoning reflects habitual, tacit processes. However, these studies show that when presented with deductive reasoning instructions, subjects can to a significant degree evaluate the arguments in a logically sound manner. They also show clearly that the extent to which people actually apply a deductive reasoning strategy is highly open to influence by verbal instruction, suggesting that rational$_2$ reasoning does indeed reflect the operation of explicit verbal processes, under some conscious control.

THE MECHANISM OF DEDUCTION: RULES OR MODELS?

We have now established our case that there is a human facility for abstract deductive competence demonstrable in the experimental psychological literature on reasoning. Human beings have been able to build on this faculty to axiomatise logic, develop mathematics and science, and create advanced technologies. Before turning to possible theoretical accounts of deduction, let us summarise what we know about this facility. First, it is fragile not robust, without special training in logic. The natural ability to reason in an explicit deductive manner is limited and much prone to errors and biases that cannot be removed by any amount of verbal instruction to reason logically. However, the deductive reasoning mode does appear to be under some degree of conscious control because people can turn it on or off in response to verbal instructions.

Of the four major theoretical approaches in the reasoning literature (see Evans, 1991), only two address the question of abstract deductive competence. The heuristic approach in general is mainly concerned with the explanation of biases and the heuristic-analytic theory of Evans (1984, 1989) specifically omits a description of the mechanism of analytic reasoning. The theory of pragmatic reasoning schemas (as in Cheng & Holyoak, 1985) is concerned with how people reason with realistic and familiar problem content where they have the opportunity to retrieve and apply schemas learned previously. This kind of theory is important because it is quite possible that people reason differently with familiar than with abstract materials. However, the theory as formulated can provide no explanation of the the general deductive competence for which we have provided evidence in the first part of this chapter.

This leaves us then with essentially the two choices discussed briefly in Chapter 1. One is the proposal that people reason by following abstract inference rules, in a restricted natural deduction version of "mental logic". The alternative is the theory of reasoning by mental models, which is particularly associated with the work of Johnson-Laird and his colleagues. We consider the merits of each approach in turn for explaining the competence we have identified.

Mental rules

The basic idea of the rules approach is that there is an in-built logic in the mind comprised of a set of primary inference rules plus a reasoning program or strategy for their application to sets of assumptions. Because the rules are general purpose and abstract, reasoning must be preceded by a stage of encoding the actual problem content into an abstract form, and succeeded by a decoding of any conclusion drawn back into the problem domain. It might appear to be only in these encoding and decoding phases that the theory has the potential to account for the hugely influential effects of thematic content on reasoning. However, in the words of O'Brien (1993, p.131), "Mental logic theorists have never claimed exclusivity" and propose that an abstract logic may co-exist with pragmatic reasoning procedures (see also Rips, 1994).

There are currently two major forms of the mental logic, or inference rule, theory which we present here only in conceptual outline (for detailed exposition and review see Evans et al., 1993a, Chapter 3). First, there is the three-part theory of Braine and O'Brien (see Braine & O'Brien, 1991; Braine, Reiser, & Rumain, 1984; O'Brien, 1993). The three components of this theory are the set of natural inference schemas, the reasoning program that applies these schemas, and the pragmatic reasoning system. The first two parts should explain abstract competence. There are simple inference rules that can be applied by a direct reasoning program and that should be immediate and easy to draw: for example, *modus ponens*. Then there are compound inference rules that require indirect reasoning by use of suppositions and are more error-prone. For example, there is no simple rule for *modus tollens*—it must be effected by an indirect line of reasoning using *reductio ad absurdum*. Given "If p then q" and not-q, one has to make a supposition of p, derive q by *modus ponens*, and so get the inconsistency of q and not-q. From that, one infers that the supposition p cannot hold and derives not-p.

The major alternative is the theory of Rips' (1983) ANDS model recently expanded and refashioned as PSYCOP (Rips, 1994). Rips' model is implemented as a working Prolog computer program and differs from that of Braine and O'Brien in being primarily aimed at proving theorems where the conclusion of the argument is known in advance. This is achieved by a combination of forward reasoning in which rules are applied to derive conclusions from premises and backward reasoning in which sub-goals are generated, thus greatly reducing the search space required by forward reasoning, in a manner analogous to the early Logic Theorist of Newell & Simon (1972). When no conclusion is specified, only forward rules can be used, which have limited competence. In fact, there are close parallels between this system and that of Braine and O'Brien: for example, the simple inference schemas of the latter are essentially similar to Rips' forward reasoning rules, and Rips' backward rules likewise involve suppositional reasoning of the kind described by Braine and O'Brien as indirect.

The mental logic or inference rule theory does account for basic deductive competence, but has serious limitations as a psychological theory of behaviour on reasoning tasks. First, as acknowledged by the inference rule theorists themselves, pragmatic influences can only be accounted for by mechanisms additional to and separate from the basic mental logic, such as invited inferences, conversational implicatures, and pragmatic reasoning schemas. Because almost all real word reasoning takes place in semantically rich contexts in which such pragmatic influences apply, it seems rather odd to us to identify an abstract mental logic as the primary reasoning mechanism whilst requiring a supplementary pragmatic theory to account for most of what actually happens! Also, we have already seen clear evidence both that the natural way of reasoning is primarily from uncertain beliefs, and that reasoning logically on the basis of a restricted set of assumptions requires a conscious and only partially successful effort by the subjects.

The second major problem for the inference rule theory concerns its account of error and bias. The strongest claim it seems that such theorists can make is to be able to specify the conditions under which errors are likely to occur: for example, when indirect reasoning procedures are required or when more steps of inference are involved (see Rips, 1989). Take the case of the Wason selection task. Inference theorists have argued that the poor solution rate on the abstract task is consistent with their theory because the task is difficult to solve by mental logical principles (Rips, 1994; O'Brien, 1993). For example, Rips argues that only forward rules such as *modus ponens*—leading to selection of the p card—can be applied, so that there is no means provided to support not-q choices, whereas O'Brien argues that not-q selections require a complex chain of indirect reasoning that few subjects are likely to achieve.

This is all very well, but the theory is telling us little about what subjects actually do. People endorse *modus tollens* less than *modus ponens*, but the only explanation for this in the theory is that the latter is a simple rule in mental logic, while the former is a compound one there and so more difficult to execute. No account is proffered for why MT is not expressed in a simple rule. We indeed showed in Chapter 1 that, for inferences from uncertain beliefs, one should more often reject the conditional when given the premises for MT than when given those for MP. But the inference rule theory has no natural way of accounting for uncertainty in the premises—it is essentially based on the idea that the premises are assumptions or suppositions.

The theory also lacks the means for explaining such clear phenomena as matching bias and negative conclusion bias that we have already argued are not response biases that can be tacked on to a competence system. In fact, none of the vast range of psychological factors that are now known to influence behaviour on the Wason selection task in both abstract and thematic versions (reviewed by Evans et al., 1993a, and here mainly in Chapter 4) can be accounted for by any part of the psychological theory of mental logic. In a way, of course, the mental rules theory could be viewed as the mirror-image of the heuristic-analytic theory in that it is explicit about the logical component of performance with little to say about the non-logical component. Because the selection task provides the least evidence of deductive competence of any reasoning problem studied in this field, it is not surprising that the rule theory is at its weakest here where the H-A theory is at its strongest. However, if the rule theory was to provide the missing analytic component it would have to provide a mechanism for competence that was both inherently plausible and able to integrate at a psychological level with the heuristic/relevance account of the non-logical component of performance. We will return to this issue following a brief survey of the rival mental model theory approach.

Mental models

The theory of reasoning by mental models, introduced by Johnson-Laird (1983), has been very successful, not least because of the energy of its advocates who have applied the theory in relevant experimental studies to all major fields of deductive reasoning research, including syllogistic reasoning, conditional and propositional reasoning, relational reasoning, and meta-deduction (see Johnson-Laird & Byrne, 1991). The theory has also been judged the most complete of the current reasoning theories in a different sense. It is the only theory to have been applied to all three major problem areas in the reasoning literature: those of deductive competence, bias, and content effects (Evans, 1991).

As we pointed out in Chapter 1, the theory of mental models itself postulates a limited kind of mental logic, with rules for manipulating mental models taking the place of natural deduction inference forms. But the inference rule theory, as this name for it suggests, is more heavily committed to logical rules than Johnson-Laird's mental models theory, and hence one can describe the difference as one of (logical) rules vs. models. In Johnson-Laird's theory, mental models consist of tokens and represent putative states of the world. The basic theory as originally applied to syllogisms and quantified reasoning (Johnson-Laird & Bara, 1984) involves three basic stages:

- Given some premises, the reasoner forms a provisional mental model representing a possible state of the world in which these premises are true.
- The reasoner then inspects the model in order to derive a provisional conclusion of a not-trivial nature (e.g. not a repetition of a premise).
- The reasoner searches for counter-examples—i.e. models in which the premises would be true and the conclusion false. If no such counter-examples are found then the conclusion is regarded as valid.

The third stage is crucial if the subject is genuinely to attempt deductive reasoning, and predictions for syllogistic reasoning are focused on this stage. For example, Johnson-Laird and Bara (1984) showed that the more alternative models the subjects need to consider, the less accurate is their reasoning—an effect that they attribute to limited working memory capacity. Similarly, the mental models explanation of the typical belief bias effect in syllogistic reasoning—acceptance of invalid but believable conclusions—is that subjects lack motivation to seek counter-examples when the initial conclusion favours belief. In moving the theory into the domain of propositional reasoning

(Johnson-Laird & Byrne, 1991; Johnson-Laird, Byrne, & Schaeken, 1992), however, the role of the third stage has become less clear. In conditional reasoning, for example, it is typically assumed that the subject represents the sentence as one or more explicit models plus an implicit model. For example, "If p then q" might be represented as:

[p]   q
...

Johnson-Laird and Byrne suggest that given the second premise p, subjects will immediately infer q (*modus ponens*), and given q they will infer p (affirmation of the consequent) unless they flesh out the representation to provide a counter-example, e.g.:

[p]   q
¬p   q
¬p   ¬q

Evans (1993b) has argued that only *modus ponens* should follow from the initial representation in which the minor premise p is exhaustively represented (indicated by the square brackets). To infer q directly from p, appears to violate the third general principle of mental model theory—namely the search for counter-examples. The point is that the presence of the implicit model "..." means that the subjects know that other situations may be consistent with the conditional, even though they have not yet thought what those situations might be. Hence, unless the premise is *exhaustively* represented it should be apparent that there could be a counter-example model to be found.

Johnson-Laird and Byrne (1993, p.194) argue against what they term "impeccable rationality" and propose instead:

> The ... notion of deductive competence rests on a meta-principle: an inference is valid provided that there is no model of the premises in which its conclusion is false. Individuals who have no training in logic appear to have a tacit grasp of this meta-principle, but have no grasp of specific logical principles ... They have no principles for valid thinking, i.e. for searching for models that refute conclusions.

What we understand Johnson-Laird and Byrne to be saying is that subjects will only draw inferences where no counter-example is present, but their competence in executing the original stage 3 of the model theory is weak. Thus subjects will not necessarily seek to flesh out models with implicit components, and will not suppress an inference simply because there could be a counter-example. It is certainly true that the characteristic error in both propositional and syllogistic reasoning is to execute "fallacies", i.e. to draw more conclusions than are strictly warranted by the premises given—a finding consistent with weak understanding of logical necessity. We have already seen that instructions emphasising necessity can reduce endorsement of fallacious conclusions and associated belief bias (Evans et al., 1994; Newstead et al., 1992), suggesting that the search for counter-examples is to some extent under conscious control.

The mental model theory appears to us to be a more complete psychological theory of reasoning than the inference rules theory in that errors and biases can be accounted for in ways that are intrinsic to the reasoning process. We have already seen one example, in the case of belief bias, where the theory can naturally incorporate the idea that search for counter-examples is curtailed when the putative conclusion is believable. Now, we have noted that rule theorists are happy to concede the presence of "response biases" that are external to and additional to the process of reasoning (e.g. O'Brien, 1993). However, we have already argued that effects such as matching bias and negative conclusion bias in conditional reasoning are not response biases, but arise as part of the effort of reasoning (see Evans et al., 1995 and in press a, for detailed experimental evidence and discussion concerning these biases). For example, if "negative conclusion bias" was really a bias to endorse negative conclusions following a process of inference, the inference rule theory would not be affected. Since it has something to do with double negation, as Evans et al. (in press a) have shown, it is a major problem; the rule of double negation, from not-not-p to infer p, is included as a primary (direct, forward) rule of inference in both the major inference rule systems we have discussed, and should therefore be immediately executed.

The concrete reasoning specified in the model theory can incorporate such an effect (although it was not predicted by model theorists). For example, *modus tollens* is difficult with a negative antecedent conditional "If not p then q". If this is represented as:

[¬p] q

...

then the minor premise (not-q) clearly eliminates the first model. In order to draw the correct conclusion p, however, the subject must appreciate that, because not-p is exhaustively represented, any other model must have a p. Due to double negation this is more difficult than when the antecedent is affirmative and [p] is the case eliminated. Here the conclusion not-p is a natural denial of a supposition.

A further attraction of the model theory for us is the ability to link with the notion of relevance. Mental model theorists are already talking about "focusing" effects in which subjects are assumed to concentrate on cases explicitly represented in mental models (e.g. Legrenzi et al., 1993). As we argued in Chapter 3, relevance is the prime cause of focusing. Hence the model theory would appear to provide the simplest solution to the missing analytic component of the heuristic-analytic theory, with heuristic relevance determining the content of the models from which inferences are then drawn in the manner described by Johnson-Laird and Byrne. Before opting for this easy solution to a very complex problem, however, we are aware of some further issues in the inference rules versus models debate that need to be aired.

Can we decide between rules and models?

The advocates of the inference rules and mental model theories themselves appear to believe that it is possible to decide who is right. For example, Johnson-Laird and Byrne (1991) are very confident that they have established the case for models, and present a number of apparent grounds for rejecting inference rules. Equally, theorists such as Rips (1994) believe that the case for their rules is unanswerable, and the model theory has been subjected to very strong attacks in the recent literature (see O'Brien, Braine, & Yang, 1994; Bonatti, 1994; and for a reply, Johnson-Laird, Byrne, & Schaeken, 1994). For a detailed review of the large range of evidence and argument that has been offered in the inference rules versus models debate see Evans et al. (1993a, Chapter 3).

For the neutral observer, trying to decide between inference rules and models on the basis of the arguments, the debate between the two can be frustrating. Both sides attribute predictions to the other approach that they then proceed—to nobody's surprise—to refute. The debate is also conducted as if it were between two precise scientific theories, capable of being clearly confirmed or disconfirmed in experiments easy to interpret, yet unfortunately this is not the case. Consider the free parameters that each side permits itself in explaining the data.

Inference rule theorists can choose what list of rules to have and what mechanisms for their application are proposed. They can attribute error to the use of complex rules, made up of indirect reasoning procedures or proofs with more steps of inference. They can allow for variance in the unspecified pragmatic processes that carry out the translation between the domain and the abstract code used for reasoning. As if this was not enough, they can also attribute variance to response biases, and to pragmatic reasoning schemas and may even suppose the use of mental models as well. It is very hard to see what would provide a means of strongly confirming or disconfirming the core of this theory.

Mental model theory has similar problems. First, there is no pragmatic theory of mental representation: the proposals concerning the contents of models are provided by argument and example rather than by full computational procedures, and are subject to arbitrary change and some inconsistency—e.g. on the subject of conditionals with negations in them (see Evans, Clibbens, & Rood, 1995). Explanations about pragmatic influences, say by thematic content on the Wason selection task, are attributed to the influence of knowledge upon model representation without specification of principles or mechanism. Next, there are no clear principles to explain when fleshing out of models will occur, and even the mechanism for deduction from a given representation is sometimes left unspecified. As an example, Evans (1993b) derived a new prediction of an affirmative premise bias from his interpretation of the mental model theory of conditionals, but there seems to be no way to establish whether this is predicted by the "official" theory.

If neither approach is fully and precisely defined in itself, then the issue of which is "correct" is going to be hard to decide on empirical grounds. The best one might achieve is to disconfirm a particular version or application of either theory. Like a hydra, however, the theories may grow new heads faster than one can cut them off. A further problem is that both approaches are forms of mental logic that are essentially similar at a deep level. Oaksford and Chater (1993, 1995) for example have used this argument in an attempt to demonstrate that both theories are subject to computational intractability problems. Oaksford and Chater's argument is that in real life we have to reason from many beliefs so that any logic-based theory will become intractable whether based on syntactic (rules) or semantic (models) principles.

Actually we would argue that Oaksford and Chater's analysis is not correct, because the focusing power of the heuristic (pragmatic, relevance) system is such as to constrain all reasoning to a small set of premises. Of course, we are also well aware that this puts the computational problem back a stage leaving us with the "frame problem" that no one currently knows how to solve. There is, however, a profound implication of this analysis for reasoning research. It suggests that the common agenda of the model and rule theorists—the search for a mechanism of deduction—is relatively lightweight. The computationally heavy and rational$_1$ part of the process lies in the highly selective retrieval and application of information from memory. Accounting for people's relatively modest, in every way, rationality$_2$ should be much easier.

It is a challenge to separate rule and model theories by empirical means, but we see some grounds for preferring the model theory approach, at least for reasoning with *novel* problems. When reasoning with semantically rich materials, we think it likely that subjects will retrieve rules and heuristics that they have learned to apply in similar contexts. We have shown earlier in this chapter that deductive competence from assumptions is associated with the explicit cognitive system, but it is fragile, always subject to errors and biases, and easily abandoned in favour of reasoning from uncertain belief. Thus the idea of an innate, mental, natural, deduction system as the core for intelligent processes, with pragmatic processes added on as an afterthought seems implausible to us.

For those who regard mental model theory as an equally strong form of mental logic, the same arguments would apply. However, its main proponents do not regard it as such, as the above quote from Johnson-Laird and Byrne (1993) clearly illustrates. We agree with them that the meagre amount of deductive competence actually achieved by subjects in reasoning experiments requires nothing more than a grasp of their semantic principle. Really all it comes down to is this: in trying to decide what must follow from some premises, people try to see what is common to all the states of affairs they can think of in which the premises are true. We find this minimalist description of human logical reasoning far more plausible than a set of innate abstract inference rules. Notice as well that it appears to have a natural extension to the case of uncertain premises. These will not be true in all possible models people can think of, but they can take account of that and try to see what follows in most of the models in which the premises are true. There is thus a way to extend mental models theory to probabilistic reasoning, and this is a big advantage it has over the rules approach (Johnson-Laird, 1994a,b; Stevenson & Over, 1995).

We have other reasons for preferring the model type theory, some of which we have already indicated. We regard it as a much more psychological theory, capable of yielding—at least in principle— accounts of the influence of pragmatic factors and biases in ways that are intrinsic to the process of reasoning proposed, and not extrinsic as in the mental model account. We are attracted also by the linkage with focusing and relevance which we see as arising from the implicit heuristic processes. Perhaps most importantly, model theory can provide a framework for understanding decision making as well as deductive reasoning (see Chapter 7). We do, however, have important reservations about the current specifications of the theory of Johnson-Laird and Byrne, which we will elaborate in Chapter 7.

NOTE

1. Strictly speaking 6.2 is not a *modus tollens* argument the conclusion of which would instead be "Therefore the letter is not not T". From a logical point of view 6.2 thus combines MT with double negation elimination. We follow the conventional terminology of the psychological rather than philosophical literature on this point.

CHAPTER SEVEN

A dual process theory of thinking

We started this book with our account of rationality, and we end it with our theory of thinking. We believe that one leads to the other in natural fashion with the dual nature of rationality being mirrored, to an extent, in dual systems of underlying thought. Let us briefly recap and round off the argument to this point.

The distinction between rationality$_1$ and rationality$_2$ was originally introduced to solve an apparent paradox of rationality (Chapter 1). This is that the human species is obviously highly intelligent, being able to achieve many practical and even abstract goals, and yet the psychological literatures on reasoning, judgement and decision making seem to be littered with evidence of error and bias. To resolve the problem, we have distinguished between people's rationality$_1$, which consists in their ability to achieve many personal goals, and their more limited rationality$_2$, which shows in their violation in many experiments of the rules of logic and decision theory. As argued in Chapter 6, human beings without special training do have some deductive competence. This modest ability, combined with their higher degree of rationality$_1$, makes it no real paradox that they have done so well, and even been able ultimately to create logic and decision theory as formal systems.

In discussing this distinction throughout the book, we have been able to show a number of reasons why people may be irrational$_2$ without being judged to be irrational$_1$. First, the normative systems may themselves be inadequate. We have pointed to the limitations both of formal logic as a standard for good reasoning (Chapter 1) and of formal decision theory as a standard for good decision making (Chapter 2). Secondly, we have shown that behaviour often appears irrational only in the sense that people fail to observe the experimental instructions, whereas the processes applied would normally be effective in everyday life (a point also made by Sperber et al., 1995). For example, a "positivity bias" may be a generally adaptive feature of thinking with a limited capacity system and yet lead to errors described as confirmation or matching biases under particular experimental conditions (see Chapters 3 and 5). We have shown (Chapter 5) that people's thinking is habitually influenced by prior belief, a tendency that can be highly rational₁ but may lead to belief biases in experimental tasks.

We are not saying that people are invariably rational₁ because any rationality is clearly bounded by cognitive constraints. Of course, people may fail to achieve their goals because they have not had the opportunity to learn the strategy required or because the task exceeds their cognitive processing capabilities. Particularly difficult to achieve are high-level and long-term goals, conceivable only in language and requiring much explicit processing. Consider the case of probabilistic reasoning. On the one hand, we have evidence that people can detect contingencies and probabilities very accurately, as measured by implicit learning methods (see Reber, 1993). On the other, the literature on statistical reasoning and judgement provides much evidence of bias and fallacious inference, particularly on unfamiliar problems that are merely described to subjects. Some of these biases can certainly have irrational₁ consequences. For example, a tendency to generalise from small or biased samples of information in novel cases will clearly lead to some poor decision making. A plausible explanation for this is that it is very difficult to abstract principles of probabilistic reasoning in a purely inductive way, without knowledge of task structure—a problem that is intrinsic to the nature of probability (see Einhorn, 1980). It is clearly important to recognise contexts where formal probability theory has to be applied to achieve effective reasoning and decision making. At the very highest level, it is essential for scientific research, but it is sometimes needed in ordinary affairs as well.

In discussing rationality in this way, we believe that some clear psychological proposals have also arisen. A major advantage of our approach is that there is no ground for making a sharp distinction between reasoning and decision making. All the tasks we have discussed in this book involve the same general stages of problem representation, judgement or inference, and decision/actions. Exactly the same psychological problems arise in accounting for reasoning and decision making. For example, we need to ask (a) how the problem information gets represented, (b) what causes people to focus selectively on some aspects and ignore others, and (c) what mechanism is responsible for the retrieval of relevant prior knowledge? There is no clear distinction either in terms of the processes applied to produce the response to the task: decision making may require explicit reasoning for example, whereas response to reasoning problems may require only intuitive judgements. We hope in particular that our extended discussion of the Wason selection task (Chapter 4) has served to illustrate the false distinction between reasoning and decision tasks. As we have shown, the most investigated single problem in the literature on "reasoning" can best be understood by an analysis in terms of judgemental and decision processes.

The most important psychological distinction, however, is the one we focus on in this final chapter—that between explicit and tacit cognitive processes. In Chapter 3, we introduced our thesis that our thinking is highly focused on what are subjectively relevant features in the task information and from memory. We argued that such focusing can be rational₁ and is achieved by preconscious and tacit processes. What we are aware of and what we think about is therefore determined mostly by tacit, implicit processes. We argued that such processes are computationally extremely powerful and operate in a very rapid and almost certainly parallel manner. In fact, we characterise our implicit system in much the same way as do neural network theorists and feel that connectionist models provide a promising approach to understanding how this system works. Such tacit systems can clearly be called, in a sense, "inferential"—for example, in applying general knowledge to specific cases. It is important, however, to distinguish such implicit inferencing from explicit reasoning of the kind discussed in Chapter 6, which involves manipulation of explicit propositional representations.

The notion of implicit processing has also been crucial in our explanation of "biases". However, we are not adopting a behaviouristic or epiphenomenalist stance in which conscious thinking serves no purpose. On the contrary, we wish to propose a dual process theory of thinking in which tacit and parallel processes of thought combine with explicit and sequential processes in determining our actions. In Chapter 6, for example, we argued both that there is evidence of deductive competence in reasoning, and therefore of a limited capacity to be rational₂, and also that such reasoning arises from an explicit verbal process. Support for the latter claim comes from the extent to which rational₂ processes, unlike rational₁ processes, are subject to the influence of verbal instructions.

Although not previously linked to a theory of rationality, the dual process theory we present has origins in much earlier theorising of the first author in the area of deductive reasoning. However, the emphasis of the theory has shifted over the years in particular with regard to the relationship between the two processes. We discuss this issue first, and then proceed to look more closely at what is known about both tacit and explicit thought processes.

DUAL PROCESSES IN REASONING: SEQUENTIAL, PARALLEL, OR INTERACTIVE?

In order to illustrate the issues involved we give a brief summary of the history of dual factor and dual process accounts of reasoning. Evans (1982) in reviewing the then state-of-the-art in the field of deductive reasoning, presented a descriptive two-factor theory with the claim that almost all reasoning tasks show evidence of a logical and non-logical component of performance. Despite all the large amount of further research that has been conducted since then, we see no reason to revise this analysis, and much of our discussion of competence and bias in Chapter 6 is built upon this dichotomy.

In the two-factor theory, logical and non-logical processes were characterised as competing processes and formalised as an additive probability model by Evans (1977b) who provided statistical evidence of within-subject conflict between the two factors, for example by showing statistical independence between selection rates of different cards on the selection task. The two-factor, within-subject conflict model was also applied by Evans et al. (1983) to explain their belief bias findings. Of particular importance were the results of protocol analyses which showed firstly that, when subjects attended to the conclusion more than the premise, they were more likely to show a belief bias. The crucial evidence for the conflict model was that these two modes of reasoning were not associated with different subjects. (Recently, however, George, 1991, has presented some evidence that subjects differ in the extent to which their reasoning is belief based.)

The descriptive two-factor theory was also cautiously linked to psychological assumptions about conscious and unconscious processes in what was termed the "dual process theory of reasoning" (Evans, 1982, Chapter 12; Evans & Wason, 1976; Wason & Evans, 1975). This theory was motivated by the need to account for discrepancies between introspective reports and experimental evidence of bias on the Wason selection task. Wason and Evans investigated the reasons people gave for choosing cards both with the usual "if p then q" conditional, and also with the form "if p then not q" where the correct choices are greatly facilitated because they are also favoured by matching bias. The striking results were for subjects who received the negative consequent conditional first. Most of course, chose p and q, but also stated that they were turning the cards to seek falsifying combinations—apparent evidence of "full insight". The same subjects, subsequently given the affirmative conditional also tended to choose p and q, and now gave verification explanations in line with "no insight".

Wason and Evans thought it implausible that subjects possessed an insight on one version and not on the other and instead proposed their dual process theory. They argued for a distinction between type 1, unconscious, and type 2, conscious processes. They proposed that matching was an unconscious type 1 process that led to the card choices and that the type 2 conscious processes served only to rationalise the choices made. Evans and Wason (1976) went on to show that subjects would happily provide a verbal justification for any common solution to the selection task that was proposed to them as the "correct" solution.

The heuristic-analytic theory of Evans (1984, 1989) has already been discussed at a number of points in this book. This theory developed the earlier dual process theory in several ways. First, the heuristic (type 1) processes were better specified as providing "relevant" problem representation, and the specific if- and not-heuristics were proposed to account for abstract selection task performance and other aspects of conditional reasoning. The analytic (type 2) processes were upgraded from a purely rationalising role to form the basis of the logical component of performance in the two-factor theory, albeit by an unspecified mechanism. This development depended on the critical insight that the Wason selection task is a most unrepresentative example of a reasoning task—one in which logical inferences, rather than relevance judgements, are rarely employed.

Though we generally regard the heuristic-analytic theory as an advance, there is a respect in which we now prefer the proposals of the original dual process theory, a name which we would now like to revive. Evans (1989) was particularly concerned to explain the evidence of biases in terms of relevance effects in problem representation. Hence the analyses of that book were mostly concerned with how tacit thought processes lead to selective representation of problem information. The impression created, however, was that the analytic processes take over where the heuristic processes leave off. This sequential model is clearly at odds with the conflict and competition model in the Evans (1982) two-factor theory. Wason and Evans, on the other hand, discussed the possibility of a dynamic interaction between type 1 and type 2 processes.

The dual process theory that we now favour is neither a sequential model nor a conflict model, but rather an interactive model. We would agree with Evans (1989) that the processes responsible for problem representation and focusing are primarily tacit. However, we also believe that inferences and actions often result from implicit processing without intervention from the explicit system. When we look at inferences drawn and decisions made it seems to us that these can reflect either tacit or explicit processes. For example, we can make a decision in a quick "intuitive" way or by conscious elaboration. Subjects on a reasoning task may make an effort at explicit reasoning in accordance with the instructions and they may succeed in deriving the conclusion in this way. Alternatively, they may give up and choose a conclusion that "feels" right. The interactive nature of the two processes lies in the fact that our conscious thinking is always shaped, directed, and limited by tacit, pre-attentive processes. For example, on the selection task not only is people's conscious thinking restricted in general to the matching cards, but their thought about the consequences of turning the cards is also limited to the matching values on the other side (Evans, 1995b; Wason & Evans, 1975). Clearly such a finding is not consistent with the idea of an implicit stage followed by an explicit stage.

We are pleased to discover that Sloman (1996) has recently argued the case for two systems of reasoning that bears many similarities to the dual process theory we support here. He distinguishes between associative reasoning—which he assumes to be based in connectionist systems—and rule-based reasoning. By rule-based reasoning he refers to symbol manipulation and does not attempt to adjudicate the debate between inference rules and mental models. We agree with him that these two theories share a common agenda that we have described as the deductive competence problem (Chapter 6). Sloman's discussion also roughly indicates an implicit/explicit distinction similar to ours. First, he argues that awareness of process is a rough if fallible heuristic for distinguishing the two processes. He argues that with associate reasoning we are aware only of the product—say a judgement—and not the process. However, he is cautious about awareness of process with rule-based reasoning, owing to the interpretational problems of introspective report (so are we, see below). The other way in which Sloman's two reasoning systems are similar to the implicit/explicit distinction is that he relates his distinction to automatic versus controlled processing. Awareness and control are, of course, two defining characteristics of consciousness. Sloman also argues that "the rule-based system may suppress the associative system but not completely inhibit it". This accords with our own analysis that conscious reasoning can overcome habitual tacit processes, but only to a limited extent (see Chapter 6).

THE NATURE OF TACIT THOUGHT PROCESSES

Discussion in this book has been focused principally on giving $rational_1$ accounts of behaviour on reasoning and decision tasks—for example by reinterpreting evidence of biases—so we have already provided much discussion of psychological processes that we regard as primarily tacit. We obviously cannot make a direct equation between $rationality_1$ as we have defined it and successful type 1 implicit processes, or between $rationality_2$ and correct, by some normative theory, type 2 explicit processes. The notions are, however, very closely correlated for reasons we will explain.

As we have argued, $rational_1$ reasoning and decision making happens when we make practical decisions that help us to achieve our personal goals. Much of the time we do this very effectively and by use of habitual type 1 processes. As indicated earlier in this book, adaptive tacit processes may be either innate or learned. We do not wish to take a strong position on the argument that cognitive processing reflects the possession of innate, specialised modules (e.g. Fodor, 1983; Chomsky, 1986) although we accept that systems such as language and visual perception could not be learned within the lifetime of an individual without a strong innate basis. We are currently unconvinced, however, that higher-level thought involved in reasoning and decision making can plausibly be accounted for in terms of specific evolutionary mechanisms (e.g. that proposed by Cosmides, 1989) and feel that many $rational_1$ actions reflect specific learning experiences of the individual. Nevertheless, the mechanism by which such learning and application comes about is clearly subject to biological constraints such as, perhaps, the first (cognitive) principle of relevance proposed by Sperber et al. (1995—see Chapter 3).

Our assumption is, therefore, that that tacit processes primarily reflect (biologically constrained) learning, and that we have learned how to do most of the things that we require to do to achieve our everyday goals. It is fully necessary that this is the case, because conscious thought is a very scarce and limited resource. The execution of the most ordinary tasks, such as travelling to work, demand extraordinary amounts of information processing, and the interaction of both very large stores of prior knowledge and very complex processing of environmental stimuli. If you do not immediately agree with this statement, then think what would be needed to design and program a robot that could—without external assistance—perform your own journey to work.[1] Yet so automated are your own processes, that you will probably not require much application at all of your conscious thinking for travelling to work, and will instead have this resource available during the journey for planning your day's activities.

As already indicated, there are occasions where to be rational$_1$ you must apply conscious resources, or type 2 processes. It is also possible to conform to a normative theory by entirely type 1 processes. We discussed examples in Chapter 2, where we pointed out that even the foraging behaviour of a bumble-bee can be seen to comply with normative decision theory. We also pointed out that, by our definition, a bumble-bee cannot have rationality$_2$. That implies having good reasons for one's reasoning or decision making, and this in turn means following rules, sanctioned by a normative theory, in which propositional representations are manipulated. In this case, not only would there have to be propositional representations, but these would have to have numerals attached to them, so that the SEU rule for calculating subjective expected utility could be followed. Surely bumble-bees do not follow any such rules, as opposed to merely conforming to them—i.e. producing behaviour in another way that gives the same result as following the rule would have.

Let us consider a human example to illustrate how closely type 1 and type 2 processes, and rationality$_1$ and rationality$_2$, can be related to each other. Our visual system is highly reliable but sometimes gives us misleading representations of the world. This system has reliable type 1, implicit processes that do not follow normative rules for manipulating propositional representations. But after processing, it presents us with a representation of the world that is sometimes inaccurate. An example would be when we are looking at a fish in water, which would have an illusory location. Now we could learn by type 1, implicit processes to compensate for this inaccuracy, just by throwing a barbed spear at some fish again and again. We would explicitly note when we had failed to spear one and try again. Eventually we could learn how to make a small compensation for our visual illusion, without however being explicitly aware of what this was, and be able to spear fish with great success. In this process we would display mostly rationality$_1$.

We could carry on and explicitly investigate the illusion and how we compensate for it. To do that, we could become fully scientific and follow logical and probabilistic rules for reasoning, in type 2, explicit processing. We would then be rational$_2$, and that would be necessary for acquiring scientific knowledge of what was going on. Even so, we would have to rely on many type 1 processes, and be rational$_1$ again, to gather our scientific data and make relevance judgements for our inferences in our investigation, and of course we would still experience the illusion no matter how extensive our scientific knowledge. We are conscious of and can control to some extent our type 2 processes, but not our type 1 processes. To clarify further the difference between implicit and explicit thought process, some valuable insights can be gained by looking at the literature on implicit learning, to which we now turn.

Implicit learning and tacit processing

Fortunately, the interesting and important field of implicit learning has recently been reviewed and discussed in two books by Reber (1993) and by Berry and Dienes (1993, and see Evans, 1995a, for an extended review and discussion of these books). One way to define implicit learning is that it occurs below a subjective threshold—the subject is unable to report what has been learned. Frequently such learning is implicit in a second sense—subjects may lack awareness that they have learned anything at all. Berry and Dienes take the stronger position that there are separate implicit and explicit cognitive systems that differ in respects other than awareness. For example, they argue that implicit learning leads to only limited and specific transfer to other tasks compared with explicit learning. They also say it gives rise to a phenomenal sense of "intuition"—a point to which we will return. The best evidence that they offer for this view of implicit learning is in control tasks of the sort studied by Berry and Broadbent (e.g. 1984). Here subjects learn by experience to control and predict systems, such as factory production, simulated on computer without acquiring verbal knowledge of how they are doing it.

Berry and Broadbent (1988) proposed that in implicit learning mode subjects store all contingencies in an unselective manner whereas explicit learning is much more focused. They suggested that explicit processing is more similar to what happens in problem solving where subjects evaluate explicit hypotheses, apply explicit rules, or manipulate mental models. They showed that implicitly acquired knowledge would transfer between similar domains but not across problems where the domain was different and only the principle was the same at a higher level of abstraction. They also found that transfer between similar tasks was inhibited if subjects were informed verbally of the connection between them, suggesting that this induced a less effective explicit mode of learning. Reber (1993) also discusses a number of examples in his own experiments where instructions inducing explicit learning strategies impede performance.

Like Berry and Dienes, Reber (1993) argues for separate implicit and explicit systems. One point on which he agrees with Berry and Dienes is that implicit learning is relatively robust—in particular, implicitly acquired knowledge is less affected by neurological damage than is explicitly acquired knowledge. This can be taken as evidence for the connectionist nature of implicit processing. Reber claims also that implicit processes are less variable across individuals and to a large degree independent of age and IQ. He uses these features to build an evolutionary argument for what he calls the "primacy of the cognitive unconscious". Tacit processes evolved first, are common with other higher mammals, and are relatively robust and invariant.

Because Reber discusses the unconscious, he feels obliged to define what he means by consciousness. He argues that although there is a sense of consciousness that is common with other animals, there is also a sense of the term—he calls it Consciousness II—which is uniquely human:

> The kind of consciousness we typically imagine when we think of our own sense of awareness is one that functions not merely to differentiate self from others but one that incorporates a large number of functions that allow us to modulate and refine the actions of self (p. 136).

He goes on to argue that in most of his experiments subjects are aware that they have learned something although they do not know what it is. He adds: "But this kind of consciousness is not really Consciousness II, it is something less well developed ... is a function that contains awareness but lacks the self-reflecting, modulating functions."

Now, if there is a uniquely human consciousness, Consciousness II, that evolved late and which is—unlike implicit systems—related to age, IQ, and so on, as Reber claims, then we should ask (a) what specifically is its function and (b) what have studies of implicit learning informed us about what this function is? We return to this point when we consider the nature of explicit thinking.

Intuitive judgement

One of Berry and Dienes' characteristics of implicit learning is that it gives rise to a phenomenal sense of intuition. "Intuition" is a term used to describe the experience of processes whose end-product only is posted in consciousness. Most human expertise is intuitive because judgements have to be exercised in complex domains with the interaction of many variables. This is why knowledge elicitation for expert systems has proved such a difficult exercise (see Evans, 1988). For example, an expert chess player thinks about only a small set of the possible moves when analysing a position, and a small set of replies and so on, thus restricting an otherwise unmanageably large problem space. However, the process by which moves are selected for consideration is tacit and unreportable. The problem is that much of the intelligence or expertise lies in these intuitive processes: better players think of better moves to consider in the first place.

Intuitive judgement has been studied extensively in cognitive and social psychology. Statistical or probabilistic judgement has been the main focus of study in the "heuristics and biases" tradition of Kahneman and Tversky. People may be asked, for example, whether a sequence appears to be random, whether two variables seem to be correlated, or which of two samples appears to give better evidence for a hypothesis. Such research is marked by widespread claims of bias: for example, people have the "gambler's fallacy" expecting sequences of random events to alternate outcomes; they see "illusory correlations" in data biased by their prior expectations and so on (see Baron, 1988; Garnham & Oakhill, 1994, for review of these literatures). Kahneman and Tversky have proposed various "heuristics" as explanations of such biases, most notably *representativeness* where judgements of probability reflect detection of similarity between features of events and hypotheses (Kahneman & Tversky, 1972b) and *availability* in which probability of single events is judged by the ease with which examples can be brought to mind (Tversky & Kahneman, 1973).

Of course, such judgements are only correctly described as intuitive if they reflect tacit processing. Kahneman and Tversky did not give a precise account of their heuristics, and in particular did not state whether these operate at a conscious or unconscious level. In the case of the availability heuristic, the processes that determine what "comes to mind" seem to be the same kind of tacit processes that we have discussed as determining selective representations in reasoning, by a combination of salience of the stimuli presented and retrieval from memory of associated and relevant knowledge and limited by processing effort. Availability must be closely related to the idea of relevance and focusing effects discussed in Chapter 3 and elsewhere in this book. The only sense in which this heuristic could be explicit is if the subject was to reason, "I can think of several examples of this event, so it must occur often." We think it more likely that availability of examples would confer an intuitive feeling of probability.

There is evidence to suggest that at least in the case of subjects lacking training in statistics, probability judgements are indeed tacit. A series of studies by Nisbett and colleagues on people's understanding of statistical principles in everyday reasoning are relevant here. Nisbett, Krantz, Jepson, and Kunda (1983, Study 4) gave subjects problems in everyday domains that involved the law of large numbers: for example, they might have to explain why players showing good form in early season sporting results do no better than the rest in the longer term. Subjects were given a choice of several explanations, one of which was the correct, statistical reason. The problems were presented in two domains—sports and acting—and the subjects had varied experience in the two domains.

What Nisbett et al. found was that a majority of subjects with experience in the domain chose the statistical explanation, whereas a majority of those inexperienced in the domain in question chose a deterministic account. This suggests that understanding of the law of large numbers can be acquired by experience, but in a *domain-specific* manner. In a separate study, Jepson, Krantz, and Nisbett (1983) asked subjects to give explanations of events in a large number of domains and classified their open-ended answers as statistical, determinate, or intermediate. Across the nine domains studied, the frequency of statistical explanations ranged from as low as 5% to as high as 93%. Bearing in mind Berry and Dienes' criterion of specificity of learning and transfer, these findings again suggest that an intuitive understanding of the law of large numbers may be acquired by tacit processing in a domain-specific manner.

In accordance with the dual process theory, just because one has initially learned to comply with a rule implicitly does not mean that one cannot come to learn it and follow it explicitly. Smith et al. (1992) have recently argued that people can follow the law of large numbers as an abstract rule. One piece of evidence they refer to comes from Nisbett et al. (1983), where subjects made appropriate use of sample size and variability when reasoning about the colour of imaginary birds and people on an imaginary island. However, we are not sure that subjects are following a rule to think about this case. After all, they are very familiar with birds and other people, and could have learned only implicitly to take account of the greater colour variability in birds than in people. All ravens may be black, but the males and females of many bird species differ in colour.

A good test, as Smith et al. (1992) also point out, would be whether teaching someone the explicit verbal principle of the law of large numbers would benefit their everyday reasoning. Fong, Krantz, and Nisbett (1986) showed that statistical answers to problems couched in everyday terms increased dramatically as a function of the amount of formal statistical training the subjects had received. Given the normal method of teaching statistics—by verbal instruction—this suggests a benefit of explicit thinking. Stronger evidence is provided by experimental training in studies in the same paper. For example, in Experiment 1 a control group without training gave 42% statistical answers; a group given (explicit) rule-based training 56%, a group given (implicit) examples-based training 54%, and a group trained by both methods 64%. The benefits of rule-based training certainly give evidence that subjects may bring explicit principles to bear in such tasks. Whether the implicit, examples-based training leads to implicit or explicit knowledge of the principle is moot. Studies of concept and rule learning show that people can learn to conform to a rule in a wholly tacit manner, but that they can be led to explicit knowledge of it, depending on factors such as the complexity of the domain and the mode of learning (see Berry & Dienes, 1993, Chapter 3).

The points discussed here illustrate that people's conformity with a rule or normative system does not necessarily qualify them as rational$_2$. However, the evidence also suggests that people can learn to follow rules explicitly and thus increase their rationality$_2$. Compare human beings again with bumble-bees. The bees' behaviour is determined by the quality of the food they get from a small number of flowers they have recently visited. They may have a very limited memory, but they do well with this heuristic in their natural environment, in part because of the variability of their food there (Real, 1991). Human beings can be much more flexible and even eventually learn to follow the law of large numbers explicitly, taking account of both sample size and variability in different circumstances. We now turn to further consideration of the explicit thinking system, which makes us far and away the most adaptable of animals.

THE NATURE OF EXPLICIT THOUGHT PROCESSES

It is clear that the major benefit of the implicit system is its vast computational power, allowing very complex acts of information processing to take place very rapidly. Conscious thought, by contrast, is slow and very limited in capacity. We have shown already that such thinking is highly focused on selected information: we may have difficulty thinking about more than one hypothesis or more than one mental model at a time. As we do not regard consciousness as an epiphenomenon, it is important to consider what functional advantage it gives to us. The answer to this can be found by considering the limitations of the implicit cognitive system, and in particular what aspects of human intelligence cannot be achieved in a tacit manner.

We have already seen that implicit systems lead to learning that is relatively inflexible and domain specific—evidence, perhaps, for the operation of innate modules. Such processes are at least in part shaped by our past history of personal learning: the perceptions, judgements, and actions they prescribe are those that are effective in the environment in which the underlying neural networks have received their training. The advantage of the dual process system is that conscious reflective thought provides the flexibility and foresight that the tacit system cannot, by its very nature, deliver. Most of the time our decision making is automatic and habitual, determined by past learning, but it does not have to be this way. We *can* make conscious decisions based upon analysis of a novel problem, projection of mental models of future possible worlds, and calculations of risks, costs, and benefits. Granted we are not very good at conscious decision making, just as we are not very good at deductive reasoning, because of severe cognitive constraints. The most striking of these is our very limited span of attention already discussed. Acquisition of effective explicit thinking skills is also very hard work, in contrast with the automatic and apparently effortless acquisition of our tacit and intuitive processes. The point is, however, that consciousness gives us the possibility to deal with novelty and to anticipate the future. We can be rational$_2$ as well as rational$_1$.

Although the concept of explicit thought links with consciousness, it is also connected with language. In making this point, we do not overlook the fact that the *mechanism* of language operates primarily at a tacit level and may well reflect the possession of innate modules (see, for example, Chomsky, 1980, 1986; Fodor, 1983). Our point is that human beings' unique possession of language is almost certainly a prerequisite for our special form of reflective consciousness—Reber's Consciousness II—and hence for our facility for explicit, rational$_2$ thought. We accept the evolutionary argument that tacit processing is shared with animals who can thus be rational$_1$, but assert that rationality$_2$ is uniquely human. We have already indicated ways in which explicit thinking is linked with verbal processes. For one thing, such thinking appears to be frequently *verbalisable*—i.e. present in verbal working memory and able to be "thought aloud". Deductive processes are, as we have shown, also highly influenced by verbal instructions. We would not go so far as to say that language is the sole medium of explicit thinking, but it is hard to see how Consciousness II would have been achieved without it. For this reason we are interested in the argument of Polk and Newell (1995) that deductive reasoning processes are verbal and very closely linked with linguistic comprehension processes.

It seems to us that the stream of consciousness is a channel of not just limited but apparently fixed capacity. We cannot increase the capacity when a problem of complexity needs to be dealt with: nor can we reduce it when there is nothing to be done. Never empty, the channel fills with daydreams or occupies itself in gossip or with the vicarious experience of a television show when it has no pressing employment. Goal-directed, explicit thinking—aimed at problem solving or decision making—is also highly demanding of effort and concentration that noticeably tires the individual. Thus we may seek to delay such tasks as filling in a tax form which require a conscious effort, and prefer activities such as idle gossip, which involve far more complex information processing, but primarily at a tacit level with the results delivered effortlessly to our consciousness.

In attempting to study the explicit system of thinking and reasoning, we must be aware of the limitations of self-knowledge and verbal reporting. These issues have been discussed in detail by Evans (1989, Chapter 5) and will be reviewed only briefly here.

Self-knowledge and verbal reports

The notion of explicit, conscious thought is bound up with the problems of introspection and verbal report. Folk psychology includes the belief that we make decisions for conscious reasons that we can report. Vast industries of opinion polling and market research are built upon this belief. People are asked, for example, not only how they will vote but why. They may be given lists of issues and asked to identify which ones are influencing their voting. Politicians and political journalists take very seriously the results of such surveys. From the perspective of the dual process theory this is all very dubious. First, many decisions and actions result directly from tacit, judgemental processes that are by definition inaccessible to consciousness. Secondly, even where explicit thought is employed, there is no guarantee that this will confer insight and accurate introspective reporting.

In the Wason and Evans (1975) study, discussed earlier, subjects were asked to give reasons for their choices. This they did, using type 2 explicit verbal reasoning, relating their actions to the experimental instructions by arguing that the cards turned could prove the rule true or false. However, this reasoning was evidently serving the function of rationalising choices caused by tacit processes such as matching bias, a conclusion supported by the recent study of inspection times and protocols reported by Evans (1995b, and in press—and see Chapter 3 in the present volume). The famous paper of Nisbett and Wilson (1977) demonstrated effects consistent with this conclusion across a range of cognitive and social psychological experiments. They argued that people have no direct or special access to their own thought processes. According to Nisbett and Wilson, when people are asked for introspective reports what they actually do is to theorise about their own behaviour. Although such self-theorising is potentially advantageous, such theories are often erroneous. Thus journalists commissioning opinion polls may be engaging in self-fulfilling prophecies. Their newspaper articles provide people with theories, for example, of why one should vote for particular political parties. When opinion polls then ask people to give their reasons for voting, these theories are delivered back.

Those who criticise introspection may find themselves attacked as anti-rationalist. (For a summary of hostile reactions to Nisbett & Wilson, see White, 1988.) For example, Fellows (1976) once accused the first author (Evans) of regarding human beings as "non-verbal animals" and went on to add:

> If Evans dismisses the subject's reports as rationalisations, then logically he must dismiss his own explanations in the same way.

This line of attack misses the crucial point about the dual process theory. The rationalisations of Wason and Evans and the causal theories of Nisbett and Wilson are clear evidence of the existence of type 2 explicit verbal reasoning. Of course, Fellows is right to say that the kind of thinking used by Evans to write the discussions of his papers is the same as that used by subjects to rationalise their choices. Both are theorising in an explicit verbal manner. However, it is the psychologist, not the subject who has privileged access in this situation. The psychologist knows the previous literature on the topic and also knows the experimental design, what subjects in other groups were doing, and much else besides. Hence the researcher will have a better chance of getting the theory right than the subject. The point is not that subjects do not reason explicitly and verbally—they evidently do—but that they lack insight into the causes of their own behaviour. Even when they give correct accounts, it can be argued that this is because they hold a good theory of their behaviour rather than direct access to their thought processes (see Nisbett & Wilson, 1977).

Now, as we have argued, we do not regard explicit thinking as simply serving to rationalise behaviour, and believe that decisions and actions can result from explicit processes. The findings discussed here, however, militate against introspective reporting as a method of studying such processes. When asked how or why they have performed an action, or to predict future behaviour, people appear to access and apply theories of their own behaviour through their explicit thinking system. Such theories are often inaccurate and cannot be relied upon. So how can we investigate the role of explicit thinking in reasoning and decision making? One method that we have already discussed (e.g. in Chapter 6) is to investigate the effects of verbal instruction on reasoning performance. Tacit thought processes, we assume, are non-verbal and not responsive to such instructions. The other method is that of verbal protocol analysis.

In considering the difference between introspective report and protocol analysis we are happy to adopt the broad position advocated by Ericsson and Simon (1980, 1984). Contrary to much popular mis-citation, Ericsson and Simon did not refute Nisbett and Wilson's arguments. They also do not expect reports to be accurate if they are (a) retrospective and (b) invite subjects to state reasons for behaviour, or to make strategy reports. What Ericsson and Simon argue for is a method of verbal protocol analysis that differs from introspection in two crucial regards. First subjects report their thoughts concurrently, not retrospectively so that the current contents of short-term memory can be reported before they are forgotten. Next, the subjects only report their locus of attention—what they are thinking about. The process of thinking is to be inferred by the psychologist, not described by the subject.

Ericsson and Simon (1984) say that such verbal reports will be incomplete because there are automatic and "recognition" processes that do not register as sequential steps in verbal short-term memory, or working memory as we might better describe it. The processes they refer to are evidently part of our type 1, tacit system. However, the processes that can be traced by verbal protocol analysis are those that make use of working memory. Protocols can reveal the locus of attention—what information is currently being heeded—and may be informative about the goals that the subject is pursuing. They also reveal intermediate products and stages of problem solving. Even tacit processes may deliver their final products to consciousness. Complex problem solving involves lots of sub-stages—e.g. by pursuit and solution of sub-goals—which register their products in reportable working memory, allowing the processes as a whole to be traced and interpreted.

With these methodological considerations in mind, we turn finally to the mechanisms of explicit reasoning, picking up from where we left the issue of deductive competence in Chapter 6.

The mechanism of explicit reasoning and decision making

In discussing the inference rules versus mental models accounts of deductive competence (Chapter 6) we indicated a general preference for the models approach on the grounds that it was more plausible and psychologically richer. However, in the context of the current chapter we must raise a serious concern about the research programme on reasoning by mental models: the neglect of the problem of consciousness and explicit reasoning. Johnson-Laird and Byrne (1991, p.39) in virtually the only reference to consciousness in their entire book on reasoning, comment:

> The tokens of mental models may occur in a visual image, or they may not be directly accessible to consciousness. What matters is not the phenomenal experience, but the structure of the models.

We find this statement very unsatisfactory and note to our surprise that in the massive body of experimental work summarised by Johnson-Laird and Byrne, none appears to include evidence based on verbal protocol analysis. Johnson-Laird and Byrne appear to be adopting an epiphenomenalist stance that just does not stand up to the evidence. First, we have shown that people only make an effort at deductive reasoning when explicitly instructed to do so. Although we welcome Johnson-Laird's (e.g. 1993) recent extension of mental model theory to the realm of induction, we must ask why the validation stage (search for counter-examples) only arises when deductive reasoning instructions are given, unless the process is in some way explicit? The evidence that belief bias can be inhibited by instructions giving extra emphasis to the principle of logical necessity (Evans et al., 1994) can be interpreted as evidence for the model theory, but only on the assumption that the effort to find counter-examples is under conscious control.

The other difficulty here is the claim that mental models occupy space in working memory—a central proposal for the explanation of differences in difficulty between syllogisms, namely that multiple model problems are more difficult than single model problems (Johnson-Laird & Bara, 1984). Now in the widely accepted Ericsson and Simon model, the contents of working memory are generally regarded as conscious and reportable. We do not argue that the process by which mental models are manipulated can be reported, but we find it most implausible that this manipulation would not manifest itself in any way in a verbal protocol. In particular, it should be possible to tell whether subjects are thinking about single or multiple models. For example, if subjects consider alternative possibilities because they have been instructed to do so, it seems to us that this must show up in a verbal protocol.

Inference rule theorists have produced verbal protocol analysis in support of their arguments for rule-based reasoning—O'Brien, Braine, and Yang (1994) and Rips (1994) provide important evidence of this type. O'Brien et al. gave their subjects relatively long reasoning problems and asked them "… to write down everything that followed logically from the premises in the order that inferences occurred to them …". The point is that the steps in the solution of one of these problems should be in a certain order if the subjects are following logical rules. Most subjects did report the predicted order in their protocols. These results do establish that the subjects are following rules in step-by-step fashion under some conscious control, and not merely conforming to logic by coming up with the logically correct overall solution in some other way. But it is more open whether they are following natural deduction rules, as the inference rule theorists would contend, or following rules for constructing mental models.

In replying to O'Brien et al., Johnson-Laird, Byrne, and Schaeken (1994) acknowledge the importance of studying the intermediate steps subjects report themselves as using in solving logical problems. Johnson-Laird et al. admit that their model theory does not yet cover the order in which people will construct models to solve problems like those in O'Brien et al., but claim that this can be done in a way consistent with the data by supposing that "… reasoners will tend to start with a premise that is maximally semantically informative …". They give simple examples of what they mean, but we would argue that they need much more than this if their theory is to make predictions precise enough to be tested by experiments like those reported by O'Brien et al. In general, Johnson-Laird et al. must introduce some definition of semantic information, or as we would say, epistemic utility, into their theory, and use that to predict the order in which subjects will construct models to tackle any given problem. That prediction could then be tested by the subjects' protocols.

Despite this current limitation of the model theory, we reiterate our view that the inference rule theory is too limited in proposing a central reasoning mechanism based on abstract natural deduction rules, which maps so poorly on to the kind of reasoning that most of us do most of the time. The theory is also poorly suited to an integrated approach to reasoning and decision making because it can have little to say about the latter, or even about valid inference from uncertain premises (Stevenson & Over, 1995). In this respect we see much greater potential for the mental models approach. Johnson-Laird (1994a,b) has at least started to extend his theory, and in a seemingly natural way, to inductive and probabilistic reasoning. This should allow him to define semantic information or epistemic utility in some way, and beyond that to specify some common mechanism underlying both deductive reasoning and general decision making. In our view, this mechanism is one for constructing and manipulating mental models of alternative possibilities, and of their plausibility and desirability.

Johnson-Laird (1994a,b) has suggested that the probability of a proposition is assessed by the proportion of mental models in which it is true. To us the idea that people often generate, enumerate, or match many possible models is implausible and stands in contradiction to the proposal that deductive reasoning is difficult when only two or three alternative models need to be considered (Johnson-Laird & Bara, 1984). Moreover, Johnson-Laird appears to presuppose that mental models are, in effect, thought of as all equally probable—i.e. any mental model counts as only one item in any proportion. People are good at learning the relative frequencies of events in the world (Chapter 2), but they have to come to think that some of their mental models are more probable than others if they are to learn which hypotheses are more probable than others from experience (Carnap, 1950; Stevenson & Over, 1995). Even when people do judge probability by the proportion of propositions in mental models or the relative frequency of events in the world, that probability would still have to be mentally represented in some other way in order to affect decision making.

We think that some decision making does take place through the explicit consideration of alternative possibilities, but we do not imagine that people make extensive use of numerals to express probabilities and utilities in their mental models. Any explicit reasoning or decision making requires the help of the implicit system, and both probabilities and pay-offs can be embodied in this system. How else could one explain the massive Skinnerian research programme with its vast accumulated evidence for the effect of alternative reinforcement schedules on animal learning? Johnson-Laird and Byrne (1993) themselves allow mental models to be "annotated" with epistemic qualifiers, and this might be enough to reflect the vague thoughts people often have of some states of affairs as more probable than others. One possibility is to treat "is more probable than" as a relation between models in the way that "is to the right of" is a relation between terms within mental models in Johnson-Laird and Byrne (1991). For decision making, one would also need a relation "is of greater value than" between mental models (Manktelow & Over, 1992).

There is still a long way to go to get a full theory of deductive competence that is integrated with one of decision making. We favour the model approach, but we want to emphasise that we do not regard the manipulation of mental models as the sole mechanism of reasoning that people employ. Where problems of a similar type are repeatedly attempted and solved, it is highly efficient for people to learn specific heuristics. Neural networks are probably the mechanism that underlies much of this learning, so that the system is behaving in an "as if" manner. In the terms we have used, the system would only comply with or conform to rules, giving the same output as these would if they really were followed by someone. It is nevertheless possible to learn to formulate a rule explicitly, like a version of the law of large numbers, and then to follow it in an explicit process, as the work of Nisbett and colleagues, discussed earlier, suggests. However, discussion of such rules, and the schemas that are sometimes used to try and express them, is beyond the scope of this book.

CONCLUSIONS AND FINAL THOUGHTS

Much can be learned about human thought by studying errors and biases, relative to impersonal normative systems, in the same way as much can be learned about human vision by studying visual illusions. It is generally misleading, however, to impute irrationality to our subjects on the basis of such errors—and their associated cognitive illusions—in laboratory tasks. Our distinction between rationality$_1$ and rationality$_2$ is made to clear up confusions and to assist with the demanding theoretical task of understanding how people think. We have argued that people have a high degree of rationality$_1$ enabling them to achieve many personal goals, but that such rationality is achieved primarily by use of the tacit cognitive system based upon biologically constrained learning. We have also argued that people have a more limited capacity to be rational$_2$ dependent on the explicit thinking system with its access to natural language and reflective consciousness.

Considering future research on the psychology of thinking, we hope that a general effort will be made to achieve theoretical integration, and see promising signs that this is beginning to happen. The emphasis on rationality$_2$ has, in our view, had a divisive influence—sustaining, for example, the unfortunate separation of the study of reasoning and decision processes. In experiments on explicit deductive reasoning tasks, the focus on this notion of rationality has also led to undue emphasis on the problem of deductive competence and the somewhat sterile rules versus models debate. We feel that researchers should first take account of the very powerful tacit processing systems that affect our judgements and inferences. We would like to see a major expansion in the programme of research here on pragmatic processes, relevance, probability, utility, and information. At the same time, attention must be paid to the ways in which the explicit cognitive system can enhance reasoning and decision making and confer the uniquely human form of intelligence. Above all, we need to raise our vision above that of understanding behaviour within particular paradigms and develop a truly general and integrated theory of human thinking.

NOTE

1. We assume here the computational theory of mind within the cognitive science aproach. We realise that some philosophers would dispute the validity of our robot analogy, but it is particularly hard to reject with respect to implicit processes. Indeed we would argue that these philosophers concentrate too much on explicit, conscious process, and wrongly assume that these are more important in thinking than implicit processes.

References

Ackerman, R., & DeRubeis, R. (1991). Is depressive realism real? *Clinical Psychology Review, 11*, 565–584.

Adams, E.W. (1975). *The logic of conditionals*. Dordrecht: Reidel.

Ajzen, I. (1977). Intuitive theories of events and the effects of base rate information on prediction. *Journal of Personality and Social Psychology, 35*, 303–314.

Anderson, J.R. (1990). *The adaptive character of thought*. Hillsdale, NJ: Lawrence Erlbaum Associates Inc.

Anderson, J.R. (1993). *Rules of the mind*. Hillsdale, NJ: Lawrence Erlbaum Associates Inc.

Audi, R. (1989). *Practical reasoning*. London: Routledge and Kegan Paul.

Ball, L.J. (1990). *Cognitive processes in engineering design*. Unpublished Ph.D. thesis, University of Plymouth.

Ball, L.J., Evans, J.St.B.T., & Dennis, I. (1994). Cognitive processes in engineering design: A longitudinal study. *Ergonomics, 37*, 1653–1786.

Bar-Hillel, M. (1980). The base rate fallacy in probability judgements. *Acta Psychologica, 44*, 211–233.

Baron, J. (1985). *Rationality and intelligence*. Cambridge: Cambridge University Press.

Baron, J. (1988). *Thinking and deciding*. Cambridge: Cambridge University Press.

Beattie, J., & Baron, J. (1988). Confirmation and matching biases in hypothesis testing. *Quarterly Journal of Experimental Psychology, 40A*, 269–297.

Berkeley, D., & Humphreys, P. (1982). Structuring decision problems and the bias heuristic. *Acta Psychologica, 50*, 201–252.

Berry, D.C., & Broadbent, D.E. (1984). On the relationship between task performance and associated verbalisable knowledge. *Quarterly Journal of Experimental Psychology, 36A*, 209–231.

Berry, D.C., & Broadbent, D.E. (1988). Interactive tasks and the implicit-explicit distinction. *British Journal of Psychology, 79*, 251–273.

Berry, D.C., & Dienes, Z. (1993). *Implicit learning*. Hove, UK: Lawrence Erlbaum Associates Ltd.

Bonatti, L. (1994). Propositional reasoning by model? *Psychological Review, 101*, 725–733.

Braine, M.D.S., Connell, J., Freitag, J., & O'Brien, D.P. (1990). Is the base rate fallacy an instance of affirming the consequent? In K.J. Gilhooly & R.H. Logie (Eds.), *Lines of thinking*. London: Wiley.

Braine, M.D.S., & O'Brien, D.P. (1991). A theory of If: A lexical entry, reasoning program, and pragmatic principles. *Psychological Review, 98*, 182–203.

Braine, M.D.S., Reiser, B.J., & Rumain, B. (1984). Some empirical justification for a theory of natural propositional logic. In G.H. Bower (Ed.), *The psychology of learning and motivation, Vol 18*. New York: Academic Press.

Byrne, R.M.J. (1989). Suppressing valid inferences with conditionals. *Cognition, 31*, 61–83.

Carnap, P. (1950). *Logical foundations of probability*. Chicago: University of Chicago Press.

Cheng, P.W., & Holyoak, K.J. (1985). Pragmatic reasoning schemas. *Cognitive Psychology, 17*, 391–416.

Cheng, P.W., Holyoak, K.J., Nisbett, R.E., & Oliver, L.M. (1986). Pragmatic versus syntactic approaches to training deductive reasoning. *Cognitive Psychology, 18*, 293–328.

Chomsky, N. (1980). *Rules and representations*. New York: Columbia University Press.

Chomsky, N. (1986). *Knowledge of language: Its nature, origin, and use*. New York: Praeger.

Christensen-Szalanski, J.J.J., & Beach, L. R. (1982). Experience and the base rate fallacy. *Organisational Behavior and Human Performance, 29*, 270–278.

Christensen-Szalanski, J.J.J., & Beach, L.R. (1984). The citation bias: Fad and fashion in the judgement and decision literature. *American Psychologist, 39*, 75–78.

Cohen, L.J. (1981). Can human irrationality be experimentally demonstrated? *The Behavioral and Brain Sciences, 4*, 317–370.

Cohen, L.J. (1982). Are people programmed to commit fallacies? Further thought about the interpretation of data on judgement. *Journal for the Theory of Social Behaviour, 12*, 251–274.

Cooper, A.C., Woo, C. Y., & Dunkleberg, W.C. (1988). Entrepreneurs' perceived chances for success. *Journal of Business Venturing, 3*, 97–108.

Cosmides, L. (1989). The logic of social exchange: Has natural selection shaped how humans reason? Studies with the Wason selection task. *Cognition, 31*, 187–276.

Cosmides, L., & Tooby, J. (1992). Cognitive adaptations for social exchange. In J. Barkow, L. Cosmides, & J. Tooby (Eds.), *The adapted mind*. Oxford: Oxford University Press.

Dennett, D. (1995). *Darwin's dangerous idea*. London: Allen Lane; The Penguin Press.

Dickstein, L.S. (1978). Error processes in syllogistic reasoning. *Memory and Cognition, 6*, 537–43.

Dixon, N.F. (1976). *The psychology of military incompetence*. London: Jonathan Cape,

Doherty, M.E., Mynatt, C.R., Tweney, R.D., & Schiavo, M.D. (1979). Pseudo-diagnosticity. *Acta Psychologica, 43*, 11–21.

Dorling, J. (1983). In philosophical defence of Bayesian rationality. *The Behavioral and Brain Sciences, 6*, 249–250.

Edgington, D. (1991). Do conditionals have truth conditions? In F. Jackson (Ed.), *Conditionals*. Oxford: Clarendon Press.

Edgington, D. (1995). On conditionals. *Mind, 104*, 235–329.

Einhorn, H.J. (1980). Learning from experience and suboptimal rules in decision making. In T.S. Wallsten (Ed.), *Cognitive processes in choice and decision behaviour*. Hillsdale, NJ: Lawrence Erlbaum Associates Inc.

Ericsson, K.A., & Simon, H.A. (1980). Verbal reports as data. *Psychological Review, 87*, 215–251.

Ericsson, K.A., & Simon, H.A. (1984). *Protocol analysis: Verbal reports as data*. Cambridge, MA: MIT Press.

Evans, J.St.B.T. (1972). Interpretation and matching bias in a reasoning task. *British Journal of Psychology, 24*, 193–199.

Evans, J.St.B.T. (1975). On interpreting reasoning data: A reply to Van Duyne. *Cognition, 3*, 387–390.

Evans, J.St.B.T. (1977a). Linguistic factors in reasoning. *Quarterly Journal of Experimental Psychology, 29*, 297–306.

Evans, J.St.B.T. (1977b). Toward a statistical theory of reasoning. *Quarterly Journal of Experimental Psychology, 29*, 297–306.

Evans, J.St.B.T. (1982). *The psychology of deductive reasoning*. London: Routledge and Kegan Paul.

Evans, J.St.B.T. (1983). Linguistic determinants of bias in conditional reasoning. *Quarterly Journal of Experimental Psychology, 35A*, 635–644.

Evans, J.St.B.T. (1984). Heuristic and analytic processes in reasoning. *British Journal of Psychology, 75*, 451–468.

Evans, J.St.B.T. (1988). The knowledge elicitation problem: a psychological perspective. *Behaviour and Information Technology, 7*, 111–130.

Evans, J.St.B.T. (1989). *Bias in human reasoning: Causes and consequences*. Hove, UK: Lawrence Erlbaum Associates Ltd.

Evans, J.St.B.T. (1991). Theories of human reasoning: The fragmented state of the art. *Theory and Psychology, 1*, 83–105.

Evans, J.St.B.T. (1993a). Bias and rationality. In K.I. Manktelow & D.E. Over (Eds.), *Rationality*. London: Routledge and Kegan Paul.

Evans, J.St.B.T. (1993b). The mental model theory of conditional reasoning: Critical appraisal and revision. *Cognition 48*, 1–20.

Evans, J.St.B.T. (1995a). Implicit learning, consciousness, and the psychology of thinking. *Thinking & Reasoning, 1*, 105–118.

Evans, J.St.B.T. (1995b). Relevance and reasoning. In S.E. Newstead & J.St.B.T. Evans (Eds.), *Perspectives on thinking and reasoning*. Hove, UK: Lawrence Erlbaum Associates Ltd.

Evans, J.St.B.T. (in press). Deciding before you think: Relevance and reasoning in the selection task. *British Journal of Psychology*.

Evans, J.St.B.T., Allen, J.L., Newstead, S.E., & Pollard, P. (1994). Debiasing by instruction: The case of belief bias. *European Journal of Cognitive Psychology, 6,* 263–285.

Evans, J.St.B.T., Ball, L.J., & Brooks, P.G. (1987). Attentional bias and decision order in a reasoning task. *British Journal of Psychology, 78,* 385–394.

Evans, J.St.B.T., Barston, J.L., & Pollard, P. (1983). On the conflict between logic and belief in syllogistic reasoning. *Memory and Cognition, 11,* 295–306.

Evans, J.St.B.T., Brooks, P.G., & Pollard, P. (1985). Prior beliefs in statistical inference. *British Journal of Psychology, 76,* 469–477.

Evans, J.St.B.T., & Clibbens, J. (1995). Perspective shifts on the selection task: Reasoning or relevance? *Thinking & Reasoning, 1,* 315–323.

Evans, J.St.B.T., Clibbens, J., & Rood, B. (1995). Bias in conditional inference: Implications for mental models and mental logic. *Quarterly Journal of Experimental Psychology, 48A,* 644–670.

Evans, J.St.B.T., Clibbens, J., & Rood, B. (in press a). The role of implicit and explicit negation in conditional reasoning bias. *Journal of Memory and Language.*

Evans, J.St.B.T., Ellis, C., & Newstead, S.E. (in press b). On the mental representation of conditional sentences. *Quarterly Journal of Experimental Psychology, Section A.*

Evans, J.St.B.T., Legrenzi, P., & Girotto, V. (submitted). The influence of linguistic context on propositional reasoning: The case of matching bias.

Evans, J.St.B.T., & Lynch, J.S. (1973). Matching bias in the selection task. *British Journal of Psychology, 64,* 391–397.

Evans, J.St.B.T., & Newstead, S.E. (1980). A study of disjunctive reasoning. *Psychological Research, 41,* 373–388.

Evans, J.St.B.T., Newstead, S.E., & Byrne, R.M.J. (1993a). *Human reasoning: The psychology of deduction.* Hove, UK: Lawrence Erlbaum Associates Ltd.

Evans, J.St.B.T., & Over, D.E. (in press). Rationality in the selection task: Epistemic utility versus uncertainty reduction. *Psychological Review.*

Evans, J.St.B.T., Over, D.E., & Manktelow, K.I. (1993b). Reasoning, decision making, and rationality. *Cognition, 49,* 165–187.

Evans, J.St.B.T., & Wason, P.C. (1976). Rationalisation in a reasoning task. *British Journal of Psychology, 63,* 205–212.

Fellows, B.J. (1976). The role of introspection in problem solving research: A reply to Evans. *British Journal of Psychology, 67,* 519–550.

Fischhoff, B., & Beyth-Marom, R. (1983). Hypothesis evaluation from a Bayesian perspective. *Psychological Review, 90,* 239–260.

Flanagan, O. (1984). *The science of mind.* Cambridge, MA: MIT Press.

Fodor, J. (1983). *The modularity of mind.* Scranton, PA: Crowell.

Fong, G.T., Krantz, D.H., & Nisbett, R.E. (1986). The effects of statistical training on thinking about everyday problems. *Cognitive Psychology, 18,* 253–292.

Funder, D.C. (1987). Errors and mistakes: Evaluating the accuracy of social judgements. *Psychological Bulletin, 101,* 75–90.

Garnham, A., & Oakhill, J. (1994). *Thinking and reasoning.* Oxford: Basil Blackwell.

George, C. (1991). Facilitation in Wason's selection task with a consequent referring to an unsatisfactory outcome. *British Journal of Psychology, 82,* 463–472.

George, C. (1995). The endorsement of the premises: Assumption-based or belief-based reasoning. *British Journal of Psychology, 86*, 93–113.

Gigerenzer, G. (1993). The bounded rationality of probabilistic mental models. In K.I. Manktelow and D.E. Over (Eds.), *Rationality*. London: Routledge and Kegan Paul.

Gigerenzer, G., Hoffrage, U., & Kleinbölting, H. (1991). Probabilistic mental models: A Brunswikian theory of confidence. *Psychological Review, 98*, 506–528.

Gigerenzer, G., & Hug, K. (1992). Domain-specific reasoning: Social contracts, cheating, and perspective change. *Cognition, 43*, 127–171.

Gigerenzer, G., & Murray, D.J. (1987). *Cognition as intuitive statistics*. Hillsdale, NJ: Lawrence Erlbaum Associates Inc.

Girotto, V., Mazzocco, A., & Cherubini, P. (1992). Pragmatic judgements of relevance and reasoning: A reply to Jackson & Griggs. *Quarterly Journal of Experimental Psychology, 45A*, 547–574.

Green, D.W. (1995). Externalisation, counter-examples, and the abstract selection task. *Quarterly Journal of Experimental Psychology, 48A*, 424–447.

Green, D.W., & Larking, R. (1995). The locus of facilitation in the abstract selection task. *Thinking & Reasoning, 1*, 183–199.

Grice, P. (1975). Logic and conversation. In P. Cole & J.L. Morgan (Eds.), *Studies in syntax. Vol 3: Speech acts*. New York: Academic Press.

Grice, P. (1989). *Studies in the way of words*. Cambridge, MA: Harvard University Press.

Griffin, D., & Tversky, A. (1992). The weighting of evidence and the determinants of confidence. *Cognitive Psychology, 24*, 411–435.

Griggs, R.A. (1983). The role of problem content in the selection task and in the THOG problem. In J.St.B.T. Evans (Ed.), *Thinking and reasoning: Psychological approaches*. London: Routledge and Kegan Paul.

Griggs, R.A., & Cox, J.R. (1982). The elusive thematic materials effect in the Wason selection task. *British Journal of Psychology, 73*, 407–420.

Griggs, R.A., & Cox, J.R. (1983). The effects of problem content and negation on Wason's selection task. *Quarterly Journal of Experimental Psychology, 35A*, 519–533.

Griggs, R.A., & Cox, J.R. (1993). Permission schemas and the selection task. *Quarterly Journal of Experimental Psychology, 46A*, 637–652.

Harman, G. (1986). *Change in view*. Cambridge: MIT Press.

Hasher, L., & Zacks, R.T. (1984). Automatic processing of fundamental information: The case of frequency occurrence. *American Psychologist, 39*, 1327–1388.

Henle, M. (1962). On the relation between logic and thinking. *Psychological Review, 69*, 366–378.

Hogarth, R.M., & Einhorn, H.J. (1992). Order effects in belief updating: The belief adjustment model. *Cognitive Psychology, 24*, 1–55.

Holyoak, K. J., & Cheng, P. W. (1995). Pragmatic reasoning with a point of view. *Thinking & Reasoning, 1*, 289–313.

Howson, C., & Urbach, P. (1993). *Scientific reasoning, (2nd edition)*. Chicago: Open Court.

Inhelder, B., & Piaget, J. (1958). *The growth of logical thinking*. New York: Basic Books.

Jackson, S.L., & Griggs, R.A. (1990). The elusive pragmatic reasoning schemas effect. *Quarterly Journal of Experimental Psychology, 42A*, 353–374.

Jeffrey, R.C. (1981). *Formal logic: Its scope and limits* (2nd edn.). New York: McGraw-Hill.

Jepson, D., Krantz, D.H., & Nisbett, R.E. (1983). Inductive reasoning: Competence or skill? *The Behavioral and Brain Sciences, 6*, 494–501.

Johnson-Laird, P.N. (1983). *Mental models*. Cambridge: Cambridge University Press.

Johnson-Laird, P.N. (1994a). Mental models and probabilistic thinking. *Cognition, 50*, 189–209.

Johnson-Laird, P.N. (1994b). A model theory of induction. *International Studies in the Philosophy of Science, 8*, 5–29.

Johnson-Laird, P.N., & Bara, B.G. (1984). Syllogistic inference. *Cognition, 16*, 1–62.

Johnson-Laird, P.N., & Byrne, R.M.J. (1991). *Deduction*. Hove, UK: Lawrence Erlbaum Associates Ltd.

Johnson-Laird, P.N., & Byrne, R.M.J. (1993). Models and deductive rationality. In K.I. Manktelow & D.E. Over (Eds.), *Rationality*. London: Routledge and Kegan Paul.

Johnson-Laird, P.N., Byrne, R.M.J., & Schaeken, W. (1992). Propositional reasoning by model. *Psychological Review, 99*, 418–439.

Johnson-Laird, P.N., Byrne, R.M.J., & Schaeken, W. (1994). Why models rather than rules give a better account of propositional reasoning: A reply to Bonatti and to O'Brien, Braine, & Yang. *Psychological Review, 101*, 734–739.

Johnson-Laird, P.N., Legrenzi, P., & Legrenzi, M.S. (1972). Reasoning and a sense of reality. *British Journal of Psychology, 63*, 395–400.

Johnson-Laird, P.N., & Tagart, J. (1969). How implication is understood. *American Journal of Psychology, 2*, 367–373.

Kahneman, D. (1994). New challenges to the rationality assumption. *Journal of Institutional and Theoretical Economics* (JITE), *150/1*, 18–36.

Kahneman, D., & Tversky, A. (1972a). On prediction and judgement. *ORI Research Monograph, 1* (4).

Kahneman, D., & Tversky, A. (1972b). Subjective probability: A judgement of representativeness. *Cognitive Psychology, 3*, 430–454.

Kahneman, D., & Tversky, A. (1973). On the psychology of prediction. *Psychological Review, 80*, 237–251.

Kahneman, D., & Tversky, A. (1979). Prospect theory: An analysis of decision under risk. *Econometrica, 47*, 263–291.

Kahneman, D., & Varey, C. (1991). Notes on the psychology of utility. In J. Elster & J. Roemer (Eds.), *Interpersonal comparisons of well-being*. Cambridge: Cambridge University Press.

Kareev, Y., & Avrahami, J. (1995). Teaching by examples: The case of number series. *British Journal of Psychology, 86*, 41–54.

Kareev, Y., & Halberstadt, N. (1993). Evaluating negative tasks and refutations in a rule discovery task. *Quarterly Journal of Experimental Psychology, 46A*, 715–728.

Kareev, Y., Halberstadt, N., & Shafir, D. (1993). Improving performance and increasing the use of non-positive testing in a rule-discovery task. *Quarterly Journal of Experimental Psychology, 46A*, 729–742.

Kirby, K.N. (1994a). Probabilities and utilities of fictional outcomes in Wason's four-card selection task. *Cognition, 51*, 1–28.

Kirby, K.N. (1994b). False alarm: A reply to Over and Evans. *Cognition, 52*, 245–250.

Klayman, J., & Ha, Y-W. (1987). Confirmation, disconfirmation, and information in hypothesis testing. *Psychological Review, 94*, 211–228.

Kroger, J.K., Cheng, P.W., & Holyoak, K.J. (1993). Evoking the permission schema: The impact of explicit negation and a violation checking context. *Quarterly Journal of Experimental Psychology, 46A*, 615–635

Kullback, S. (1959). *Information theory and statistics.* New York: Wiley.

Laming, D. (in press). On the analysis of irrational data selection: A critique of Oaksford & Chater. *Psychological Review.*

Legrenzi, P., Girotto, V., & Johnson-Laird, P.N. (1993). Focusing in reasoning and decision making. *Cognition, 49*, 37–66.

Levi, I. (1984). *Decisions and revisions.* Cambridge: Cambridge University Press.

Lichtenstein, S., Fischhoff, B., & Phillips, L.D. (1982). Calibration of probabilities: The state of the art to 1980. In D. Kahneman, P. Slovic, & A. Tversky (Eds.), *Judgement under uncertainty: Heuristics biases.* Cambridge: Cambridge University Press.

Lopes, L.L. (1991). The rhetoric of irrationality. *Theory and Psychology, 1*, 65–82.

Love, R.E., & Kessler, C.M. (1995). Focusing in Wason's selection task: Content and instruction effects. *Thinking & Reasoning, 1*, 153–182.

Lowe, E.J. (1993). Rationality, deduction, and mental models. In K.I. Manktelow & D.E. Over (Eds.), *Rationality.* London: Routledge and Kegan Paul.

Maachi, L. (1995). Pragmatic aspects of the base-rate fallacy. *Quarterly Journal of Experimental Psychology, 48A*, 188–207.

Manktelow, K.I., & Over, D.E. (1990a). *Inference and understanding.* London: Routledge and Kegan Paul.

Manktelow, K.I., & Over, D.E. (1990b). Deontic thought and the selection task. In K.J. Gilhooly, M. Keane, R.H. Logie, & G. Erdos (Eds.), *Lines of thinking, Vol. 1.* Chichester: Wiley.

Manktelow, K.I., & Over, D. (1991). Social roles and utilities in reasoning with deontic conditionals. *Cognition, 39*, 85–105.

Manktelow, K.I., & Over D.E. (1992). Utility and deontic reasoning: Some comments on Johnson-Laird & Byrne. *Cognition, 43*, 183–186.

Manktelow, K.I., & Over, D.E. (1993). *Rationality: Psychological and philosophical perspectives.* London: Routledge and Kegan Paul.

Manktelow, K.I., & Over, D.E. (1995). Deontic reasoning. In S.E. Newstead & J.St.B.T. Evans (Eds.), *Perspectives on thinking and reasoning.* Hove, UK: Lawrence Erlbaum Associates Ltd.

Manktelow, K.I., Sutherland, E.J., & Over, D.E. (1995). Probabilistic factors in deontic reasoning. *Thinking & Reasoning 1*, 201–220.

Markovits, H., & Nantel, G. (1989). The belief bias effect in the production and evaluation of logical conclusions. *Memory & Cognition, 17*, 11–17.

McClelland, A.G.R., & Bolger, F. (1994). The calibration of subjective probabilities: Theories and models 1980–94. In G. Wright & P. Ayton (Eds.), *Subjective probability.* New York: Wiley.

Mynatt, C.R., Doherty, M.E., & Dragan, W. (1993). Information relevance, working memory and the consideration of alternatives. *Quarterly Journal of Experimental Psychology, 46A*, 759–778.

Newell, A., & Simon, H.A. (1972). *Human problem solving.* Englewood Cliffs, NJ: Prentice-Hall.

Newstead, S.E., Pollard, P., Evans, J.St.B.T., & Allen, J.L. (1992). The source of belief bias in syllogistic reasoning. *Cognition 45*, 257–284.

Nisbett, R.E., Krantz, D.H., Jepson, C., & Kunda, Z. (1983). The use of statistical heuristics in everyday inductive reasoning. *Psychological Review, 90*, 339–363.

Nisbett, R., & Ross, L. (1980). *Human inference: Strategies and shortcomings of social judgement*. Englewood Cliffs, NJ: Prentice-Hall.

Nisbett, R.E., & Wilson, T.D. (1977). Telling more than we can know: Verbal reports on mental processes. *Psychological Review, 84*, 231–295.

Nozick, R. (1993). *The nature of rationality*. Princeton: Princeton University Press.

O'Brien, D.P. (1993). Mental logic and irrationality: We can put a man on the moon, so why can't we solve those logical reasoning problems. In K.I. Manktelow & D.E. Over (Eds.), *Rationality*. London: Routledge and Kegan Paul.

O'Brien, D.P., Braine, M.D.S., & Yang, Y. (1994). Propositional reasoning by mental models? Simple to refute in principle and in practice. *Psychological Review, 101*, 711–724.

Oakhill, J., & Johnson-Laird, P.N. (1985). The effect of belief on the spontaneous production of syllogistic conclusions. *Quarterly Journal of Experimental Psychology, 37A*, 553–570.

Oakhill, J., Johnson-Laird, P.N., & Garnham, A. (1989). Believability and syllogistic reasoning. *Cognition, 31*, 117–140.

Oaksford, M., & Chater, N. (1993). Reasoning theories and bounded rationality. In K.I. Manktelow & D.E. Over (Eds.), *Rationality*. London: Routledge and Kegan Paul.

Oaksford, M., & Chater, N. (1994). A rational analysis of the selection task as optimal data selection. *Psychological Review, 101*, 608–631.

Oaksford, M., & Chater, N. (1995). Theories of reasoning and the computational explanation of everyday inference. *Thinking & Reasoning, 1*, 121–152.

Oaksford, M., & Chater, N. (in press). How to explain the selection task. *Psychological Review*.

Over, D.E., & Evans, J.St.B.T. (1994). Hits and misses: Kirby on the selection task. *Cognition, 52*, 235–243.

Over, D.E., & Manktelow, K.I. (1993). Rationality, utility, and deontic reasoning. In K.I. Manktelow & D.E. Over (Eds.), *Rationality*. London: Routledge and Kegan Paul.

Peterson, C.R., & Beach, L.R. (1967). Man as an intuitive statistician. *Psychological Bulletin, 68*, 29–46.

Platt, R.D., & Griggs, R.A. (1993). Facilitation in the abstract selection task: The effect of attentional and instructional factors. *Quarterly Journal of Experimental Psychology, 46A*, 591–614.

Politzer, G., & Nguyen-Xuan, A. (1992). Reasoning about conditional promises and warnings: Darwinian algorithms, mental models, relevance judgements or pragmatic schemas? *Quarterly Journal of Experimental Psychology, 44*, 401–412.

Polk, T.A., & Newell, A. (1995). Deduction as verbal reasoning. *Psychological Review, 102*, 533–566.

Pollard, P. (1982). Human reasoning: Some possible effects of availability. *Cognition, 12*, 65–96.

Pollard, P., & Evans, J.St.B.T. (1980). The influence of logic on conditional reasoning performance. *Quarterly Journal of Experimental Psychology, 32A,* 605–624.

Pollard, P., & Evans, J.St.B.T. (1981). The effect of prior beliefs in reasoning: An associational interpretation. *British Journal of Psychology, 72,* 73–82.

Pollard, P., & Evans, J.St.B.T. (1983). The effect of experimentally contrived experience on reasoning performance. *Psychological Research. 45,* 287–301.

Pollard, P., & Evans, J.St.B.T. (1987). On the relationship between content and context effects in reasoning. *American Journal of Psychology, 100,* 41–60.

Popper, K.R. (1959). *The logic of scientific discovery.* London: Hutchinson.

Popper, K.R. (1962). *Conjectures and refutations.* London: Hutchinson.

Real, L.A. (1991). Animal choice behavior and the evolution of cognitive architecture. *Science, 253,* 980–979.

Reber (1993). *Implicit learning and tacit knowledge.* Oxford: Oxford University Press.

Reich, S.S., & Ruth, P. (1982). Wason's selection task: Verification, falsification, and matching. *British Journal of Psychology, 73,* 395–405.

Rips, L.J. (1983). Cognitive processes in propositional reasoning. *Psychological Review, 90,* 38–71.

Rips, L.J. (1989). The psychology of knights and knaves. *Cognition, 31,* 85–116.

Rips, L.J. (1994). *The psychology of proof.* Cambridge, MA: MIT Press.

Ryle, G. (1949). *The concept of mind.* New York: Barnes & Noble.

Savage, L.J. (1954). *The foundations of statistics.* New York: Wiley.

Sen, A. (1990). Rational behaviour. In J. Eatwell, M. Milgate, & P. Newman (Eds.), *The new plagrave: Utility and probability.* New York: W.W. Norton.

Shafir, E. (1993). Choosing versus rejecting: Why some options are both better and worse than others. *Memory & Cognition, 21,* 546–556.

Shafir, E., & Tversky, A. (1992). Thinking through uncertainty: Non-consequential reasoning and decision making. *Cognitive Psychology, 29,* 449–474.

Shafir, E., Simonson, I., & Tversky, A. (1993). Reason-based choice. *Cognition, 49,* 11–36.

Shanks, D.R. (1995). Is human learning rational? *Quarterly Journal of Experimental Psychology, 48A,* 257–289.

Simon, H.A. (1957). *Models of man: Social and rational.* New York: Wiley.

Simon, H.A. (1983). *Reason in human affairs.* Stanford: Stanford University Press.

Sloman, S.A. (1996). The empirical case for two systems of reasoning. *Psychological Bulletin, 119,* 3–22.

Slote, M. (1989). *Beyond optimizing.* Cambridge: Harvard University Press.

Smedslund, J. (1970). On the circular relation between logic and understanding. *Scandinavian Journal of Psychology, 11,* 217–219.

Smedslund, J. (1990). A critique of Tversky and Kahneman's distinction between fallacy and misunderstanding. *Scandinavian Journal of Psychology, 31,* 110–120.

Smith, E.E., Langston, C., & Nisbett, R. (1992). The case of rules in reasoning. *Cognitive Science, 16,* 1–40.

Smolensky, P. (1988). On the proper treatment of connectionism. *Behavioral and Brain Sciences, 11,* 1–23.

Sperber, D., & Wilson, D. (1986). *Relevance.* Oxford: Basil Blackwell.

Sperber, D., Cara, F., & Girotto, V. (1995).   Relevance theory explains the selection task. *Cognition, 57*, 31–95.

Stevenson, R.J., & Over, D.E. (1995). Deduction from uncertain premises. *Quarterly Journal of Experimental Psychology, 48A*, 613–643.

Strack, F., Argyle, M., & Schwarz, N. (Eds.) (1990). *Subjective well-being*. Oxford: Pergamon Press.

Taylor, S.E., & Brown, J. D. (1988). Illusion and well-being: A social psychological perspective on mental health. *Psychological Bulletin, 103*, 193–210.

Tversky, A., & Kahneman, D. (1973). Availability: A heuristic for judging frequency and probability. *Cognitive Psychology, 5*, 207–232.

Tversky, A., & Kahneman, D. (1980). Causal schemata in judgements under uncertainty. In M. Fishbein (Ed.), *Progress in social psychology*. Hillsdale, NJ: Lawrence Erlbaum Associates Inc.

Tversky, A., & Kahneman, D. (1986). Rational choice and the framing of decisions. *Journal of Business, 59*, s251–s278.

Tversky, A., & Shafir, E. (1992). The disjunction effect in choice under uncertainty. *Psychological Science, 3*, 305–309.

Van Duyne, P.C. (1976). Necessity and contingency in reasoning. *Acta Psychologica, 40*, 85–101.

von Winterfeldt, D., & Edwards, W. (1986). *Decision analysis and behavioural research*. Cambridge: Cambridge University Press.

Wason, P.C. (1960). On the failure to eliminate hypotheses in a conceptual task. *Quarterly Journal of Experimental Psychology, 12*, 129–140.

Wason, P.C. (1966). Reasoning. In B.M. Foss (Ed.), *New horizons in psychology I*. Harmondsworth: Penguin.

Wason, P.C. (1968). On the failure to eliminate hypotheses... A second look. In P.C. Wason & P.N. Johnson-Laird (Eds), *Thinking and reasoning*. Harmondsworth: Penguin.

Wason, P.C. (1969). Regression in reasoning? *British Journal of Psychology, 60*, 471–480.

Wason, P.C., & Brooks, P.G. (1979). THOG: The anatomy of a problem. *Psychological Research, 41*, 79–90.

Wason, P.C., & Evans, J.St.B.T. (1975). Dual processes in reasoning? *Cognition, 3*, 141–154.

Wason, P.C., & Johnson-Laird, P.N. (1972). *Psychology of reasoning: Structure and content*. London: Batsford.

Wetherick, N.E. (1962). Eliminative and enumerative behaviour in a conceptual task. *Quarterly Journal of Experimental Psychology, 14*, 246–249.

Wetherick, N.E. (1993). Human rationality. In K.I. Manktelow & D.E Over (Eds), *Rationality*. London: Routledge and Kegan Paul.

Wharton, C.M., Cheng, P.W., & Wickens, T.D. (1993). Hypothesis-testing strategies: Why two goals are better than one. *Quarterly Journal of Experimental Psychology, 46A*, 743–758.

White, P.A. (1988). Knowing more than we can tell: "Introspective access" and causal report accuracy 10 years later. *British Journal of Psychology, 79*, 13–46.

Wittgenstein, L. (1953). *Philosophical investigations*. Oxford: Basil Blackwell.

Author index

Ackerman, R., 34, 97
Adams, E.W., 19
Ajzen, I., 100
Allen, J.L., 111, 128
Anderson, J.R., 15, 18, 53
Argyle, M., 35
Audi, R., 14
Avrahami, J., 105

Ball, L.J., 31–32, 59
Bar-Hillel, M., 100
Bara, B.G., 68, 126, 133, 158, 160
Baron, J., 1, 4, 60, 96, 104, 108, 122, 151
Barston, J.L., 3, 110
Beach, L.R., 6, 98, 101
Beattie, J., 60, 122
Berkeley, D., 6
Berry, D.C., 10, 51, 149–150, 152–153
Beyth-Marom, R., 98, 104
Bolger, F., 33
Bonatti, L., 136
Braine, M.D.S., 11, 17, 100, 130–131, 136, 158
Broadbent, D.E., 149
Brooks, P.G., 59, 102, 106

Brown, J. D., 34, 97
Byrne, R.M.J., 1, 12–13, 108, 113, 133–134, 136, 138, 158–160

Cara, F., 47, 61
Carnap, P., 160
Chater, N., 5, 52, 88–91, 137
Cheng, P.W., 58, 73, 78–79, 105, 120, 122, 130
Cherubini, P., 58
Chomsky, N., 147, 154
Christensen-Szalanski, J.J.J., 6, 101
Clibbens, J., 58, 122, 137
Cohen, L.J., 4, 6, 100
Connell, J., 100
Cooper, A.C., 33
Cosmides, L., 29, 78–79, 147
Cox, J.R., 58, 75, 125

Dennett, D., 78–79
Dennis, I., 31
DeRubeis, R., 34, 97
Dickstein, L.S., 126
Dienes, Z., 10, 51, 149–150, 152–153
Dixon, N.F., 96

Doherty, M.E., 39–40, 42, 65
Dorling, J., 88
Dragan, W., 40, 65
Dunkleberg, W.C., 33

Edgington, D., 19, 83
Edwards, W., 27
Einhorn, H.J., 115, 142
Ellis, C., 92
Ericsson, K.A., 52, 157–158
Evans, J.St.B.T., 1, 3–4, 6–7, 10,
    17, 20, 31, 35, 40, 48–51, 55–61,
    70–71, 74–75, 80–81, 84, 86–93,
    100, 102, 104–113, 121–128, 130,
    132–138, 144–146, 149–150,
    155–156, 158

Fellows, B.J., 156
Fischhoff, B., 34, 98, 104
Flanagan, O., 7
Fodor, J., 147, 154
Fong, G.T., 152
Freitag, J., 100
Funder, D.C., 6

Garnham, A., 1, 111, 151
George, C., 37, 112, 114, 129, 144
Gigerenzer, G., 33–34, 78, 98,
    100–101
Girotto, V., 47, 58, 61, 70, 125
Green, D.W., 61, 91, 93, 107, 122
Grice, P., 46–47
Griffin, D., 33
Griggs, R.A., 58, 74–75, 122, 125

Ha, Y-W., 41, 104, 106
Halberstadt, N., 105
Harman, G., 10, 22, 42
Hasher, L., 34
Henle, M., 5, 11
Hoffrage, U., 33
Hogarth, R.M., 115
Holyoak, K.J., 58, 73, 78–79, 120,
    122, 130
Howson, C., 21, 32, 37, 84, 97,
    114–115
Hug, K., 78
Humphreys, P., 6

Inhelder, B., 11

Jackson, S.L., 58
Jeffrey, R.C., 13, 115
Jepson, C., 90, 151–152
Johnson-Laird, P.N., 12–13, 20,
    54–55, 61, 68, 73–74, 104, 108,
    111, 126, 130, 133–134, 136, 138,
    158–160

Kahneman, D., 30, 35, 48, 80–81,
    99–100, 151
Kareev, Y., 105
Kessler, C.M., 61, 91–93, 107, 122
Kirby, K.N., 75, 79–80, 84–88
Klayman, J., 41, 104, 106
Kleinbölting, H., 33
Krantz, D.H., 90, 151–152
Kroger, J.K., 58
Kullback, S., 41
Kunda, Z., 90, 151

Laming, D., 89
Langston, C., 23
Larking, R., 61, 91, 107, 122
Legrenzi, M.S., 73
Legrenzi, P., 61, 67, 70, 73, 125, 136
Levi, I., 40
Lichtenstein, S., 34
Lopes, L.L., 4, 7
Love, R.E., 61, 91–93, 107, 122
Lowe, E.J., 13, 70
Lynch, J.S., 56, 104

Maachi, L., 100–101
Manktelow, K.I., 7, 43, 74–75,
    78–80, 160
Markovits, H., 111
Mazzocco, A., 58
McClelland, A.G.R., 33
Murray, D.J., 98, 100–101
Mynatt, C.R., 39–40, 42, 65–68, 70,
    107

Nantel, G., 111
Newell, A., 131, 154
Newstead, S.E., 1, 92, 105, 111,
    125, 127–128, 135
Nguyen-Xuan, A., 78
Nisbett, R.E., 23, 90, 96, 108, 120,
    151–152, 155–157, 161
Nozick, R., 8, 22

O'Brien, D.P., 11, 17, 100, 130–132, 135–136, 158–159
Oakhill, J., 1, 111–112, 151
Oaksford, M., 5, 52, 88–91, 137
Oliver, L.M., 120
Over, D.E., 7, 18, 37, 43, 74–75, 77–80, 84, 86, 88–90, 106, 112–113, 128, 138, 159–160

Peterson, C.R., 98
Phillips, L.D., 34
Piaget, J., 11
Platt, R.D., 122
Politzer, G., 78
Polk, T.A., 154
Pollard, P., 3, 48, 75, 86–88, 90–91, 93, 102, 107, 110–111, 124–125, 128
Popper, K.R., 20, 97, 103, 114

Real, L.A., 28, 153
Reber, A.S., 10, 34, 36, 51, 142, 149–150, 154
Reich, S.S., 125
Reiser, B.J., 130
Rips, L.J., 11–13, 130–132, 136, 158
Rood, B., 58, 137
Ross, L., 96, 108
Rumain, B., 130
Ruth, P., 125
Ryle, G., 51

Savage, L.J., 31, 64
Schaeken, W., 134, 136, 159
Schiavo, M.D., 39, 65
Schwarz, N., 35
Sen, A., 34
Shafir, D., 105
Shafir, E., 62–65, 69
Shanks, D.R., 70
Simon, H.A., 31, 52, 131, 157–158
Simonson, I., 62

Sloman, S.A., 10, 23, 146
Slote, M., 31
Smedslund, J., 5
Smith, E.E., 23, 152
Smolensky, P., 50
Sperber, D., 46–49, 52, 61, 92–93, 142, 147
Stevenson, R.J., 18, 37, 112–113, 128, 138–139, 160
Strack, F., 35
Sutherland, E.J., 79

Tagart, J., 54–55
Taylor, S.E., 34, 97
Tooby, J., 29, 79
Tversky, A., 30, 33, 48, 62–65, 69, 80–81, 99–100, 150
Tweney, R.D., 39, 65

Urbach, P., 21, 32, 37, 84, 97, 114–115

Van Duyne, P.C., 86
Varey, C., 80
von Winterfeldt, D., 27

Wason, P.C., 6, 22, 48–49, 54, 56–57, 60, 65–66, 69, 71–72, 74, 104, 106–108, 120–122, 125, 132, 137, 144–146, 155–156
Wetherick, N.E., 84, 104–105
Wharton, C.M., 105
White, P.A., 156
Wickens, T.D., 105
Wilson, D., 46–47, 49, 52, 61
Wilson, T.D., 155–157
Wittgenstein, L., 46
Woo, C.Y., 33

Yang, Y., 136, 158

Zacks, R.T., 34

Subject index

ACT model, 53
Ad hominem argument, 8–9
ANDS model, 12, 131
Availability heuristic, 48, 151

Base rate fallacy, 48, 99–103, 107
Bayes' theorem, Bayesian inference,
    38–40, 97–98, 109, 114–116
Belief bias, 3, 95, 102, 109–115,
    116–117, 144
    instructional effects, 110,
    127–129, 158
    mental model theory, 112, 133
Bias, definition of, 2
Book bag and poker chip task,
    96–97
Bounded rationality, 31–32

Calibration, 33
Chess playing, 19, 150–151
Citation bias, 6
Computational intractability, 5, 52,
    137
Conditional reasoning, 11–12,
    17–18, 113–114, 128–129
    competence and bias in, 120–125
    relevance effect in, 54–60

conditional inference task,
    123–125, 132
    see also Wason selection task
Conditionalisation, strict and
    Jeffrey, 114–115
Confirmation, 20
    confirmation bias, 20, 42, 56, 95,
    103–109
Connectionism, see Neural Networks
Conscious thinking, consciousness,
    48, 51, 121, 150, 154–155, 161

Decision theory, 27–36, 72–73,
    75–77, 64, 148
    see also Bayes' theorem
Declarative knowledge, 53
Depressive realism, 33–34
Diagnosticity, 38–43
Disjunction effect, 63–64
Disjunctive reasoning, 105
Dual process theory of reasoning, 49
Dual process theory of reasoning,
    144–147

Engineering design, 31–32
Epiphenomenalism, 52
Epistemic goals, 36, 40, 88

Epistemic utility, 36, 40–43, 159
Evolutionary arguments, 34–35, 51, 78–79, 154
Expected information gain (EIG), 88–91
Expert systems, 11, 150
Explicit cognitive processes, 10, 153–161
see also Conscious thinking
Explicit knowledge, 29, 51
External validity issue, 6–7, 100

Focusing effects, 151
in decision making, 67–68
in reasoning, 61, 91
Frequencies, judgements of *vs* probabilities, 34

Gambler's fallacy, 151
Goals,
personal, 25–29, 52, 81
sub-goals 26, 33
epistemic, *see* epistemic goals
Gricean maxims, 46–47

Heuristic-analytic (H-A) theory, 49–51, 58–60, 122, 130, 132, 145

Illusory correlation, 151
Implicit learning, 34, 142
and tacit processing, 10, 149–150
Inference rule theory,
see Mental Logic
Information,
measured by diagnosticity, 41
measured by uncertainty reduction, 88–91
Innate modules, 147, 153
Introspective reports, 53, 146, 155–157
Intuitive judgement, 150–153
Invariance, problem of, 30–31

Language, 154, 161
Law of large numbers, 151–152, 161
Likelihood, 39
Logic, 5–6, 10–14, 16–21, 26, 29–30, 119
Loss aversion, 80

Matching bias, 55–57, 61, 105, 122–123, 155
implicit *vs* explicit negation, 57–59, 123, 125
Mental imagery, 53
Mental logic, 10–12, 23, 124, 129–132, 135–138, 158–159
Mental models, 12–14, 20, 23, 61, 68, 82, 107–108, 112, 124, 129–130, 133–138, 158–161
Military incompetence, 96–97
Mutual manifestness, 47

Negations paradigm, 55–56
Negative conclusion bias, 123–125
Neural networks, 50–51, 154, 160
Normative systems, 4–5, 26–27, 148

Optimality in decision making, 15
Objective probability, chance, 32
Overconfidence, 33

Popperian philosophy, 20–21, 97, 103, 106, 114
Positive test heuristic, 106
Positivity bias, 106, 142
Practical reasoning, 14–16
Pragmatic reasoning schemas, 122, 130
Pragmatics,
in discourse, 46–49
see also pragmatic reasoning schemas
Principal principle, 32–33
Probabilistic reasoning, 142, 159–160
Problem solving, 157
Procedural knowledge, 53
Pseudo-diagnosticity, 38–40, 65–67, 107
relevance account, 66–67
PSYCOP model, 12, 131–132

Rational analysis, 53, 88–91
Rationality, two kinds, 7–10
Raven's paradox, 83–84, 121–122, 125
Reasons for decisions, 8–9, 62–63
Relevance, 10, 138, 151
and pragmatics, 46–49
principles of relevance, 46–49

and tacit processing, 49–51
and goals, 52
in selection task, 57–62, 80–83, 92
in decision making and
    judgement, 62–68
in the base rate fallacy, 100
Representativeness heuristic, 151
Rules,
    following, 9, 12
    complying with (conforming to), 12

Satisficing, 31–32
Self-knowledge, 155–157
Subjective expected utility (SEU),
    27–29
Subjective probability, 27–28, 32–34,
    37–38, 81–82, 85–88, 89–90
Syllogistic inference, 3, 109–113,
    125–129, 133, 135, 158

Tacit (implicit) cognitive processes,
    10, 22, 29, 138, 143, 145,
    147–153, 161
    and relevance, 48–52
    tacit knowledge, 51
Theoretical reasoning, 14–16
Training studies,
    logic training, 120–121
    statistical training, 151–153
Two-factor theory of reasoning, 144

Uncertainty in premises, 36–37,
    112–115
    see also belief bias
Utility, 27

Verbal protocols, 5, 155–159
Visual perception, 50

Wason 2 4 6 task, 104–108
Wason selection task,
    general, 6, 65, 71–73, 101, 104,
        107, 125, 132, 143
    negations paradigm and matching
        bias, 56–58
    card inspection times, 59–60, 71,
        155
    deontic selection task, 73–82
    indicative selection task, 83–93,
        120–122
    thematic facilitation effect, 74–75
    scenarios, 75, 77, 125
    decision theoretic analysis, 75–77,
        79–82, 84–91
    cheater detection, 78–80
    counter-examples, cueing of,
        91–93, 122
    logic training, 120–121
Working memory, 154